Steeltown, USSR

A CENTENNIAL BOOK

One hundred books
published between 1990 and 1995
bear this special imprint of
the University of California Press.
We have chosen each Centennial Book
as an example of the Press's finest
publishing and bookmaking traditions
as we celebrate the beginning of
our second century.

UNIVERSITY OF CALIFORNIA PRESS

Founded in 1893

Steeltown, USSR

Soviet Society
in the Gorbachev Era

Stephen Kotkin

UNIVERSITY OF CALIFORNIA PRESS

Berkeley / Los Angeles

University of California Press
Berkeley and Los Angeles, California

© 1991 by
The Regents of the University of California

Library of Congress Cataloging-in-Publication Data
Kotkin, Stephen.
    Steeltown, USSR : Soviet society in the Gorbachev era / Stephen
Kotkin.
        p.   cm.
    Includes index.
    ISBN 0-520-07353-3 (cloth)
    1. Magnitogorsk (R.S.F.S.R.)—Politics and government.
2. Perestroĭka—Russian S.F.S.R.—Magnitogorsk.   3. Soviet
Union—Politics and government—1985–   I. Title.
DK651.M159K68   1991
947'.87—dc20   90-11310
                                                                              CIP

Printed in the United States of America
1   2   3   4   5   6   7   8   9

For my mother and the memory
of my father, who stuttered

Contents

Photographs Following Page 117

Preface

Behind the Urals, more than half a century after the construction of the colossal steelworks of Magnitogorsk, the local populace still calls the smoke from the works the "bouquet of Magnitka." The bright orange tint of the clouds rising above the forest of smokestacks confers a sense of majesty on this mammoth center of old-style industrialism, one of the vehicles for the USSR's rise to superpower status—and for its decline.

Although debate about *perestroika* (restructuring) in the Soviet Union focuses on Moscow, the country's reform stage to the world, perhaps something can be learned from venturing into the provinces. At one time synonymous with Soviet industrialization and the "building of socialism," Magnitogorsk today is a prime expression of the realities that called forth the current reform and of the impediments that restrain it.

■　　■　　■

Two-thirds of the Soviet Union's 285 million people live in cities. When we call to mind cities in the USSR, we are apt to think of Moscow, Leningrad, Kiev, or perhaps even Tashkent. But there is another urban USSR, one composed of small- and medium-sized industrial towns. In the more than seventy years since the October Revolution, some twelve hundred new urban settlements have been created, the majority of them industrial centers. Magnitogorsk was one of the first.

Magnitogorsk gets its name from Magnetic Mountain (in Russian, *Magnitnaia gora*), a popular expression given to an unspectacular outcrop of five semicircular hills that contained some of the richest and most accessible iron ore in the world. At Magnetic Mountain, just beyond the southern tip of the Urals in the wide-open steppe, as far to the east of Moscow as Berlin is to the west, secure from the threat of foreign invasion, the Soviet government decided to build the world's largest and most technologically advanced iron and steel plant.

Founded in 1929, Magnitogorsk instantly became the symbol of the revolutionary remaking of society that the October Revolution had promised. By 1932 this monument to Joseph Stalin's leadership was already producing pig iron and by 1933, steel. The transformation of the Soviet Union from a predominantly agrarian to a predominantly industrial country was under way.

While the great factory churned out pig iron and rolled steel, the two hundred thousand inhabitants of the town lived mostly in barracks, tents, and mud huts. There was almost no sewage system or running water; there were few street lights and virtually no paved streets. The workers, the vast majority of whom were yesterday's peasants, marched off to work carrying pictures of Stalin and singing the "Internationale." They worked sixteen-hour shifts, often without warm clothes and without enough to eat. In the heroic and chaotic days of the 1930s, Magnitogorsk was a frontier boomtown on a grand crusade.

By 1939 the Magnitogorsk Works was producing 10 percent of the Soviet Union's steel—at a site that a decade earlier had been barren. A few years later, this eastern steelmaking center played a vital role in the Great Patriotic War, especially after the chief industrial regions to the west were captured by the rapidly advancing German Wehrmacht. Magnitogorsk produced 50 percent of the steel used to make tanks during the war.

The sacrifices people made in building the plant during the 1930s stood them in good stead for the even greater sacrifices they were called upon to make during the war effort. Memories of the war in Magnitogorsk, as in all of the USSR, are palpably alive, a great source of anguish and of pride.

After the war the steel plant continued to expand, together with a large wiremaking factory that had been uprooted and evacuated to Magnitogorsk during the war. The euphoria of victory quickly gave way, however, to the enormous challenges of postwar reconstruction. Just as there had been severe food shortages in the city during the countrywide famine of 1932, so there were again, fifteen years later. Housing remained primitive. As late as the early 1960s more than half the population still lived in barracks.

By the end of the 1980s, Magnitogorsk had become an industrial city of 438,000 people. Although its population is not large, it possesses what is now the largest steel complex in the world: the Magnitogorsk Works produces almost as much steel each year, sixteen million tons, as Great Britain does. But the revolutionary dream for an industrial and technological revolution that was supposed to produce a better way of life has faded.

Today Magnitogorsk finds itself in the midst of a severe housing crisis; with a municipal economy struggling to feed, clothe, and provide services for its people; with a bloated bureaucracy nevertheless unable to regulate or even measure a pervasive "second" economy; and with a population awash in alcohol and overwhelmed by lung and other respiratory diseases. Meanwhile, the development of heavy industry, the crowning achievement of the revolution, has reached a dead end: the mighty steel plant has turned into a wheezing dinosaur.

■   ■   ■

Although Magnitogorsk is a working-class town, at one time it was recognized as an international showpiece, used by Soviets and foreigners alike to demonstrate the robust health of the USSR at a time when the capitalist West was mired in the Great Depression. In fact, some of the leading Western engineering and industrial firms designed and helped build Magnitogorsk, and the city contained a sizable foreign community in the 1930s.

A special settlement called Amerikanka was created for the influx of foreign engineers and consultants. It was composed of cottages whose designs were lifted straight out of an American architectural magazine, affording the foreigners what were then unheard-of comforts: private sleeping quarters, indoor plumbing, hot water, even volleyball and tennis courts for summer recreation. Before long, however, the foreigners were asked to leave, at least in part because of a shortage of convertible currency with which to pay them. A new Soviet elite soon moved into the cozy cottages and built more, somewhat plusher ones that had gardens and were cordoned off by steel gates, so that they resembled little estates. By 1933 most foreign specialists had left Magnitogorsk, although a few hundred skilled workers remained. One of them was John Scott.

In 1932 Scott, disgusted by depression America, left the University of Wisconsin, took a welding course at the General Electric plant in Schenectady, New York, and made his way to Moscow, where, he imagined, a new world was being built. From there he was immediately dispatched to Magnitogorsk, where he lived and worked to build that new world until 1937, first as a welder and then as a chemical operator. Scott later described his Magnitogorsk experiences in a superb book, *Behind the Urals: An American Worker in Russia's City of Steel*. First published in 1943, Scott's memoir is still regarded as the classic firsthand account of daily life under Stalin.

Scott wrote his book during World War II at a time when the Wehrmacht's lightning advances into Soviet territory had been halted and what many thought would be a total Soviet defeat had come to look like an improbable Soviet victory. In *Behind the Urals* he argued that the secret to the Soviet Union's ability to withstand the Nazi onslaught lay in the experience of Stalinist industrialization: a ruthless, but ultimately necessary, crash program of building factories and training hundreds of thousands of "new" people to work in and manage them, combined with the far-seeing location of these factories in the Urals beyond enemy reach. Scott's admiration for the hardy folk he met in Magnitogorsk was eclipsed only by his awe at the genius and iron will of Stalin, whom Scott credited with conceiving and implementing this industrialization strategy.

Scott was enamored of Stalin's ability to "get the job done" but became appalled by the baffling, seemingly pointless murder of many of the country's most talented engineers and managers. After the terror of 1937 and 1938, when many people he knew to be innocent were arrested, a disillusioned Scott repudiated his Communist sympathies. In 1941 he, his Russian wife, and their two young children departed the USSR for America after a four-year struggle with Soviet authorities to secure permission for Maria Scott to leave.

During the war Scott put his considerable knowledge of Soviet industry east of the Urals to work for the Board of Economic Warfare, which, like the Office of Strategic Services, was a forerunner of the CIA. In the postwar period, the former Communist propagandist became, like many of his generation, an evangelical anti-Communist. He became involved in efforts to organize Soviet émigrés in Europe and was a founder of the anti-Communist Radio Liberty. Included among his personal papers, which were donated after his death in 1976 to the State Historical Society of Wisconsin, are memoranda he wrote in the 1950s con-

firming the alleged Communist proclivities of certain American journalists.

As an editor for Time-Life for three decades, Scott traveled extensively and wrote a number of books warning of the dangers to the
United States and Europe of the appeal to developing nations of the
Soviet Union, which offered what Scott thought to be a successful, if
costly and bloody, model of economic modernization. In addition to
encouraging U.S. involvement in developing nations, Scott spoke everywhere, from U.S. Army bases abroad to PTA meetings in rural Con-
necticut, of the need to counter the Communist menace in places such
as Vietnam.

∎   ∎   ∎

For a long time after Scott left, Magnitogorsk was officially "closed"
(even, it seems, to foreigners from socialist countries). The city was re-
opened in the early 1980s, coincidentally just after the last people had
moved out of barracks housing. But outside of a handful of industrial
consultants and managers, few foreigners chose to avail themselves of
the opportunity to go there. In the spring of 1987, as part of a ten-
month research trip to the USSR, I asked and received permission to
visit Magnitogorsk. According to local authorities, I was the first American to spend time in the city in forty-five years.

During that stay in Magnitogorsk I lived in one of those cottages in
the original American settlement, on a quiet, shady lane tucked away in
a birch grove to the north of the steelworks. Two live-in maids were
assigned to the premises. A large kitchen, a telephone, a color television
set, and other luxuries were at my disposal.

At first, as virtually no foreigners ever visited the city and no public
announcement had yet been made of my presence, there was absolutely
no reason to suspect that I was not a Soviet citizen. True, I speak Russian with an accent, but so do approximately half the people living on
Soviet territory. My anonymity was a terrific advantage, enabling me to
mix in public without rigmarole, at least for a while.

Then when word spread that a young American was in the city, everyone, it seemed, wanted to meet me and to ask me questions. People
would find me at the local archive, where I worked every weekday from
9:00 to 5:30. They would be waiting for me at the special cafeteria at
the time I usually showed up; or they would be waiting for me at night,
outside the locked gates of my five-bedroom cottage, sometimes past
midnight. The phones at whatever institution I was expected to be vis-

iting would ring nonstop. For the inhabitants of Magnitogorsk I was a unique source of information about life in the United States and in Europe and, more surprisingly, about the history of the USSR and especially of Magnitogorsk. Moreover, I brought with me certain objects that otherwise would never have been seen by most of the locals: a Japanese automatic-focus camera, a Japanese laptop computer, zip-locking plastic bags, and pictures of my life in California. In short, my popularity, in part a result of Russian hospitality and warmth, ought also to be understood as reflecting the geographical and cultural isolation in which the people of Magnitogorsk lived.

Understandably, there was great concern among my hosts at the city's Mining and Metallurgical Institute about what I might see, what I might learn, with whom I might speak, and where I might go. At most, they were accustomed to giving visitors the two-hour *pokazuka* tour (that is, a tour of model institutions and well-coached people). But here they were confronted with someone who would be staying two months and who knew the Russian language and their city well enough to function independently of their supervision. And yet, the very people supervising my stay in the city and charged with "controlling" that stay through schedules, rules, and official escorts were also worried about what I would later say to the outside world. Given these ambiguities, few officials ever figured out how best to handle me and my endless string of unprecedented entreaties.

Their twin concerns—to limit what I would see and do and to make sure I left with positive impressions—led to some hilarious and contradictory behavior on the part of officials: scolding me one minute, flattering me the next; giving me lectures on what to say in front of an audience, then granting me special access to city officials. For the most part, however, requests to visit a court, school, factory, sobering-up station, and hospital were met with extreme suspicion and interpreted as confirmation that this American visitor was interested solely in discrediting the Soviet system. With rare exceptions, all such requests were refused. Not wanting to anger my hosts, I avoided attempting to visit such institutions without an official chaperone, instead making the most of the opportunities that came my way. In the end, virtually everything I was able to see and do in 1987 came about only after prolonged struggle and maneuvering.

Once they let me in the city, the authorities could not really control me, if only because of their own people's curiosity. I was able to meet Magnitogorsk inhabitants easily, and I developed a large number of acquaintances and friends. Not all of my escorts, however, were chosen by me. The administration of the Mining Institute provided a large and varied group of people to take care of me. Some of these people were genuinely helpful. Others were far more of a hindrance, and still others pretended friendship while at the same time asking probing and inappropriate questions about my activities. All of these people, some heroically, others nefariously, performed the dual function of assisting and keeping tabs on me.

Around town there was considerable suspicion of "the American." Accusations of "spy" were commonly heard from all sorts of people, most of whom were unable to imagine how anyone "permitted" by his own government to travel abroad could *not* be a spy. Meanwhile, it soon became apparent that phones were being tapped. A number of people not on the approved "plan" who nevertheless met with me—often accidentally—were visited by the security police, questioned extensively, and usually intimidated from further contact. A few individuals who went out of their way to be friendly were sent out of the city by the authorities until the end of my stay. That police officials sought to determine whether an American on an official exchange deep in Soviet territory was a spy was, sadly, fully warranted by past experiences and known (if unacknowledged) practice.

·   ·   ·

Strange as it might now seem, I went to Magnitogorsk in 1987 with the intention not of recording its present but of studying its past. But the archives closed at 5:30, after which I had little choice but to confront the upheavals of today. The extraordinary fact that I had been granted permission to be there, and that I was witnessing something special taking place, struck me with great force. Soviet society was opening up, not only to the outside world but to itself. As busy as I was with my historical work on the Stalin era, it became impossible not to become equally caught up in what was happening under Mikhail Gorbachev.

The next year, 1987–88, while home in Berkeley, California, writing my doctoral dissertation, I applied to return to Magnitogorsk on the academic exchange for 1988–89 and was accepted. In April, almost exactly two years after my first trip, I was back. The contrast was astounding. No cottage or official friends this time; I stayed in the apartment of a Soviet family. No schedules, plans, and bureaucratic entanglements; hospitals, courts, party meetings, and, finally, the famed steel plant all opened their doors to me. My presence, far from startling anyone, became a matter of course.

During my two two-month visits to Magnitogorsk, I read almost every issue of the daily city newspaper from March 1985 until June 1989 and many other local publications. And I had the opportunity to talk to hundreds of people. The limitations of this study stem less from traditional problems with access than from deficiencies in my own energy and imagination.

My walks in the Magnitogorsk cemetery, where I saw names I recognized from my research, and my walks through the streets, where I stumbled upon old, sometimes abandoned buildings in which important events in the city's life had taken place, combined with my readings on Magnitogorsk's past to provide me with a special relationship to the city. Furthermore, the city's manageable size enabled me to become familiar with virtually the entire community in a reasonable period of time.

And yet Magnitogorsk can be difficult for an American to get a handle on. It is a place where surface is nothing and depth is everything, where the simplicity that is visible disguises the complexity underneath, where blending in is considered preferable to standing out. Most uncanny for an American, one can drop in on friends at any time, day or night, and be welcomed utterly; soon, "failure" to drop by regularly becomes a cause for reproach and jealousy, as one is suspected of having been elsewhere (it is inconceivable that a person could prefer to be alone).

As an American, I found my life in Magnitogorsk disorienting for other reasons, too. It is a city without restaurants and cafés, without take-out eateries, all-night convenience stores, or supermarkets. It is a city in which disposable diapers or food processors, not to mention personal computers, seem like artifacts of a science fictional world. It is a city in which the chances of traveling abroad are probably not much better than those of winning the lottery.

At the same time, Magnitogorsk is a working-class city without unemployment or even the fear of being laid off, without a sizable and visible underclass, without a conspicuous elite or wealthy class, or for that matter without any manifest personal wealth at all. It is a city without traffic jams and parking nightmares—indeed, there are few cars. It is a city without guns and other lethal weapons, where murder and other violent crimes are uncommon and, even more strikingly, uncelebrated events. It is a city where people do not fear walking alone at night, where children can be left to play outside without the threat of being kidnapped. Above all, it is a city with Pepsi but without the Pepsi generation, without yuppies who can have it all, without even the illusion of being able to have it all. And television plays a minor role in the lives of the people.

.   .   .

In the pages that follow I have adopted a documentary approach to telling the story of Magnitogorsk in the Gorbachev era. I am not so foolish as to think that someone from a different country, not to say a different person from America, would have written anything like the same book. By documentary I mean that through the extensive use of quotation, I have sought as much as possible to let the people of Magnitogorsk speak for themselves.

My method for gathering conversations, in addition to exhaustive reading of the local press, involved immersing myself in the society and becoming a sponge, absorbing as many different voices as Magnitogorsk had to offer. I rarely passed up one of the scores of invitations from people to join them in their homes, and I told of my life as I inquired of theirs; or, encountering people haphazardly on streets or buses, in shops or institutions, I asked questions, then wrote down almost everything that was said. Not everyone with whom I crossed paths was met randomly. Of the two dozen or so individuals I most wanted to interview, only a couple refused, and their refusals, although regrettable, did not substantially interfere with my ability to cover the issues as they suggested themselves and as I understood them.

No theme considered significant by the Magnitogorsk newspaper has been omitted from the discussion. No person interviewed by me has been left out, unless that person merely repeated what someone else had to say (this amounted to fewer than half a dozen people). Obviously, I could not include everything that everyone said, but I made sure to convey each person's principal thoughts and, if possible, his or her way of thinking.

In formal and informal settings, I spoke with the city's chief architect, his predecessor, the mayor, various party functionaries, the local priest, teachers, students, labor camp survivors, original settlers, Komsomol activists, engineers, night school students, soldiers back from Afghanistan, young writers, nearby collective farmers, old men at a retirement home, shoppers at the market, local artists and theater people, archivists, the editorial staff and reporters of the city newspaper, steelworkers, and others. In all the outpouring of news and information to the outside world on the Soviet Union under Gorbachev, these voices, the voices of the full range of society in the Russian republic, have yet to be assembled and heard together.

The juxtaposition of voices in this book reflects both what I heard and what local journalists claimed they heard. Sometimes the comments from various people made at group meetings have been used separately. Lengthy discussions with locals, all of whom were made aware of my purposes, deeply influenced my understanding of how best to present their story.

It was not possible to learn everyone's identity, but people's names, when known, are used, with certain exceptions (such as a worker quoted in chapter 1, members of his family quoted in chapter 4, and a party official quoted in chapters 3 and 5, all of whom remain anonymous). Because all quotations in the pages that follow are of conversations that I participated in or that were cited in the city newspaper, footnotes to interviews and newspaper articles have been omitted. Other notes have been kept to a minimum.

Rendering the experience of Magnitogorsk inhabitants in English posed certain challenges. The literal English equivalents for such Russian concepts as *apparatnym putem* (done in an apparat-like way), *dukhovnaia zhizn* (spiritual life), and *kommunalka* (communal apartment) fail to convey the cultural richness and the many associations of the original. Nevertheless, my practice throughout was to translate the Russian as literally as possible, making (infrequent) exceptions only for idiomatic expressions. It is my hope that any awkwardness encountered in quotations reflects a similar failing in the Russian.*

I have divided the book into six chapters: chapter 1 deals with economic *perestroika;* chapter 2, with *glasnost* (openness) or ideological change; chapter 3, with the reformation of the party and the rise of informal groups; chapter 4, with the sluggishness of change seen through the reforms' impact on everyday life; chapter 5, with the attempt to reinvigorate the reform process with competitive elections; and chapter 6, with the revival of historical memory, which, appropriately, affords a glimpse beyond the short term. Although the Soviet re-

* No method of transliterating Russian words into the Latin alphabet is entirely satisfactory. For the names of people from Magnitogorsk I have followed the Library of Congress conventions, with the exception that diacritical marks have been omitted. For the names of well-known individuals, however, I have opted for commonly used English spellings. Thus, the reader will encounter Evgenii Terletskii, but Joseph Brodsky (not Iosif Brodskii).

forms have been distinguished by their comprehensiveness, thereby giving an indication of the systemic nature of the trouble and the enormity of the tasks at hand, they proceeded in a rough sequence from ideology to economics to politics. In ordering the chapters, however, I thought it best to begin with the economy, which remains the crux. I have provided an afterword in lieu of a conclusion; a map and a select chronology of events precede the text.

The period under study is roughly that from spring 1985 until summer 1989 and the watershed Congress of People's Deputies. The congress involved the first competitive elections in the USSR since just after the October Revolution and marked an implicit switch by the Soviet leadership from reform of the Communist order to hesitant but fateful moves toward that order's transcendence. Not long after the congress, the avalanche in Eastern Europe began, thereby further clarifying the (unintended) significance of *perestroika:* termination rather than revitalization of Communist regimes. For these reasons, Gorbachev's rule constitutes a distinct historical era, even if he should eventually leave the political scene.

As they groped for an understanding of the turmoil threatening to engulf their country, the inhabitants of Magnitogorsk sometimes turned to me for information and analysis. Yet other than historical data culled from archives and libraries, everything I had to say, if not already current, soon became so as a result of the deluge of ideas and images reaching the city through the Soviet media. My presence may in certain instances have accelerated the reception of specific ideas, but a larger process with its own momentum was taking place.

To be sure, there is no substitute for face-to-face contact, but I was not the only Westerner with whom the people of Magnitogorsk had lively discussions during the period under study. In the summer of 1988 thirty-two American guides accompanied an exhibit of American life that toured Magnitogorsk for five weeks. And after May 1987, Celestine Bohlen, then a reporter for the *Washington Post,* Bill Keller of the *New York Times,* Ann Cooper of National Public Radio, Jane Corbin of the BBC, and others visited, looking for insight into the progress of Gorbachev's reforms in Stalin's city of steel.

■   ■   ■

"It is said that cities are the face of an epoch," wrote A. M. Pankov, former Magnitogorsk party secretary, in the foreword to the city's guidebook published in 1978. "Contemporary Magnitogorsk to a remarkable degree reflects the epoch of socialism." Pankov's apt comment, made at the height of Brezhnev-era confidence, remained accurate a decade later, but by then it had acquired an entirely different significance.

Five years into *perestroika* it became clear that the epoch opened by the 1917 October Revolution and consolidated by Stalin's 1929 Revolution from Above was drawing to a close, to virtually everyone's profound surprise. And just as the story of Magnitogorsk encapsulated the formative period of Stalinism, so the experience of this Soviet steeltown in the Gorbachev era reliably reflects the accelerated decomposition of that system brought on unremittingly by the efforts to mend it.

During my second stay in Magnitogorsk I was able to visit the still officially "closed" city of Cheliabinsk, the capital of the province in which Magnitogorsk is located, for three days. Although more than twice as large as Magnitogorsk, Cheliabinsk, a city of almost exclusively heavy industry, offered an excellent foil—not only physically but socially and politically—for understanding Magnitogorsk. My experience in Cheliabinsk suggested, among other things, how widespread the patterns encountered in Magnitogorsk were.

Cheliabinsk was not my only basis of comparison, however. My four months in Magnitogorsk formed part of two trips to the Soviet Union totaling sixteen months. I spent most of that time in Moscow, although in addition to the Urals I was able to visit virtually every major region of the country, including most of the fifteen national republics that rim it. Unlike what I saw in Cheliabinsk, developments among the border nationalities offered a striking contrast to what I observed in Magnitogorsk.

From the Baltic Sea to the Caucasus Mountains political movements aimed at dismantling the Soviet system rode the powerful wave of nationalism, fusing the goal of an exit from the union with that of an exit from communism. The world watched in awe as Communist party rule crumbled and independent political groups of varying orientation assumed power in Estonia, Latvia, Lithuania, Georgia, Armenia, and Azerbaijan. Similar forces were at work, although not always with quite the same goals or results, in Moldavia, the Ukraine, and Central Asia.

By contrast the largest Soviet republic, Russia, seemed far behind—until the banner of Russian nationalism was taken away in 1990 from anti-Semitic chauvinists and made a vehicle for anticommunism by the parliamentary opposition. And yet in the urbanized parts of the Russian republic, only the largest cities—Moscow, Leningrad, Sverdlovsk, Novosibirsk, and perhaps one or two others—offer a slightly different picture of the course of the Gorbachev reforms from the one presented in this book. Moreover, those differences, above all in the breakthroughs achieved by oppositional political groups, only confirm the lesson of Magnitogorsk—namely, that if the real task before the country is not restructuring the Communist system but dismantling it, alternative political structures—to say nothing of economic ones—do not automatically arise.

In this regard, superseding Communist party rule would be only a first step. Developments in Moscow, mind-boggling as they have been, carry an uncertain prospect for the resolution of Magnitogorsk's myriad problems. And these problems—obsolete industry, ecological devastation, dilapidated or nonexistent infrastructure, declining living standards, and deteriorating health—beset more than one thousand similar cities with almost one hundred million combined inhabitants. Ultimately, whatever happens in the contests for power in the capital and between the republics, the dilemmas posed by industrial cities with large working-class populations will remain, forming both the backdrop for central political struggles and a daunting stumbling block for all who would dare to lead the country out of crisis.

■   ■   ■

To witness the drama of the Gorbachev reforms as they unfolded in a medium-sized provincial industrial city in the second half of the 1980s was an astonishing opportunity, one made possible by a particularly favorable convergence of circumstances over a number of years.

This project grew out of my doctoral work in history at the University of California, Berkeley, where I had the greatest of fortunes to be trained by Reginald Zelnik, whose scholarship and professional conduct have had a profound impact on me. At Berkeley Martin Malia impressed upon me his views on the Soviet phenomenon with captivating analytical rigor during what turned out to be a three-year conversation in his office, a tradition that has been periodically revived. I am grateful for his guidance and comments on this manuscript. Ever since my 1985 visit to Columbia University's Harriman Institute, Mark von Hagen has bestowed on me not only his incomparably wide knowledge and appreciation of twentieth-century Russia but also a loving and much-needed friendship. His suggestions for the afterword were invaluable. The late Michel Foucault enthusiastically took a group of us at Berkeley under his wing, freely sharing the riches of his fertile and playful mind while always maintaining the utmost gentleness and personal modesty. More than any other, this experience continues to shape my thinking.

My travel to the USSR was funded and sponsored by the International Research and Exchanges Board, which, notwithstanding the enormous increase in demand, generously provided me with a second extended visit soon after my first. I also wish to acknowledge my gracious Soviet hosts, particularly the now defunct Ministry of Culture, Moscow State University, and the Magnitogorsk Mining and Metallurgical Institute. In between trips to the Soviet Union I received substantial financial assistance from the Social Science Research Council, from the Princeton University Committee on Research, and from the Alan Sharlin Memorial Fund and the Center for Slavic and East European Studies at the University of California. The Berkeley Slavic Center published an early essay version of this book in its occasional papers series.

Most of this book was written in the hothouse environs of the Princeton University history department. Of my many colleagues who questioned, provoked, goaded, and otherwise encouraged me in my pursuits, I owe a special debt to the following: Mark Mazower, who in exchange for reading an excruciatingly primitive draft of virtually the entire manuscript extracted the price of having me read half a dozen versions of his article about Nazi carnage in a Greek village; Arno Mayer, who taught me about twentieth-century Europe and after reading early versions of three chapters frightened me into digesting my material more; Peter Mandler, who provided frequent and indispensable counsel and comradeship as well as an intriguing intellectual parallel in his study of nineteenth-century British aristocrats adept at devising ways to cling to power in a rapidly changing world; Gyan Prakash, who could be counted on to ask poignantly disarming questions and to offer cherished computer assistance and who worked to rescue the afterword; Philip Nord, who took seriously my half-coherent ramblings about nineteenth-century Europe in the Russian mirror; and Dan Rodgers, whose mouth curled at the corners only slightly at the endless questions of a first-time assistant professor and who went out of his way to ease my arrival into the department. From the Friday morning faculty seminars to the intellectual banter and good-natured needling practiced with virtuosity in the corridors and the lounge, Dickinson Hall was a powerful stimulant indeed.

Few authors could have enjoyed greater support than I was privileged to receive from Jim Clark and Sheila Levine of the University of California Press. Their incisive editorial comments went right to the heart of the manuscript, straightening out even the order of the chapters. I also benefited from the remarks of two anonymous referees retained by the press and from the expert copyediting and assistance of Jan Kristiansson and Amy Klatzkin. Steven Forman offered helpful comments, and Kindy Kemp made a map of Magnitogorsk out of some vague and constantly shifting instructions. Joyce Howe collaborated heroically on the index.

I owe an enormous intellectual debt to Bill Keller, the *New York Times* Moscow bureau chief, whose elegantly written dispatches from the USSR, distinguished by their unprecedented range of coverage and uncanny depth of insight, permitted me to follow closely and comprehend more fully developments in the Soviet Union from a great distance. Bill applied his enviable skills to Magnitogorsk in two articles and further shared his thoughts with me in conversation.

In Magnitogorsk I encountered the assistance and goodwill of virtually an entire city, as will become evident from the text. Here I wish to acknowledge the indispensable assistance of Valerii Kucher, Viktor Shraiman, Galina Osolodkova, Oleg Vilinskii, Tatiana Leus, Nina Kondratkovskaia, Mikhail Lysenko, Vilii Bogun, Anatolii Sorokin, and the factory's photographer, Anatolii Kniazev. Volodia Mozgovoi and his two beautiful children and Zhena Terletskii and his family provided the fullest of evenings in their sparest of apartments. Most of all, Zhena and Tamara Vernikov took the unusual and risky step of inviting me into their home, asking nothing but my company in return, extending their hospitality even as they allowed me full independence. While they both spent many hours listening to my ravings, Zhena was further occupied in cajoling meetings for me over the phone. To all the people of Magnitogorsk who befriended me, I can hope only that should any of you one day duplicate my inquiry in an American town, you will meet with the same warmth and generosity of spirit I was afforded.

Lastly, my thanks to Ann Chun for her understanding and support over many years.

Select Chronology

	Soviet Union	Magnitogorsk
1917	October Revolution	
1918–20	Civil war	
1921–28	New Economic Policy	
January 1924	Death of Lenin	
1929–41	Stalin's Revolution from Above, crash industrialization	Magnitogorsk founded
1930–33	Collectivization, dekulakization, famine	Some 40,000 dispossessed kulaks arrive in Magnitogorsk
December 1934	Assassination of Leningrad party boss Sergei Kirov	
January 1935		Suicide of Magnitogorsk party boss Beso Lominadze
1937–38	Great Terror	Thousands arrested in Magnitogorsk
1941–45	Great Patriotic War	Magnitogorsk furnaces produce half the steel in the country used to manufacture tanks Magnitogorsk becomes a "closed" city
March 1953	Death of Stalin	

	Soviet Union	*Magnitogorsk*
1956	Khrushchev's "secret speech" denouncing Stalin	
1964	Khrushchev ousted	
Early 1980s		Magnitogorsk is technically "opened"
1982	Death of Brezhnev	
1984	Death of Andropov	
1985	Death of Chernenko	
March 1985	Gorbachev becomes general secretary	
April 1985	Central Committee plenum announcing new course	
June 1985	Beginning of antialcohol campaign	
February 1986	Twenty-seventh Party Congress adopts the program of *perestroika,* or "restructuring"	
Early 1986	Emergence of *glasnost:* Appointments of new editors at *Ogonek* (V. Korotich) and *Moscow News* (Y. Yakovlev) Visits by Gorbachev to unions of writers and filmmakers	
April 1986	Chernobyl nuclear disaster: pressure to extend *glasnost*	
October 1986		Article "Hotel" in Magnitogorsk newspaper
December 1986	Release of Andrei Sakharov from exile in Gorky	
Early 1987	Beginning of publication of long-banned works, such as Anatoli Rybakov's *Children of the Arbat* Release of Tengiz Abuladze's anti-Stalin film *Repentance* Laws permitting cooperatives	
April–May 1987		*Author's first trip to Magnitogorsk*

	Soviet Union	*Magnitogorsk*
June 1987	Central Committee plenum on "radical" economic reform Outpouring of criticism of command economy from intellectuals	
Summer 1987		First cooperatives begin operating in Magnitogorsk
Fall 1987		Formation of "informal" political group Counter Movement
Early 1988	Explosion of violence in Nagorno-Karabakh, predominantly Armenian enclave in Azerbaijan, springing threat of nationalist unrest on Soviet leadership	
April 1988	Geneva accords on phased withdrawal from Afghanistan	
June 1988	Nineteenth Party Conference in Moscow	
July 1988		"Information USA" exhibit in Magnitogorsk Political leaflets distributed under cover of darkness by Magnitogorsk underground movement GIMN
November 1988		Thirty-third conference of the Magnitogorsk party organization
January 1989		Riots at Magnitogorsk drying-out prison reported in city newspaper
January–May 1989	National election campaign for seats to new Congress of People's Deputies	Magnitogorsk gains four deputies
April–May 1989		*Author's second trip to Magnitogorsk*

	Soviet Union	*Magnitogorsk*
April 1989	Violent breakup of demonstration in Tblisi, Georgia	
May–June 1989	Congress of People's Deputies, gavel-to-gavel live television coverage	

■   ■   ■

June 1989	Solidarity landslide victory in Polish elections following roundtable agreement
November 1989	Berlin Wall breached
December 1989	Violent overthrow of Nicolae Ceausescu in Romania

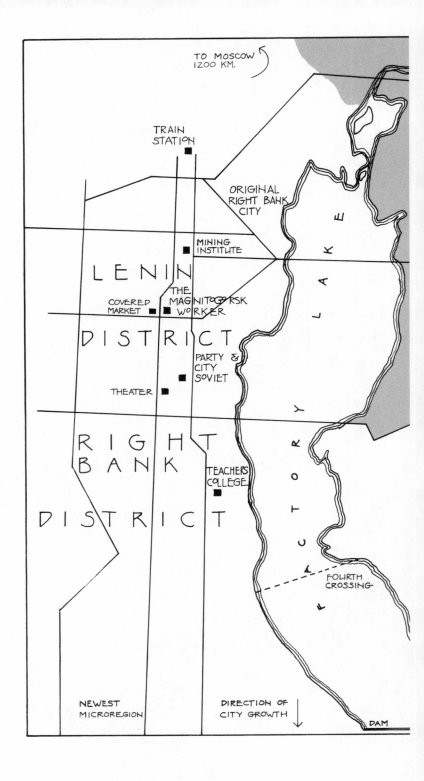

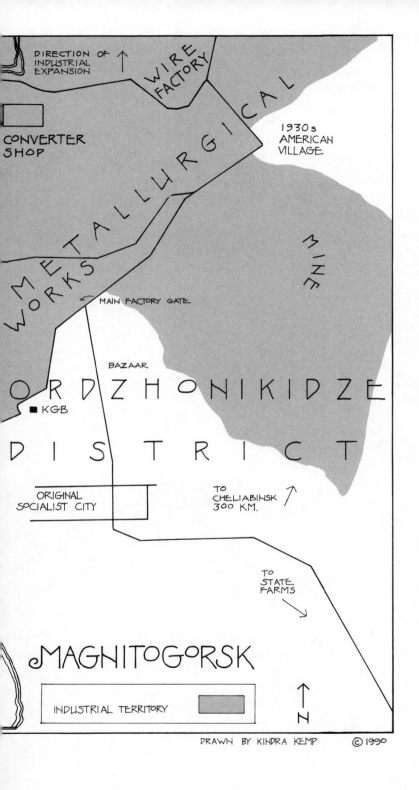

DIRECTION OF
INDUSTRIAL
EXPANSION ↑

WIRE
FACTORY

CONVERTER
SHOP

METALLURGICAL

WORKS

MAIN FACTORY GATE

1930s
AMERICAN
VILLAGE

MINE

BAZAAR

ORDZHONIKIDZE

■ KGB

DISTRICT

ORIGINAL
SOCIALIST CITY

TO
CHELIABINSK
300 KM. ↑

TO
STATE
FARMS ↘

MAGNITOGORSK

INDUSTRIAL TERRITORY	

↑
N

DRAWN BY KINDRA KEMP   © 1990

CHAPTER ONE

The Steel Cage
The Politics of Economic Restructuring

A mural depicting the heroic history of metallurgy—from its invention through its role in the defeat of the invading Nazis—stretches across the length of the main gate to the world's largest steel plant. Above the mural in giant letters is the slogan, "The Business of the Party Is the Business of the People."

Forty-three kilometers around, the Magnitogorsk Works, a dense mass of smokestacks, pipes, cranes, and railroad track, consists of 130 shops, many of which are as large as whole factories. "Steel plant" would be an inadequate description of the complex formed by an ore-crushing and ore-enriching plant, a coke and chemical by-products plant, 10 gigantic blast furnaces, 34 open-hearth ovens, and dozens of rolling and finishing mills. The Magnitogorsk Works produces more steel each year than Canada or Czechoslovakia and almost as much as Great Britain.

The metallurgical complex dominates city life in every way. The works owns apartment buildings in the city housing two hundred thousand people, eighty-five children's institutions, several hospitals, a number of nearby resort complexes, and an entire agricultural system of state farms and greenhouses in the surrounding countryside. It manages its own food service, which serves hundreds of thousands of meals a day. It owns and operates the city's mass transit system, ferrying its employees and those of every other enterprise to and from work.

1

Signs of industrialism are everywhere, from the multicolored and un-breathable air to the many young men wearing bandages or walking with a limp. The intimate connection between the factory and the city is expressed in the names of city streets and districts, while the roar and smoke and smell of steelmaking can be sensed from any part of the city twenty-four hours a day.

Magnitogorsk was built at the site of one of the country's richest and most accessible iron-ore deposits, which by virtue of its location in the Urals region lay beyond the reach of an invading army. By 1938, less than a decade after construction began, the core of the Magnitogorsk Works was in place. Further work was halted until the war necessitated abrupt expansion. Additions to the plant continued throughout the 1950s and 1960s, when by replicating itself on the basis of its 1930s design the plant doubled in size to reach its current proportions. By the early 1970s, however, the great mountain of iron ore was exhausted; "they ate it," as the locals say. The steel plant must now import iron ore from other regions. (It has always had to import its energy source, cok-ing coal.) Moreover, in the age of long-range bombers and space tech-nology, Magnitogorsk is no longer invulnerable, and it remains far from most of the markets where its products are consumed. To top it all off, there are serious problems with the plant's operation.

To be sure, Magnitogorsk supplies steel to many of the leading branches of industry in the USSR, including the military, and exports to thirty-five (almost all formerly socialist) countries. Yet although the factory seems to have no trouble maintaining or even increasing the quantity of steel it produces, recently, according to experts within the factory, it has had trouble meeting the quality standards of its custom-ers, and even greater problems are anticipated.

Ivan Romazan, the director of the Magnitogorsk Works, noted in an interview with the national Komsomol (Communist League Youth) newspaper in 1989 that "more than one-half of all fundamental equip-ment has been in use for more than thirty years." Two years earlier, Iurii Levin, deputy director for economic affairs, had been more blunt. "The factory," Levin told a correspondent for *Pravda*, "has the largest assem-blage of obsolete equipment in the country."

■   ■   ■

Nikolai Gurzhii, Magnitogorsk's director of trade, was graduated from the local Mining Institute, after which he went to work in the steel plant, where he became active in the Komsomol. Soon he moved to the city party committee bureaucracy. He spent seven years in the party's trade department and since 1980 has worked in the local soviet's trade apparatus.

"The supply for Magnitogorsk forms part of the overall plan for the Cheliabinsk region [*oblast*] drawn up in Moscow," he explained during an interview in his office. "The authorities in Cheliabinsk divide up their allocation to all cities under their jurisdiction according to the number of inhabitants of each place. Within the region there are no special designations affording privileges to a city because of its size, contrary to widespread belief. In each case the precise number of inhabitants of a locality determines its supply.

"The goods assigned to Magnitogorsk are then assigned by us to the retail networks of each of the three city districts strictly according to the size of their populations. Nevertheless, certain adjustments are made for age (districts with disproportionately old or young people require a greater supply of goods appropriate to their specific needs).

"The centralized supply system does not satisfy everyone's needs. People are not starving, they're not naked, but they're not satisfied. Here on average, we can supply 80 percent of food products (as determined by scientifically established consumption norms) and 75 percent of industrial goods. The shortfall is called our 'scarcity level' [*uroven defitsita*]."

According to Gurzhii, one could get a sense of what a "scarcity level" means by considering the availability in the city of both money and goods. "As of today," he disclosed, "savings banks in Magnitogorsk contain enough money in deposits so that people could, if they wanted to, buy up half of everything we currently possess in stores and warehouses." He conceded that the situation was even more serious if one took into account that a significant portion of the goods on hand had long languished unsold and was thus essentially dead inventory.

"At low fixed prices all desired goods are sold as they appear," Gurzhii explained. "There's nothing left on the shelves, and people hold onto large sums of money they cannot spend. Theoretically, decontrolling prices would mean that the shortages would 'disappear' because with the bidding war expected to occur, not everyone presently purchasing goods would be able to afford them. Thus, lifting price controls, with so much money available, would cause runaway inflation in the short run and severely damage the poor." He might have added that if producers proved incapable of responding adequately, devastating social dislocation would have been caused without any positive benefit.

"Meanwhile, we have nothing for a rainy day. How long would we last if suddenly all incoming supplies ceased? We do have a small reserve of industrial goods. But absolutely no food reserve. None. Forget about reserves. We currently have in Magnitogorsk 60 percent of the city's calculated need for shaving cream. Sixty percent. There's nothing in the shops, and there hasn't been for how long. What people are shaving with I'd like to know."

Much of Gurzhii's efforts were devoted to what he called "correcting the mistakes of the plan," which he did by sending his own agents around the country in search of wholesale goods. He claimed that he had developed regular commitments with several extraplan suppliers, "although 'contracts' are routinely broken." Trade in planned goods amounted to 470 million rubles in 1988; during the same year, extraplan activity reached 65 million rubles. Gurzhii emphasized that "all this is entirely up to us. We are not obliged to travel." In addition to dealmaking, Gurzhii's office, with a staff of seventeen, oversaw a city trade network with hundreds of stores and almost ten thousand employees. Although public eateries fell outside his jurisdiction, his office supplied them with milk products and investigated problems called to his attention.

One of his biggest headaches was trying to coax large local enterprises, such as the steel plant and the two separate wire factories, to produce goods not provided to the city by the central supply network. "They don't show initiative in these matters. We beg them to help us. They do not manufacture products our city needs without prodding. The pressure approach is the only one that produces results."

Even those locally produced products mandated by central plans remained largely unavailable in the city. Central directives required that more than 85 percent of output at the Magnitogorsk steel plant's sizable furniture factory be shipped out, despite the severe shortages in Magnitogorsk. The city's sewing factory, the largest in the country, turned over for local sale 2 percent of output. The city received the same 2 percent of output from the local shoe factory.

"People in trade in the West worry about how to sell goods. We are preoccupied with trying to obtain goods to sell. We travel fifteen hundred kilometers to the Belorussian republic to buy shoes made in Magnitogorsk," Gurzhii remarked, holding his head in his large hands.

■   ■   ■

Sergei Chudinov, my escort for a tour of the Magnitogorsk Works in May 1989, occupied the position of deputy secretary for ideology of the factory's party committee. In response to my barrage of probing questions before the van for the factory tour arrived, Chudinov rattled off information randomly and in an indifferent manner, pausing intermittently to allow me to catch up with my notetaking.

"Of the factory's sixty-three thousand employees," he began, "about fifty-four thousand actually work on the factory grounds. The rest can be found in the nurseries and farms owned and operated by the plant. Pay at the plant averages 310 to 330 rubles a month [about 50 percent, or 100 rubles, above the average for the city]. Blast furnace operators and steel smelters earn up to 650. Some engineers make even more. The director probably makes about 2,000.

"The plant produces some sixteen million tons of steel annually. Up to one thousand loaded rail cars a day come and go. 'Interruptions' of major raw materials—iron ore, coking coal, metal—are extremely rare. There are no problems with the quantitative supply of either water or energy. Sometimes the availability of more trivial items presents a problem. Foreign customers rarely purchase finished product like rolled steel. They are much more interested in pig iron and blooms. But the ministry severely limits what the plant may sell abroad. The metal, we are told, is needed at home.

"Consumer goods, chiefly furniture and kitchen items, account for around 2 percent of output. Soap is currently being manufactured in one of the rolling mills from oils. The state farms under our jurisdiction work a sown area of twenty thousand hectares and contain more than thirteen thousand pigs and six thousand cows. We produce twenty-five kilos of meat and ninety-six kilos of milk per worker annually. From our greenhouses we receive a large supply of vegetables, which can be seen at the lunches served in factory canteens.

"Employees can buy all the meat they can afford on factory territory. The same goes for butter. Through the trade union organization between ten thousand and twelve thousand places are available each year at summer camps for employees' children. Not all summer camps are the same, however. It's pretty much impossible to get a spot at one of the plant's preferred lakeside bungalows during the summer. Any other time of year, there's no problem. The number of trips abroad has been declining. This year there are 230 to 250 twelve-day trips to socialist countries for the whole plant. For those lucky enough to get one, the trade union pays 70 percent of the cost. The number of trips to capitalist countries is too small to mention."

When I asked Chudinov to name the biggest problems at the plant today, he responded immediately. "There are two. One, the difference between the conditions of work and the pay for it. Either we sharply improve conditions, or we sharply raise pay." Were workers complaining? "People are posing very sharp questions," he let out, smiling and shaking his head. "This did not happen before. Previously, it would have been considered a revolt."

The other issue he singled out was the environment. "This is problem number one," Chudinov said, suddenly getting extremely serious. "With the existing equipment, either you stop production or you destroy the air. That's the situation. And you have the plan and bonuses to consider. That's why they violate the directives about reducing pollution. The solution is related to the reconstruction." Reconstruction of the plant, he added, would cost an estimated 3.5 billion rubles and take until the year 2000.

The factory's party organization boasted almost nine thousand members and candidate members, only eighty of whom, including Chudinov, sat on the party committee. Yet far from seeing himself as a member of a privileged group, Chudinov at first expressed ambivalence about his status. He had worked two years as a shop boss, a job he said he preferred. "As a shop boss you see the results of your work; the metal is packed up and shipped out," he explained. "It's easier to do your job. Sometimes with party work, you wonder whether if you weren't there, anything would be different."

But he was there, along with the rest of the large factory party organization. After a moment of reflection, he added that "we [party workers] definitely do some good. When a shop goes to pieces, it's always because 'they stopped working with people,' as we say. Discipline falls, and so on. I guess party workers are like sociologists and psychologists. We work with people. It's much harder, however." The van arrived.

■   ■   ■

The city soviet's trade agency had a special market department with six employees who oversaw the city's two "peasant" markets: a highly organized indoor market on the right bank, selling food grown on private plots, and an outdoor bazaar on the left bank, selling anything and everything. Prices at both markets were allowed to fluctuate in response to supply and demand.

A trip to the bazaar revealed a large selection of high-quality boots, coats, and shoes; sporting goods; windshield wipers, gaskets, whole carburetors, even a fleet of uncannily well-preserved secondhand automobiles. Prices, however, were significantly higher than in state stores.

"People constantly come to us to complain of high prices," Nikolai Gurzhii acknowledged. "But the only way to influence prices at the markets is to sell more goods through state stores or [state] cooperative trade (which accounts for only 4 million rubles out of nearly 500 million total sales), where prices fall between those in state stores and those at the free markets. If we tried to mandate lower prices, people would stop producing, and prices for the remaining goods would climb still higher."

At the right-bank food market, he continued, "we can ask for the documents of anyone selling something, inquire where the food came from, establish that the person selling food grew it himself. But that's it. As for the other market, anyone can legally sell his or her own property, either at secondhand stores (which may take up to 7 percent commission) or at the left-bank flea market. It is illegal to sell new products at markets that are not self-made. Anything you yourself produce you can sell at whatever price you can get. But you must actually have produced the entire good. If you buy a t-shirt at a state store, affix a picture of Michael Jackson, and sell the shirt for five times what you paid, this is speculation. The product was not entirely self-produced."

．　　．　　．

Assaulted by a rush of swirling smoke and deafening noise, I, a first-time visitor to the Magnitogorsk Works, worriedly asked what had happened. Had there been an explosion? "No," I was told matter-of-factly, "we're fulfilling the plan." Although the fact that the steel plant is operating can be verified from anywhere in the city, the factory gates symbolize a divide in the consciousness of those who have witnessed steelmaking firsthand and those who have heard about it but through no lack of effort cannot really imagine what it is like—until at last they set eyes on it.

Crossing the gate is like entering the bowels of a huge animal. A thick webbing of pipes crisscrosses above one's head. Dark, heavy smoke circles between the pipes. Even out in open space, it is impossible to see the sky. A forest of tall structures, rising to heights of one hundred meters, overwhelms a mere human. Below lie graveyards of discarded metal, piled up accidentally yet in such a way that they seem to form suggestive shapes. Breathing becomes extremely difficult, so concentrated is the smoke, so noxious the chemical stench.

Inside blast furnace no. 10 flames shoot up into the air. Drafts of heavy smoke blow intermittently. Orange rivers of pig iron flow through canals, directed by metal rods held by human figures wrapped from head to toe in heavy clothing drenched in soot. The temperature of the rushing orange lava reaches sixteen hundred degrees Celsius. Heated air moves up and down in waves, producing a surreal view. The brightness and temperature make it possible to stand there observing only for a few seconds at a time. Much closer to the heat, the workers put in eight-hour shifts. The sea of hot iron surges into seventy-ton ladles that carry it away. The cascading metal is so hot that it sustains a permanent fire on top. Sparks flow continuously into the air in a kind of mock holiday display. After the entire process is finished, the canals are cleaned. Within two hours, it starts up again.

Open-hearth shop no. 1 by itself produces almost eight million tons of steel a year—an incredible figure made more believable by the ear-shattering noise, which makes it virtually impossible to hear this information. Electric cranes drag along tracks running from one end to the other of the aircraft-hangar-sized shop, pausing to push metal into roaring furnaces. Open hearths permit the worker to "look" inside and regulate the steelmaking process as it unfolds. In this way the worker can attempt to assert control over the chemical content of the steel and hence influence its quality. Yet twenty meters from the furnace it seems barely possible to endure the heat. Although summers are hot in Magnitogorsk, conditions in the shop improve considerably. The glass covering the structure housing the equipment is removed, opening it up to the sky and allowing for ventilation.

Between shops there was time for more questions. Could it be very safe to work here? Without hesitation Chudinov ticked off the following grim figures: "In 1987 there were fourteen deaths at the Works; in 1988, around ten; five months into 1989, there have been three." How long did people last in such conditions? "Some work twenty-five, thirty years. They cough and wheeze, spit out black gobs. They're special people, strong folk. Everyone knows who they are."

∎   ∎   ∎

Gurzhii took a deep breath and let out a sigh. "Here no one is interested in producing. We see what goes on abroad. They do whatever they want; they produce like crazy. On the other hand, we 'do everything for the people.' We build and build, and there are no goods for our people. How many decrees and proclamations? No goods, no equipment, no packaging, no containers for transporting goods. Our machine-building industry produces millions of tons of machines a year, for how many decades now? Where are they? What are they making? Try to buy even the simplest machine. It's disgraceful. Seventy years we live like this.

"At city enterprises no one is interested in his work. People don't work for their own city, but for 'Uncle.' There is no desire to do better, to produce more. We can't keep it, so why bother? This nonsensical situation applies throughout the Russian republic. In the Ukraine and the Baltic republics, there is a different system. There, local needs are satisfied first. In Russia, the center is not interested in our problems.

"We go to the manufacturers, show them our needs. They claim they can't help us. They don't have the resources, don't have the personnel, don't have the technology. Maybe not this year, okay, we'll wait until next year. Not next year either. They offer us no prospects. It's hopeless. How can it be that we have needs and yet no producer is in a position to fulfill them?

"It's no use appealing to the central trade authorities. The whole process usually culminates in one of their 'studies of demand.' They then include this in the reports of their work and receive bonuses for it! Our sewing factory is plastered over with posters of outstanding workers; you can't buy an article of clothing in our stores.

"We torture employees in trade. Their situation is intolerable. They work like animals, all the while cursed and denounced. They receive the lowest pay, they work all by hand, without proper technology, and they suffer nothing but abuse. What is this?

"Why do the planners punish people in trade? They give us a plan for 100 percent of consumption norms, yet we get goods for only 75 percent. Of course we can't meet the plan. We lose our bonuses. Public opinion is aroused against us. Isn't this real wrecking? The planners are economists. They know the consequences of their actions. If there are no goods, there will be no trade. You don't have to be a genius to figure it out. Yet for seven years in a row we have been given a plan that we could not under any circumstances fulfill. What the hell kind of plans are they throwing in our faces? Who benefits from this?

"All of this is offensive. War has been declared against all of this, but they do not allow us to work. The USSR Ministry of Trade, the Russian republic Ministry of Trade, the Cheliabinsk Regional Trade Management—they don't actually 'trade' anything. All they do is get in the way, hinder us, load us with inane regulations and contradictory orders. They gave us independence in law, but in practice they take it away. We are forced to comply with their orders; we are under their domination. If we resist, they fight us through their control over the banks; they withhold money, etc.

"I get a huge package of documents from the higher authorities every day. Just to read them takes up half my day and ruins my mood. I often spend the rest of the day filing official complaints to the trade authorities about themselves. They passed a law prohibiting us from going to Moscow to the ministry to try to solve our problems. Now we can do it only at our own expense, which we do. Then they ask us why we did not ask them for permission to come! But we paid for the trip!

"I need to go all the time to bang the table, both to Moscow and to Cheliabinsk, where they do absolutely nothing, aside from piling up paper. There are in fact three steps—the Cheliabinsk Regional Trade Ministry, the Russian republic Trade Ministry, and the USSR Trade Ministry—before I can get to Gosplan [the State Planning Commission]. Everyone has an apparat of thousands. I see all this with my own eyes. We could live without their flood of paper. How to disperse these ministries—that is the main problem facing the country today."

■   ■   ■

When first built in the 1930s, Magnitogorsk was hailed as one of the most modern steel plants in the world. No more. "We had some Japanese here," said Vadim, a rolling-mill worker, to a visiting American journalist in the summer of 1988. "We said, 'Tell us, how far behind are we?' They said, 'Forever. You're behind us forever.'"

Plaintive calls for the total overhaul of the Magnitogorsk plant began more than twenty-five years ago. But reconstruction was perennially postponed, and the factory was called upon to make do with what it had: shore up a bit here, patch things together there, in short, give itself a sort of artificial respiration. The factory employs many more repair workers than steel smelters.

The delay in reconstruction was not caused by ignorance of the problems or lack of proposed solutions. "There is a veritable sea of different plans," acknowledged Nikolai Panishev, professor of mining and metallurgy at the Magnitogorsk Mining Institute, in an interview in 1987. Panishev drew attention to a monograph published in the 1970s that outlined in detail the kind of reconstruction to be done. The dilemma at the plant arose more or less as a direct result of government policy. Despite the more than adequate profits for reconstruction generated by the plant, the Ministry of Ferrous Metallurgy repeatedly decided to forego the gigantic capital reinvestment required to reequip—until just recently.

A quarter century after it was first deemed urgent, large-scale reconstruction of the Magnitogorsk Works finally began with the building of a gigantic new steelmaking shop, a BOF converter, to replace the ancient open-hearth ovens. Even factory officials admitted, however, that the new converter shop, which was due to begin partial production in 1989, represented only the beginning of a long and very expensive process. A second converter was tentatively planned. Several larger and more efficient blast furnaces were envisioned to replace most of those in operation, but construction was put off. New rolling mills appeared necessary, at the very least, to replace those in operation since the 1930s.

The funds for reconstruction were to come out of the profits of the factory, part of the new policy of "self-financing." Magnitogorsk in fact was one of the first enterprises in the country to embark on reconstruction through its own financial resources, when it was put on self-financing in 1985. Nevertheless, what self-financing meant in practice remained unclear. The factory was still obliged to turn over its profits to the ministry, which then decided what percentage to return to the factory. In 1988 the factory requested to keep thirty kopecks for each ruble of its profit, but the ministry returned only fifteen. And those fifteen kopecks had to finance not only reconstruction and the building of new shops, but workers' housing, schools, medical care, the city's transport system, and so on. Factory management was livid.

A controversy over the dispute broke out in the central press in the spring of 1987. The ministry was taken to task for "starving" the plant in its hour of great need, as well as having denied for almost three decades persistent and urgent requests for reconstruction. After supplying the country with so much steel for so many years, Magnitogorsk felt cheated, the article noted. One manager divulged with considerable bitterness that "other enterprises in ferrous metallurgy receive back more than thirty kopecks per ruble of profit. In a way, we are punished for our profitability. Our profits are used to subsidize the many inefficient plants operating at a loss." Decentralization of the Soviet economic system remained no less important, in his view, than the technological reconstruction of the steel plant.

■   ■   ■

Laws permitting "individual labor activity" for certain groups of the population (retirees, students, housewives, people with disabilities) and private businesses (called "cooperatives") were issued by authorities in Moscow in late 1986 and early 1987. Significantly, an announcement in the Magnitogorsk newspaper in the spring of 1987 that a group of musicians had formed one of the city's first cooperatives, far from endorsing individual initiative, struck a threatening tone.

"The creation of a musician's cooperative will end all sources of nonworking [sic] income, which until now was accrued by so-called orchestras, crooks that played funerals," explained a city official in charge of culture. "Now," he cautioned the public, "only musicians from the cooperative are to play funerals." His words were echoed by G. A. Stekolshikov, a judge who warned that "the 'organs' were going to verify all those engaged in individual labor activities." It seemed a curious way to promote individual and collective enterprise.

A short while before, a group from one of the city's iron-cement products factories had founded Magnitogorsk's first cooperative: Obelisk, makers of gravestones. Standard metal grave markers made by state agencies predominated in the two existing city cemeteries. The cooperative members had promised not only stone but quality work at an affordable price (270 rubles).

Obelisk got off the ground relatively quickly, primarily because of the support its members received from their patron-employer, iron-cement products factory no. 1, which leased them space and equipment and provided supplies. "Not for free, of course," wrote the newspaper. "Marble, cement, metal—all at retail prices, which were twice as high as wholesale. Nevertheless, the benefits were mutual."

In sixteen months of operation, the coop produced a profit for the factory of 61,000 rubles. A further consequence of the coop's work was the reconstruction of the cemetery. Moreover, the coop's price for a gravestone had fallen from 270 to 230 rubles. Then all of a sudden, in November 1988, the iron-cement factory director, citing the pressure to meet his yearly production plan, declared that he needed the space back. According to a local journalist, however, someone at the factory overheard the director say, "Why keep a coop when you can do it yourself?"

■   ■   ■

Planning, Soviet economists readily admit, is a tricky business. For example, there are, as Boris Rumer observed in his excellent monograph on the Soviet steel industry, more than one million sizes and shapes of rolled steel required by Soviet firms.* It is impossible to predict in advance the exact proportions of each size or shape that each firm will need. Usually, a range is provided. But because every plant's performance is measured by the aggregate weight of output, a plant gets more "credit" for producing heavier strip. Unfortunately, there is a greater need for the thinner varieties.

When customers are forced to choose between the thicker strip or nothing at all, they accept the thicker variety. Perhaps they can barter the thicker strip. Most likely, they will end up machining the strip to the desired thickness. Much metal thereby goes to waste. Thus, the planning system, conceding its own limitations by suggesting a range of strip to producers, ends up encouraging production of greater quantities of metal than the planning agency itself deems necessary to meet specified needs.

Nevertheless, although a customer may be forced to shave off a significant portion of the structural metal shapes it is allocated, Soviet machines, tractors, and refrigerators are heavier than otherwise equivalent Western counterparts. A number of reasons account for this phenomenon, but a primary cause must be that the performance of machine-building firms is measured not by profits but by overall output tonnage.

Measured in gross output, the Soviet Union produces more than 20 percent of the world's steel. Yet Soviet firms, especially in the machine-building branch of the economy, ritually bemoan the desperate shortage of steel. Can the world's leading steel producer simultaneously be suffocating its steel-consuming industries?

Someone familiar with market economies might surmise, as Boris Rumer suggested, that the Soviet Union exports a significant volume of its steel. In fact, it would like to export more steel than the current pittance it does, especially for payment in hard currency, if only that steel's quality made it competitive on the world market. Perhaps in an expanding economy, demand for steel is just outstripping domestic capacity. As it turns out, however, the Soviet economy is not growing, or at least not growing very much. And in any case, intensive production, or "storming," at peak periods demonstrates that the Soviet steel industry does not operate at or near full capacity most of the time.

If neither insufficient capacity nor excessive exports explain the ostensible paradox of impressive production totals alongside a perpetual steel

* *Soviet Steel: The Challenge of Industrial Modernization* (Ithaca: Cornell University Press, 1989).

hunger, what does? The planned—or, more accurately, "command"—economy itself.

Soviet firms are not allowed to purchase steel directly from other firms. Instead, they put in "bids" for metal to the State Supply Commission (Gossnab). Because a firm knows it will receive less than it requests, the firm logically asks for more than it otherwise might need, secure in the understanding that it will not suffer for higher costs because an enterprise need not make a profit to stay in business. Gossnab tries to anticipate this upward bidding and almost always allocates less than requested, but without the lever furnished by cost, the commission invariably finds the task of disciplining enterprises impossible.

Rumer pointed out, however, that if the pressures on the demand for metal resulted simply from Gossnab's ignorance of real production needs, the problem could perhaps be alleviated. But firms experience repeated interruptions in the supply of even the metal they have been allocated. Naturally, they seek to insure themselves against potential disruptions by maintaining "reserves." Together with the absence of cost considerations, the operation of the central allocation system thus creates an unlimited demand for metal.

To buttress the point, Rumer cited an investigation undertaken during 1981 and 1982 of three hundred industrial enterprises in Moscow, all of which were found to have large metal reserves. The authors of the published investigation asserted that "stockpiling" at some plants had created artificial shortages at others. In fact, the investigators failed to find a single plant where shortages existed. Instead, reserves at all plants were found to be accumulating from year to year, thereby putting great stress on already inadequate storage facilities. Often supposedly scarce metal was simply "stored" outside in huge, undifferentiated heaps, where it naturally rusted.

■   ■   ■

Cooperatives in Magnitogorsk have no better friend than the city newspaper, which has conducted a vigorous campaign on their behalf. "They appeared according to the laws of social reality," the newspaper wrote in a long article on coops in 1988. "They will aid the state, do what the state cannot do. They are not only economically but socially beneficial, raising people's initiative and independence. True, some of this activity took place earlier, but now it has become lawful. Thus, consumers will be protected, illegal activities and speculation will be ended, and taxes will be paid."

All the same, letters demanding the immediate closing of the cooperatives deluged the newspaper. "It's no secret," wrote one person, "that under the guise of cooperation assembled those who for a long time before the birth of coops lived on unearned income, engaging in speculation and black marketeering. Coops are equally unseemly. And they gouge. Who needs these profiteers?"

M. N. Afanaseva wrote an anguished letter denouncing coops. "What will these cooperatives bring? . . . We have small pensions, we are not included in the group of war invalids, and so we do not have their privileges, as if we are guilty for coming out of the battles whole. What's more insulting—we fought, we worked without respite, and what do we have to show for it? Can you compare our income with coops? . . .

"Recently I observed how strong men, twenty-five to thirty-five years old, trade in watermelons. I inquired how much they pull in for a day's 'work' in the fresh air, not having to swallow the dust and smoke of the factory shops. 'To hell with you and your open hearths and blast furnaces,' one openly answered. 'What does one make there? Here I'll sell something, the boss'll come by, and out of the receipts he gives me fifty rubles cash.' " Afanaseva claimed she waited until the end of the day and "sure enough, he got his money.

"So I began to wonder, who will take the place of today's cadres at the works if everyone flees to sell watermelons? Youth today are literate. Do they want to swallow smoke for peanuts? And what about us, with our miserly pensions, if coops gouge for everything? How can our powerful and rich motherland allow them to mock honest, working [sic] labor?" Added the reporter: "She is far from alone in her opinions."

Indeed, conversations overheard by that same reporter at the left-bank flea market indicated considerable displeasure:

"How much are the jeans? What? You get that kind of money? You don't want to stand at the bench; you don't know how such money is really made."

"Aren't you ashamed to charge that much for a rag? Did you sew it yourself? You could pull a plow and yet you sit behind a sewing machine like a broad."

"They untied the hands of these privateers, and now they dream about Rockefeller. They live off us."

The newspaper tried to reason with its readership, pointing out that "coops pay the state a fee to rent a space at the market. They are assessed charges for utilities. As for raw materials, they must search high and low, rummaging through what state enterprises throw away. This waste they turn into useful items. All these factors go into the price. If you don't like the price, don't buy!" To consumers with few options, such words are insulting.

Special blame for harassing the coops was assigned by the newspaper to the city bureaucracy, which "remains unwilling to make available its own retail facilities. Instead, it smothers coops in paperwork." Members of the tilemaking coop Mozaika (Mosaic) complained bitterly of having to fill out innumerable forms and obtain endless stamps and signatures. "They cannot alter any product or service without forms and permission; plus there's a negative mood against them."

Notwithstanding those obstacles, prices for cooperative goods were already dropping, the newspaper asserted, and their quality was high. "Take the example of this pair of pants here. Isn't this what we dreamed of? Fashionable pants, and quality, too? But instead, we call these people 'new Nepmen,'* hunters after big money. If only everyone who said such things was rounding up junk and turning it into usable consumer goods! All our problems would be solved!"

■   ■   ■

Not simply the country's largest producer of steel, the Magnitogorsk Works was the most profitable enterprise in the ferrous metallurgy branch of the national economy. In 1988 the enterprise was officially 800 million rubles in the black. In 1989 operating profits topped 1 billion.

Nevertheless, in a command economy it is nearly impossible to determine a firm's "actual" profitability. Price controls on key raw materials and transport subsidies mean that, say, a steel mill, especially a remote one, benefits from state-set lower costs. (Magnitogorsk received seven hundred wagon loads of coal a day, many from as far away as two thousand kilometers, and almost an equal number filled with iron ore.) At the same time, however, the plant provided its workers with low-priced lunches and operated extensive day-care and resort facilities at a loss. What was most critical, a market system might come up with a price lower than the one set by the ministry for Magnitogorsk steel—if

---

* Nepmen is a derogatory term for the postrevolutionary "bourgeoisie" that purportedly arose in the 1920s as a result of the so-called New Economic Policy (NEP), under which certain types of private trade were made legal again.

any of its customers, given a choice of imported steel, would still buy from Magnitogorsk.

No one knew how much of Magnitogorsk's yearly output of sixteen million tons of steel represented its own defective output sent back a second time through the steelmaking process. What became clear was that much steel whose quality was considerably below the modest parameters set by planners was being shipped, becoming defective inputs in the machine-building industry, which in turn manufactured defective machines . . . designed to make more steel. Yet what looks like "production for production's sake" might as well be termed "production for employment's sake." To produce sixteen million tons of steel, the Magnitogorsk Works employed more than sixty thousand workers. By comparison, the USX plant in Gary, Indiana, the most modern, large, integrated American mill, produced eight million tons with seven thousand workers.

Not all of the enormous difference in work force size should be attributed to lower productivity, however. Part of the reason for the bloated work force at the Magnitogorsk Works derived from the fact that deficiencies in the central allocation system led the plant to devote substantial internal resources to the manufacture of machines, tools, and spare parts indispensable to the plant's operation. Similarly, a huge supply of workers had to be kept to cope with the strains on outmoded and overtaxed equipment. Moreover, the rhythms of industrial activity were such that an enterprise had to retain a padded work force year round to be able to "storm" at the end of production periods to meet draconian plan targets—the contingency upon which everyone's fate at a plant hung.

Demanding ever more workers, the steel plant, located in a city with a birthrate that had been declining for years, found itself incapable even of keeping pace with retirements. Inmigration was never sufficient to make up the difference. Much of the factory's reconstruction and related work was being carried out by several thousand Polish workers "on loan" from Nowa Huta, the Soviet-inspired steel complex near Cracow. Meanwhile, recruitment pitches could be seen all around town.

Like all large Soviet enterprises, the Magnitogorsk plant promised a recruit not only a secure monthly wage but medical care, housing, and subsidized leisure in the form of theaters, movie houses, sport clubs, and resorts—regardless of the profit margins, in good times and bad. Moreover, the steel plant's shops, in the words of one factory official, were "not simply places to work but communities through which not just housing but furniture are distributed. Workers vacation, not with spouses, but with co-workers."

An individual established himself or herself in the community not by purchasing a home in a particular neighborhood but by landing a job in a favored shop. "The shop or work unit is an entire social milieu," the official explained. "It's not a job, but a life." In short, the steel plant was not really a "business"; rather, it was an industrial welfare agency.

■　　■　　■

Lider (Leader), a sewing cooperative, was made up of twenty-one people, most of them former housewives. They made clothing sold wholesale to the state trade network. Unfortunately, they lamented, the local authorities had begun "detaining" payment. "So now we sell in Moscow," one woman remarked. "We get paid right away, and we get more money." The coop claimed a total value of production for the first quarter of 1989 of 100,000 rubles.

"We hunted and found a decrepit basement that was always under water; otherwise it was absolutely empty," explained the coop chairman. "We went to the sewing factory for equipment. At first, we rented. Then we purchased some. They sold us only machines that did not work. We had to fix them ourselves. If the factory director had not been well disposed to us, we could not have gotten off the ground. There was nowhere else to obtain equipment.

"It was very hard at first. We had no money, no experience. We bought a manual from a Baltic coop on how to organize and run a business. A 195 ruble investment. We're grateful. The state puts out nothing, and we can't buy foreign materials.

"Our biggest headache is raw materials. We know the stuff just lies in state warehouses as dead inventory. They don't do anything with it, but they can't (or refuse to) sell it to us. We go through hell to pick up what we can. There are millions of stupid rules." The coop chairman himself often worked at a sewing machine. An educated man, he recalled that he had been in line for a desk job with a title. "I left to form the coop. It's interesting work. There's room for initiative. It's just here they don't like businesspeople very much."

BIS, one of the first coops formed in the city, consisted of four young expert radio mechanics who had known each other a long time. They put forward a proposal in April 1987 to repair radios and hi-fi equipment. Approval by the city soviet came three months later.

After obtaining state approval, BIS rented a single room from a state firm, in which the members put down a floor and created a small storage closet. "To get a space you must hook on with an existing enterprise," one explained during a visit. "But they are not interested. What's in it for them? In fact, when you think about it, we are their competitors."

Refusing to apply for a loan from the state-controlled bank, each member contributed a small stockpile of spare parts and junk radios and then set out for more than a month to roam the country in search of more. "We really had to scrape and hustle to find supplies to open up the business," one member recalled. "We had hoped to produce our own finished products," another explained, "but it was too tough to obtain the parts on a continual basis. So we stuck to repair work. We do TVs also.

"Twenty rubles for a TV, fifteen for a radio—those are our rates, independent of the amount of work necessary. We promise service within one week. If you want it done faster, you pay slightly more. We offer a three-month guarantee on parts and labor: whatever goes wrong, we'll refix it free of charge.

"Sometimes we must refuse an item for repair, especially if it's very old. Often, it's just not worth fixing, or it can't be fixed. Owners often get angry. 'You're supposed to fix it,' they say. 'Twenty rubles.' What they bring in—you can't believe your eyes.

"We often improve on the technology of Soviet-made equipment during the course of repairs. Our hardest job is repairing Japanese and West German stereos with Soviet parts. There's no alternative.

"Our first year we worked seven days, fourteen hours a day. It's grueling work, but we all prefer it. We're the same age, share similar views, work together. There's no one hanging over you. You don't work to feed superfluous people. No one tells you what to do.

"We want to form our own trade union, organize payments for health care, put together a retirement plan. Now we make three hundred rubles a month salary and another one hundred ruble dividend from profits. Not much, but it's something. It's just we have no freedom. I have the money but I can't buy soap. I've saved; I want to travel abroad. It's not possible—no foreign currency.

"We did fifty thousand rubles' worth of business last year and expect to do the same this year. We're small. Of course, we have dreams. We want to expand, do bigger jobs. But we're concerned. We're not sure of the situation. The laws have changed a couple of times already. We used to pay 5 percent tax; now it's 30. Who can predict what will happen?

We're much more afraid of the Ministry of Finance than of any racketeers." If there was any extortion or money laundering associated with cooperatives going on in Magnitogorsk, he suggested without elaborating, it was not being done by racketeers.

■   ■   ■

No part of a Soviet factory is more lively than the supply department. One afternoon while I was seated in the office of Iosif Susel, the chief of supply for the Magnitogorsk wire factory, the phone rang incessantly. The factory's customers throughout the country were calling to learn of the status of their orders.

Iosif assured everyone that the goods would be on their way, soon. And before he let anyone off the line, he ran down a laundry list of goods and supplies needed by his own factory. Almost all conversations ended with the words, "I see, I see, well, we wouldn't be against you sending us a wagon load of such-and-such, sure, I understand, ball bearings. Don't work too hard. Speak to you soon."

In twenty minutes, Susel closed half a dozen deals. In such a way the wire factory fulfilled its plan. The fruits of his labor could be seen not only in the shops but in factory canteens and workers' apartments. Little of this activity was legal. "Sure he does it," remarked Mikhail Lysenko, Magnitogorsk's mayor, shrugging his shoulders and extending his hands outward when told of Susel's wheeling and dealing. "Romazan does it. They all do it. But technically speaking, it's hooliganism."

■   ■   ■

Zhest (Gesture), a Magnitogorsk cooperative opened for operation in 1988 as a subsidiary of the firm Garant (a short form of Garantiia, or Guarantee), headquartered in Cheliabinsk, specialized in scrap metal. "There's an almost unlimited market," explained Ivan Agalakov, a former employee of the Ministry of the Interior and the coop's chairman. "We help everyone fulfill their plan.

"We buy all the metal we can get our hands on, rework most of it so it's usable, and then sell it to thirsty enterprises. We've also branched out into catering. We bring in food to enterprises for employees, so they have something to eat and don't waste a lot of time looking. Our coop also provides assistance to firms with transportation problems. Where there's a need, we find and satisfy it.

"We just leased the entire local shop of Garant. They gave us a free hand. We retained all the workers but got rid of most of management. Everyone began working longer hours; now there's two shifts and work on weekends. We abolished the shopwide hour-long lunch break. Workers lunch in shifts so the shop stays in operation. Wages went up, but productivity rose much faster.

"In eight months in 1988, on revenues of 1.7 million, we turned 473,000 rubles profit for Garant. We're now the top shop in this branch of industry in the entire province. This year our revenues may top 4 million, and all profit above 473,000 rubles we keep. We also leased another enterprise for 1,000 rubles a month. We have so much metal, we want to begin manufacturing consumer goods.

"But there's a lot of mistrust. The big steel plant had a problem. They didn't have enough good scrap for the open hearth. We offered our services. Of course, our own costs compel us to charge more than the state-set price for scrap, but hey, that's business. Management refused to buy from us. Never mind that their furnace went idle. I brought in our books. I showed them our costs.

"The state price for scrap is 12.80 rubles a ton. They're educated men. They know we can't provide scrap at that price, yet they claimed they couldn't find a legal way to pay for the difference between the state price and ours [about double]. So we sold the lot to an eager firm in nearby Bashkiria.

"Recently, we bought an old, unused steamer as part of our plan to organize a little leisure on our own Ural River. The market is there: a cruise, some music by a band, a little fishing, even weddings. We'd clean up, and people would kill to get such a service. But the local authorities are dragging their feet. They're scared out of their minds by such new initiatives. State firms pay six kopecks a liter for fuel. They want to charge me thirty. I can't stomach it when people curse coops for putting the squeeze on. Who's doing the squeezing?

"I know the boat idea will take off, but still I worry about sinking money into it. What kind of taxes can I anticipate? What kinds of rules and stipulations are they going to attach? If you want to know, we have no faith in tomorrow. They might just take away your business. What's to stop them?"

▪   ▪   ▪

"Speculation" is one of the nastiest words in the Soviet vocabulary. Lately, it's been applied with particular enmity to the large contingent of Polish *Gastarbeiter*. Nikolai Gurzhii explained the situation.

"We are obliged to provide the visiting Poles with 100 percent of norms (not just the 75 or 80 percent we do for our own people). Moreover, the Poles earn an average of five hundred rubles a month, and they cannot take them home with them. They must spend all their rubles here. Thus, they buy up anything they can then resell back home in Poland: items such as refrigerators, television sets, electrical equipment, dishes, glasses, and so on. They empty the stores here, and they even complain that there are no goods for them to buy with all their money." This spending had not created the shortages of such goods in Magnitogorsk, Gurzhii pointed out, but neither had it helped matters.

As for the Poles, whom he did not blame for their purchasing zeal, "there is another side to their presence here. They bring in lots of goods from Poland to sell in Magnitogorsk, especially cosmetics and perfume, some of which have been imported into Poland. And they bring them here in large quantities, wholesale-size allotments." At this point, he lifted his head for emphasis, adding that "for some reason our customs agents allow this." The Poles then offered the highly desired goods to the commission stores, which were dutybound to accept them. "We receive numerous complaints that this is speculation," stated Gurzhii. "But it's out of our hands."

Faced with such indignities, beleaguered Magnitogorsk consumers, under the auspices of the city newspaper, formed the Society for the Defense of Consumers' Rights in the spring of 1989. Two dozen men and women, frustrated, angry, but determined to take a stand, participated in a roundtable discussion. "Lately we speak a great deal about a law-based state," the newspaper wrote in announcing the new group. "This is no accident, for many of us hit up against the absence of rights literally every step of the way. Perhaps the people with the greatest absence of rights are consumers. One after the other goods that are necessities disappear from the shelves. . . . And the most pathetic thing of all, the consumer has absolutely no way to influence the process."

Suggestions were many: perform laboratory tests on products to uncover poor quality; for rude behavior, rather than take away a salesclerk's bonus, send "her" to a course on proper etiquette; boycott the products of the city's lone meat factory until the sausage quality improved. When one person recommended introducing more laws to guarantee product protection, a lawyer in the group pointed out that many such laws already existed, with little effect.

"What will we be able to do in Magnitogorsk?" asked M. Beliaev, a pensioner, who wondered if forming a consumer society was not a little premature. "In Moscow it is easier. There, in the last analysis, you can approach the ministry. Out here whose door can we knock on?" Others were resolute, however, and launched the "voluntary" organization dedicated to "defending the rights and interests of consumers," in the words of the published charter. The detailed document, specifying the rights and duties of members, dues payments, and organizational structure, in many ways resembled the charter of the Communist party. What effect the new "union" could have in protecting consumers remained unclear.

•   ■   •

Perestroika entailed, along with the creation of a small cooperative sector, a series of major reforms of the all-important state sector. For the first several months of 1987 the Magnitogorsk Works buzzed with talk of the new inspection agency, Gospriemka, the creation of which was the first in a series of measures aimed at reforming the centrally controlled economic system.

Granted far-reaching powers to improve the quality of industrial goods, the controllers of Gospriemka encountered a storm of protest when rejection of poor quality output threatened to lower gross production totals and thereby reduce bonuses. "They come in all high and mighty and tell us our metal is no good, that's it, no bonuses," one steelworker remarked in an interview in 1989. "Do they give us new equipment? Do they give us quality iron ore to work with? Do they ease up on the plan targets? They're bloodsuckers. One more layer of bloodsuckers for us to feed."

By midyear, attention had shifted from Gospriemka, which was quietly phased out, to the new Law on State Enterprises, issued in June 1987. The law redefined the relationship between enterprises and ministries and allowed enterprises what looked on paper like more independence. But Magnitogorsk managers quickly learned that the new law meant something different in practice.

"Soon we figured it out," one high-level manager recalled. "They 'eliminated' the imposed plan targets and gave us 'state orders' instead. These were supposed to be lucrative for us, and they would allow some room for taking other customers' orders. Yet we were not permitted to compete for more desirable orders or to decline those suggested to us. And we received compulsory state orders for what amounted to almost 100 percent of our production capacity. What state orders? It was the same Gosplan chokehold. In fact, if you want to know, Gosplan has grown even stronger because the need to deal with more and more shortages requires greater and greater crisis management."

Then, beginning in January 1988, the steel plant went on full *khozraschet,* Lenin's term for profit and loss considerations at enterprises in a nationalized economy. A Magnitogorsk factory official explained the new practice to a reporter: "Earlier, the factory paid penalties for failing to supply customers' orders, for unauthorized changes in the type of product delivered, or for poor-quality goods out of gross revenues calculated before they were sent to the state budget. Thus, since it was the state's money that was 'lost,' no one paid much attention to the fines. Now penalties come out of that part of the profit the plant is allowed to keep. Penalties for the first eleven months of 1987 amounted to 17 million rubles. One nine-story apartment building costs us 1.23 million rubles. This is what *khozraschet,* the 'holiest of the holy,' is all about."

At the same time, however, said the official, the ministry pressured the plant into putting forth a "counterplan" for 1988 production above Gosplan targets. "Such a squeeze for quantity will lead to great waste and thus heavy penalties. They put us on *khozraschet* and say we can keep some profits, but then they force more production out of us. The ministry does not want to let the plant out of its control." Like its predecessors Gospriemka and the Law on State Enterprises, *khozraschet* failed to raise quality either directly or indirectly (by granting greater independence and flexibility to factories).

One might wonder if anything had changed in Magnitogorsk as a result of the reforms of the economic system. Opinions varied. "The struggle with the ministry has come out into the open, and factory management has been emboldened by the new candor to press its case forcefully," contended Evgenii Vernikov, managing editor of the city newspaper. "Before, no one would ever have dared to challenge the ministry, let alone do so in public."

Nikolai Kuklinov, party secretary for the city's principal industrial district, had a different answer. "The main new factor is the steep decline in industrial discipline. That's what *perestroika* has brought. It's harder and harder to coax people into working. Meanwhile, the battle with the ministry occupies the front pages." Factory managers echoed Kuklinov's remarks, adding that the ministries had become even stronger.

■   ■   ■

In February 1988 the newspaper reported that the newly opened dental coop, Ulybka (Smile), was moving to a facility at the wire factory, which had also agreed to buy equipment for the coop. But at the end of the year a new cooperative law categorically outlawed health-related cooperatives. Barely off the ground, Ulybka closed up shop.

In response to a general feeling of insecurity exacerbated by the closings mandated by the December 1988 modification of the cooperative law, Anatolii Sorokin, chairman of a small cooperative, led a successful movement to found a local union of cooperatives. During a series of interviews in May 1989, Sorokin explained that in November 1988 a group of coop chairmen from Magnitogorsk went as observers to a provincial coop conference in Cheliabinsk. When they came back to Magnitogorsk, they gathered representatives from sixty-five of the city's cooperatives into a union, the December "ambush" providing the final push. "Not all coops in the city supported the move," acknowledged Sorokin, who was elected chairman, "but now that the union has been formed, our relations with local soviet authorities have improved."

Sorokin claimed that the union hoped to organize classes for bookkeeping, "one of the most poorly understood and underrated aspects of business. We want eventually to be able to help members with the supply of raw materials and equipment, produce or at least distribute product catalogues . . . for ideas. We're opposed in all this by the coop 'manager.' These people offer business consultation and training for a fee. We think this is valuable, but it ought to be done under the union, in a more societal orientation, rather than solely for economic gain."

According to Sorokin, as of May 1989 Magnitogorsk had "220 registered coops, 60 percent functional, but not a single truly powerful one." By his count only a dozen or so coops actually "stand on their own feet." These coops did everything from reworking defective metal discarded by the steel plant to repairing television sets and aiding in apartment swaps. "In the food industry, no one has been so successful. They're just not very stable. Recently, Shashlyk, a small eatery, was shut down. There were numerous violations of tax laws. A number of other ventures have also been forced to close.

"There are so many people interested, but those who really work are few. Many get involved and then leave. They want money, but they don't want to work. They're shocked to discover what's involved in building a business. Meanwhile, people on the street curse those of us who stick it out. As soon as you tell someone you work in a coop, an abyss opens up. You become like a leper.

"There's no competition yet among coops, but there is plenty between coops and state enterprises. State enterprises have begun to reevaluate the question, Why should they provide space, raw materials, and equipment to coops that will produce better quality products at less cost? But from the point of view of coops, it's very difficult to compete with state enterprises, given their size, resources, and official position.

"We pay taxes: 2 percent the first year of operation, 4 percent the second. Then this year the laws changed. Our assessment jumped to 35 percent across the board. It's crazy. We need legal representation, legal guarantees. Taxes have to be assessed so as to encourage business, not smother it.

"We're regulated. There's a set of rules and regulations. You have to have a certain assortment of goods, for example. It doesn't seem to matter whether anyone wants to buy the full range; you must stock what the authorities think a business with your profile should stock. And you can't sell goods that cost more than one hundred rubles, regardless of what it costs to make them or whether people are willing to pay such prices. To tell you the truth, the rules are awfully stupid.

"And they keep proliferating. Now if a coop buys raw materials at state prices, it must sell finished products at state prices, notwithstanding any additional work or improvements that might be made on the design. Such rules simply kill one's desire to work. It's just these kinds of things that wiped out the supply of goods from the state stores in the first place. It's hard to believe, but they're doing it again."

■   ■   ■

"We still have to beg them for what we get," Mayor Mikhail Lysenko complained of central authorities. "For decades we waited for a fourth crossing over the Ural River to our most populous district. Now with the converter, we're finally getting the crossing. But we also need water. The city is out of water. I screamed and carried on, banged the table; they gave all sorts of excuses. In the end, the deputy minister promised two million rubles. What we must go through to get back tiny handfuls of our own money.

"After we browbeat them, they caved in and allowed [the steel plant] to engage in barter deals with foreign firms. We're negotiating with the Yugoslavs to build a furniture factory and with the Chinese to build a beer factory. We had delegations go back and forth. Then I get a new decree. No longer will we be allowed to deal directly. All of a sudden we must go through a new bureaucracy in the regional capital for overseeing foreign trade. What do we need them for? We're not capable of making deals ourselves? We do all the legwork, yet we will have to get their permission. And for this privilege we must pay them a fee."

Lysenko's remarks were later amplified by his friend and collaborator, Nikolai Gurzhii. "We know what needs to be done and how to do it, but we're trapped by central organs," Gurzhii complained. "Give the localities complete freedom. This is fully possible within socialism. Socialism will not be destroyed. The central state simply cannot supply every person. We can do it if permitted. All power to the soviets. We must have real power, not paper power. That power must be economically based. Control over resources—this is the only foundation for politics.

"Metal is very scarce, and it is possible to obtain a lot for it. Finally the steel plant has been allowed by the ministry to make legal deals with its above-plan production. But whatever they can get goes for their own workers, of course. This raises dissatisfaction in the city. The city serves the factory with schools and the militia, but the factory serves only its own. The city soviet is demanding its share from the factory in the current negotiations with foreign firms in Yugoslavia and China to exchange metal for consumer goods.

"By the way, this is something. China has overtaken us! We have invited the Chinese here to help us make consumer goods! They might build a beer factory for us. In the old days, we built factories for them. We fly into space, no one knows how we managed, yet we can't put anything in the stores. But that we made it into space shows the potential of our country.

"We have to put a stop to this Moscow farce [*kukhnia*], throw out the do-nothings. Khrushchev began this process; then they put an end to him. We're standing in place. Recently they allowed us a little breathing room. They revealed the problems. But can they finish the matter? We're waiting, waiting. Where and how to move. And the longer we wait, the more we'll pay. We need decisive steps. Enough half-measures, enough scouting.

"The situation is clear. We need action. The people are strong. They can endure. We've been through a lot. We can struggle for a number of years, as long as we are sure that there is a possibility for improvement. So far all we see are more and more rules, more and more paper, more and more levels of administrators. Only the bureaucracy at the top thrives on the half-measures. We're locked in a steel cage."

■   ■   ■

From discussions with numerous Magnitogorsk workers about their lives a striking consensus emerged. They spoke about the same themes, with similar emphasis and emotions. Of four workers I interviewed at great length in the security of their homes, one, a skilled worker, middle-aged, from one of the city's largest factories, had the most to say.

"How much evil has accumulated! It hurts to think about it. What's changed? We're more dependent than ever on the shop bosses and functionaries. Everything is scarce, so you get things only by distribution . . . if you're down on the list. When your turn comes, *they* let you know.

"If you work hard, they demand from you. You get lots of attention. They make a son of a bitch out of you. You have to get up in front of everyone and make speeches; they give you medals with pompous names. So it's best to stay quiet, not attract attention to yourself. Once in a while, you work like a bull; the remainder of the time, you rest.

"These worker-heroes—it's a lie, a fiction. There's nothing natural about them, 100 percent artificial. They find such people early on, the ones who 'pull the one blanket toward themselves.' They get apartments earlier, various privileges. Then we read all about how in the West, the bourgeoisie control the workers by creating a worker aristocracy!

"I studied Marxism-Leninism. You could read the book right side up or upside down. Whichever way suited you best at that moment. If you needed to justify something, no problem: the theory was at your service. Party-mindedness, they call it: the cleverest manipulation technique ever invented.

"Now we have democracy. We 'elect' our shop boss. Some bloodsucker comes into the shop and makes an oily speech: 'The fellows talked me into running for shop boss,' he begins. We look at each other. Who the hell would try to talk *him* into being *our* boss! Demagogy has increased beyond belief.

"No one makes a move until we see where the power lies. As soon as it is clear, we all quickly take that side. We're completely dependent on them. Food, clothes, apartments, furniture, day care, summer camp, vacations—everything is allocated by them according to their lists, with which they rule over our lives. Everyone has something to lose. It might seem you have nothing, but they take something away, and you have even less.

"This apartment, I waited eighteen years for it. During that time we lived four in one room. No one remembered what color the walls were. You couldn't see them, they were so covered with our belongings stacked up to the ceiling. I worked and struggled and endured all manner of humiliation for eighteen years for this pathetic, unexceptional new apartment. It makes me sad and angry to think about it. How much evil has accumulated! I have so much on my soul."

On the balcony, we looked across the manmade lake to the steel plant, whose mammoth structures ran as far as the eye could see in both directions along the opposite shore; stationary clouds of smoke perched above the forest of smokestacks. Even at this distance the sheer size of the metallurgical monster was overwhelming.

"We built it all right. We worked, we toiled, we built. And now they can't figure out what the hell we built! No one knows what to call it: barracks socialism, Stalinism, totalitarianism. You could spend the rest of your life thinking about it, but you'll never come up with the right name. What we built—it's unnameable."

A co-worker guest approached us on the balcony. "I heard that there are eighteen million bureaucrats in Moscow. Can you believe it! That's Russia! We have to get rid of them all. But you try and you can't do it. You can't get loose from them. And here, in this place, we can't get rid of ours either." He returned to the living room, where hospitality was available.

"He's an idiot. Don't pay any attention to him, a fool. But that's not the main thing. The main thing is that he has integrity. He'll never betray me. There are so many stoolies everywhere, especially at work. These days we talk much more, and you wonder if there are even enough stoolies to go around. Alas, there are.

"Many years ago I worked without sparing myself. My boys did the work of four brigades. Then they made someone else a boss. We did the best work; the other guy got the prize. A blabbermouth, he made speeches, applied for admission to the party. It makes you want to pull down the whole system with your bare hands.

"While growing up I understood nothing. Only later did I reflect on how fear is instilled in us. It was passed on to me from my parents, who repeatedly told me not to say certain things, that it would be bad for them if I did. I didn't understand why, but I loved them, so I obeyed. Then I find myself saying the same thing to my kids. We were born decades after the so-called terror, yet we're afraid. We're dependent.

"I read every day about our city's pollution problems and the devastation of our health. Earlier they were silent about this. Then I go to work and get a double bonus for violating our ecological norms, which are none too strict to begin with. The end of the month, and especially the end of the quarter, we crank so much to meet the plan that we make a mockery of the pathetic cleansing devices that have been installed.

"They force you to violate the technical norms for the machinery in order to increase quantities, exceed the plan targets for bonuses. The boss personally issues the order. But the machine invariably breaks down, or repairs are needed earlier than expected. You did it. If they want, they nail you for negligence, or worse. You speak up at a meeting or in the shop—they lower the boom. We know it's impossible to go on this way. The nerves can't take much more. I smoke like a furnace. My blood pressure is bad. My friends are dying of cancer—maybe I'll get it too.

"*Perestroika,* you say? I have a family, children, grandchildren. They want to go away for the summer. What can you say to them? Daddy told the boss he didn't like the way he was being treated, so this year and for the next couple of years no one is going anywhere.

"Now they 'post' the scarcity lists so you can see where you stand on the line, say, for housing. But soon you find that the people moving into the new apartments across the way weren't even on the list. Those on the list continue to wait. Only a handful of names are removed in a year. We see: the lists are a show; they look nice on the wall when it comes time for the bosses to account for themselves to the even bigger bosses.

"You can't buy anything nowadays without coupons. You have the money, but without the coupons they don't sell anything to you. The more we hear the word *perestroika,* the more goods are no longer for 'open' sale but can be bought only with coupons, the more power they have over us.

"Coupons are distributed by the trade union, by the Komsomol, by the party. They announce in the shop that soon there will be so many coupons for such and such goods. Who gives them out and when, to whom, what becomes of them—it's all a mystery. Only when my wife learns whose wife is selling cosmetics at black market prices do we discover who got the coupons.

"At first there was some hope. We felt we could breathe at last. It was a release. Now I don't know. I'm tired, even though I'm not old. And anyway, how can you live only on faith? We're boxed in." He lowered his head, took a deep breath, sighed, and suggested we rejoin the women inside. "I feel better. It's good to talk."

■   ■   ■

"Raduga (Rainbow), a carpentry cooperative with sixty members, including a dozen artists, obtained a loan from Rolling Mill Assembly, a state firm. Rolling also provided a rent-free facility and no-cost transport. At first Raduga made children's furniture and little tables. Soon the coop moved into the repair and redesign of apartment interiors. The coop operated a full year without turning a profit. Turnover was more than 100 percent. "They came for easy work, fast money," explained one member during my visit. "Those who are not afraid to work stayed."

In 1989 the group began to take on bigger jobs, such as a customized interior of a multistory office building. The chairman claimed that the coop was doing about thirty to fifty thousand rubles of business a month. "We're not even mechanized," he laughed. "It's all artisanal. But what demand! Orders are accumulating.

"We work exclusively for state enterprises. They're the only ones with building materials. They provide the materials, we do the plaster work, the bathrooms, the floors, the decorations. If we had our own materials, we could do eight hundred thousand rubles a month. As it is, we're idle a lot. Thank God we have good relations with Rolling. They're allowing us to expand."

Vostok (East), a cooperative specializing in glasswork from windows to furniture, was created in 1987 at iron-cement products factory no. 2. Given a storage room, the coop members themselves installed lights, glass, and heating pipes. The newspaper emphasized that all five members, whose average age was twenty-five, had completed their military service.

"At first," the newspaper wrote, "they worked sixteen hours a day to try to get the business going. Only after almost two years did they begin to earn four hundred rubles per month. They signed a five-year rental agreement for the shop, adjacent to which they decided to construct their own retail outlet."

The host factory director pointed out that in comparison with the factory's annual output of more than one million rubles' worth of goods, the coop produced goods worth eighteen thousand rubles. "Thus far it has made primarily a symbolic contribution to our work. The key for us is in the stimulation, the sense of people becoming self-interested in their labor." He added that the factory included the work of the coop in its own five-year plan. Mutual benefit was the message, although much was left unspecified.

In particular, what the factory director forgot to mention, and the newspaper neglected to ask about, was where the profits of the fledgling cooperative were going. But a member of another cooperative speculated that more than symbolic value was behind the new attraction that cooperative ventures seemed to be having on managers of state enterprises.

"They [managers of state factories] are now taking the initiative," this insider related. "Recently Romazan [director of the steel plant] decreed the formation of a cooperative at the Magnitogorsk Works. In such a way economic managers have discovered yet another method, indeed perhaps even a better one, to go around the ministry's strictures and allocate resources to the plant's benefit. We need not assume, by the way, that managers are excessively modest when it comes to apportioning rewards for their own efforts in the new ventures." Meanwhile, cooperatives such as Raduga and Vostok were flourishing.

■   ■   ■

In a sign of the growing frustration with the imperious behavior of the Ministry of Ferrous Metallurgy, the Magnitogorsk newspaper broke ranks and openly challenged the ministry's long-term reconstruction program as a plan to guarantee the "built-in obsolescence of the steel plant" and called for informed discussion. A. Bigeev, chairman of the steelmaking faculty at the Mining Institute, responded first, defending the ministry's decision to build the BOF converter in a long article, "The Magnitogorsk Works at the Crossroads of the Twenty-first Century."

According to Bigeev, a converter offered numerous advantages over the present open-hearth furnaces: better pollution control, more mechanization and thus better working conditions, higher productivity, and cheaper steel. He admitted that electrical furnaces, rather than converters, were the most advanced technology in the world, yet Bigeev noted that the Urals was poor in electrical energy. BOF was the way to go.

Curiously, while defending the converter, Bigeev noted that it would replace only half the open-hearth ovens in operation, and yet he came out against the construction of a second converter. "It would forever doom the Magnitogorsk Works to the position of being technologically second-rate," he revealed, appearing to undermine his own arguments in support of the one converter currently under construction. Worse, Bigeev neglected to specify what kind of technology, if not a second converter, ought to replace the rest of the open-hearth ovens. Here he ignored the issue, but in an earlier article detailing the deadly pollution emitted by the open hearths, he lamented that they would continue operating for "not a few years" (that is, presumably many).

In concluding his article, Bigeev asked, "Why make metal at all?" The mere fact that he felt such a question needed to be answered was telling, but his response—"because it is the key to civilization"—seemed vague and elusive. V. Kuchmii, also a member of the faculty of the Mining Institute, challenged Bigeev's entire presentation in a rejoinder.

The USSR, Kuchmii wrote, produces 161 million tons of steel a year, compared with only 75 million by the United States. "Do we really need all the steel we make?" he wondered. "We have seventy times more harvesters than the U.S., yet we buy grain from them. What good is so much steel? Is it possible to speak of the objectivity of a metal shortage and the necessity of constantly producing more? I don't think so. The shortage is a result of overuse and inefficiency." Kuchmii implied that the open-hearth ovens scheduled to remain in operation after the completion of the converter ought to be shut down and not replaced. No rebuttal appeared.

Whatever plans may have been down the road, many people in Magnitogorsk had already begun wondering openly about just what to expect from the one converter. Aside from angry complaints about betrayal by suppliers of the project, however, information about the course of the converter construction was limited to propaganda releases about construction targets being met ahead of deadlines. In response to my inquiries, one knowledgeable local specialist called my attention to a May 1989 article in the popular national weekly *Ogonek* about a recent attempt to attack many of the problems besetting the Soviet steel industry by the construction of a new plant equipped entirely with the latest in foreign technology.

As reported by Viktor Zhuk and Mark Shteinbok, in the town of Zhlobin, located in the republic of Belorussia, Voest Alpine, an Austrian firm, undertook to build a "miniplant" that required less capital and time to construct and that could fill orders for smaller quantities of specialized steel. The agreement also stipulated that two companion plants, in Rybnitsa in Moldavia and in Komsomolsk-na-Amure in the Far East, would be built simultaneously by Soviet teams.

The volume of the building to house the plant in Rybnitsa turned out to be twice as large as that in Zhlobin. In Komsomolsk, the building housing the plant turned out to be three times larger. The Austrian firm, used to paying for land, sought to use as little as possible. In Rybnitsa, the Soviet team used twice as much land. Moreover, the team chose prime land with superb topsoil, all of which was ruined. The Austrians, although they built in an empty space, removed the entire layer of topsoil and set it aside for agricultural uses.

Aside from the fact that the Austrians felt no need to "pad" the quantity of work, their excavators were equipped with devices that when turned on automatically began recording the volume of work. The Soviets sought and were given one of these devices, which was sent to one of their own factories for imitation. It disappeared. Inquiries were met with a shrug of the shoulders and a suggestion to forget about it because Soviet excavator operators would have vandalized the meters as soon as they were installed.

The Austrian-built plant was finished by a work force of fewer than two thousand, in what the journalists felt was incredible speed and without any acceleration, or "storming," as completion neared. In contrast, both at Rybnitsa and at Komsomolsk more than six thousand workers were frantically storming to rush completion. The latter two plants turned out to be more than one year behind schedule.

The Austrians devised a gradual timetable for breaking in the new plant and specified an optimal production level. The Soviet workers and management immediately set about trying to increase "tempos" and "exceed" capacities. Upon learning the prescribed output of a piece of equipment, the Soviet's first response invariably was, "Can it do more?" Not surprisingly, equipment was broken, which led to unscheduled downtime and loss of pay. Workers in such shops fled to others, where the same processes were under way and could be expected to produce equally self-defeating results. Many of those who had succeeded in securing apartments quit the factory altogether.

Soviet planners had insisted on using only imported technology for the plant, a move designed to lift the whole industrial branch up to the level of this new plant. Consequently, when the machinery began breaking down, there were no spare parts. In fact, under normal conditions the plant would be expected to require some three million gold rubles' worth of spare parts a year to operate. But the plant's output could not be expected to be sold for hard currency—who would buy Soviet steel when Western or Japanese steel was available?—so there was no way to insure operation even given normal wear and tear. Soon makeshift spare parts were being manufactured by artisanal methods at the plant itself by an unplanned-for repair staff of thirteen hundred, thereby adding to the firm's payroll and thus to the price of its steel.

The contract specified that the Soviets would be responsible for building apartments to house the plant's work force. By the time sections of the plant began operations, there were many thousands of people on waiting lists for housing. Observing this, the Austrians proposed to build all the required housing quickly for payment in foreign currency. And the Yugoslavs made a more attractive barter offer. Neither was acted upon. As one Soviet official commented, "Who would want to live in our apartments if there will be imported ones?" As a result, for a long time to come most workers will not live in any apartments.

The journalists noticed that the faucets for the imported sinks in the washrooms were missing. Foremen who were supposed to communicate with crane operators and others by walkie-talkie instead did so by shouting, frequently to no avail. The walkie-talkies, like the faucets, had been ordered and received. As it turned out, however, bosses, who were already connected to each other by a telephone system between offices, talked to each other by walkie-talkie. It was more fun.

Even though the two journalists acknowledged that the Zhlobin plant operated better than all other Soviet plants in its branch of industry, they pointed out that it would never achieve the level permitted by the technology. The implication of the exposé seemed to have been that only a radical transformation of the command economy into an economy regulated by markets and profit would begin to alter the behavior of firms and individuals, raise the quality of Soviet steel across the board, and eliminate the inexhaustible demand that leads to ineradicable shortages. But the question of how the country would face the necessity of reducing overall output, closing old and inefficient plants, and developing cheaper, lighter, and more durable substitutes for steel, such as aluminum and plastic, was not addressed.

•   •   •

Given the exhaustion of local raw materials, the Magnitogorsk factory's isolated geographic position, and the obsolescence of the plant's technology, one may wonder why the plant has not been abandoned in favor of a new one in a different location. Yet the factory is tied to its location by the substantial housing stock it has built up. Such commodities do not come cheaply in the Soviet Union. Moreover, a government predicated on notions of social justice cannot very well throw the more than sixty thousand people at the plant—not to mention those employed in town—out of work. "It will never happen here, never," protested Mayor Lysenko, himself a former steelworker. "For us to close such a plant for narrow economic concerns is unthinkable. Forget it."

And Magnitogorsk is more than just a huge steel plant. It is one of the very powerful symbols of the October Revolution itself; of the rise of backward peasant Russia to the status of an industrial and military superpower. Dismantling Magnitogorsk would be costly in Soviet terms and, in effect, tantamount to repudiating one of the bases of the regime's legitimacy and the achievements of the revolution.

After decades of delay, replacement of obsolete equipment has finally begun, but it has been proceeding slowly and may, because of the drawn-out nature of the process and the sheer size of the technological stock, condemn the plant to permanent obsolescence. Mounds and mounds of Magnitogorsk steel—the basis for the city's existence—continue to pile up at stockpiles around the country, rusting under the open sky. Meanwhile, more and more steel is being produced in Magnitogorsk, even as the product satisfies fewer and fewer of the plant's customers, which have no choice but to accept shipments, driven as they are to produce more and more machines.

Worse yet, despite Magnitogorsk's huge industrial base, with its pool of skilled labor and abundance of raw materials, Soviet laws and economic priorities have conspired to restrict the development of a consumer and service economy. This state of affairs has given rise to a major shadow economy of tacitly condoned illegal activities without which the official economy could not function. While the official supply network shows itself incapable of effective expansion, the protomarket shadow economy demonstrates an extraordinary capacity to fill in the growing gaps. No one is more adept at dealmaking in the shadows than the supply managers of state enterprises and the chief of the city's trade network. But they are the first to ridicule the manifest illogic of an economic system that simultaneously forbids and compels people to engage in market activities.

Although the need for some kind of radical change has grown ever more urgent, through 1989 effective economic reform remained elusive. Despite certain minor adjustments, the steel plant continued to be held in the vise of the Ministry of Ferrous Metallurgy. Raw materials were being centrally allocated, prices for the factory's wares were set by central planners, and customers for finished products were designated from above. As factory officials were hectored by central authorities to improve quality, they were also pressured for even more output, which resulted in more and more lower quality steel. Moreover, under the pressure of the various reform measures thus far implemented, the change that had occurred was in the direction of chaos and breakdown. Worst of all, the huge administrative bureaucracy targeted for reduction maneuvered to benefit from the flux, using it as a pretext to further tighten its grip on the economy.

In Magnitogorsk the attempt at radical reform of the state economic sector has brought to light what the reformers originally did not envision: the discovery that the problem lies not solely in old technology or excessive centralization but in the nature of the command economic system itself. Nevertheless, the task of not merely adjusting the economic mechanism but of superseding it confronts reformers with a vastly more daunting challenge, one of a political nature that they have hesitated to take up even though the prevailing system has been irreversibly unhinged by their efforts to fix it.

"The administrative-command economy has been thoroughly discredited," remarked one Magnitogorsk economist, "but not yet replaced." Indeed, despite all the talk about marketization and privatization, by the end of 1989 neither had been tried at the steel plant. For Magnitogorsk, this indecision was both blessing and curse. Not only would marketization and privatization fail to solve all of the problems of the Magnitogorsk Works; such measures could very well lead to the plant's demise. In the meantime, at the Magnitogorsk plant working conditions remain infernal, steel quality continues to decline, pollution defies description, and the new technology belatedly being introduced—only a fraction of what is needed—functions within an economic system that rewards inefficiency as it keeps tens of thousands employed.

Even though a fundamental transformation of the traditional state sector of the economy still looms on the horizon—such a change would be a mixed blessing for Magnitogorsk—efforts to promote a complementary cooperative (or private) sector have yielded halting results, in part because the dominant state sector remains largely unchanged. Given the endemic shortages, procuring ordinary raw materials to run a business can be done only through the state allocation system. Most cooperatives have discovered that their existence is utterly dependent on the goodwill of state enterprises. Indeed, cooperatives have sprung up not in the much-needed sphere of food and services, but within the interstices of industrial firms eager for any help they can get to meet plan targets and just as eager to pocket some of the profits.

Magnitogorsk's handful of independent private entrepreneurs have encountered a bewildering, ever-changing, and arbitrarily applied set of regulations enforced by local officials keen to exercise their authority over the fledgling businesses but less enthusiastic about promoting their success. Railing against the chokehold applied to their city by central ministries, city authorities turn around and choke the fledgling cooperative businesses under their supervision.

Nor has the hostility of the local population toward cooperatives, a hostility based on a mixture of blind resentment and a tendency toward leveling, shown any signs of abating, despite Herculean efforts by the city newspaper. Frustrated and feeling utterly powerless in the midst of chronic shortages, low-quality goods, and the higher prices charged by the coops, a small group of consumers under the newspaper's sponsorship have formed a "union" to defend their interests. But organizing a boycott in a situation of state monopoly is obviously self-defeating, while no amount of additional inspections will raise the quality of goods produced by firms supplied with defective inputs and unchallenged by competition.

Bucking the odds, members of Magnitogorsk's functioning cooperatives have pressed on, surmounting the difficulties inherent in starting any business while managing with the additional burden of an unpredictable and unfriendly business environment. Entrepreneurial skills and a capacity for hard work, both erroneously thought to have been forever eradicated by the Communist economic system, have been reasserted. More than that, cooperative members speak with one voice about the dignity and sense of freedom that have more than made up for the hassle, humiliation, and hard work. The contrast in their attitudes with those of the utterly demoralized workers at the steel plant could not be more striking.

The state-run supply system, inefficient as it is in serving elementary needs, remains the dominant one in Magnitogorsk and is a source of immense power in the hands of those who control it. Cooperatives are few, dependent, and mostly small. Yet there appears little doubt that were a freer hand extended to private business, an additional form of social stratification, one very different from the present system of privileged access based on connections and influence, would arise—with far-reaching political consequences. The business of the people may turn out not to be the business of the party.

CHAPTER TWO

Glasnost
A City Newspaper Rises,
a Theater Declines

On a clear day in the spring of 1987, Mikhail Lysenko, chairman of the Magnitogorsk city soviet, drove with me to a concrete platform perched on a hill overlooking the original left-bank "socialist city." From there Chairman Lysenko, who prefers to be known by the English term *mayor*, pointed to the open area below, where the barracks in which he had grown up once stood. When my attention turned away from the city, what seemed like a barbed-wire enclosure and a guard tower came into view. "Is that the prison?" I asked. Momentarily stunned, the mayor, known for his outspokenness, blurted out, "We have no prison."

On another spring visit two years later I learned that in January 1989, the *Magnitogorsk Worker* had reported that the previous month disturbances (*besporiadki*) took place at the city's two drying-out prisons (*lechebno-trudovoi profilaktorii*, or LTP). Covering a full page of the over-sized-format, four-page daily, the article, "Zone of Risk" by Vladimir Mozgovoi, not only confirmed for the first time the existence of prisons in the city but described those institutions in detail. What is more, the incident giving rise to the article was the first political uprising in the city's sixty-year history.

As reported, on Wednesday, 14 December, at LTP 1, seventy-two people were involved in three attempted breakouts, the third one "virtually successful": some actually made it outside—but only momentarily, as "force was answered with force," Mozgovoi wrote cryptically, implying that those who escaped had been caught.

At around the same time, a few kilometers down the road at LTP 4 (the other two evidently remained peaceful), the "patients," returning for checkup after the evening political classes (where aid for Armenian earthquake victims was discussed), amassed at the gates, shouted and insulted staff and guards, and demanded their release. Refusing a proposal to delegate fifteen to twenty representatives to be taken by bus to the city soviet to meet with officials, the patients crashed the gate. More than two hundred people got outside and began marching toward town, "partially armed, partially drunk," according to Mozgovoi. "Force was used against them." Seven staff members reportedly were hurt. Injuries to patients were not mentioned.

The next day, back at LTP 1, the patients did not show up for work, and they refused to meet with city or regional officials. Instead—something the local daily, out of modesty, neglected to mention—the striking patients demanded the newspaper's participation in any talks aimed at a resolution of the conflict. They vowed to call a halt to their siege only upon the arrival of the city's top journalists. The patients felt that such a meeting offered a chance to air grievances that in the new era of *glasnost* would reach a wide and attentive audience—public opinion. A new locus of power in the city had arisen.

At the meeting between patient-prisoners and journalist–public representatives years of enforced public silence were drowned in an outpouring of emotional invective. "The conditions here are akin to those for prisoners," one patient was quoted as saying. Another claimed he "took a smoke in the hallway, and they stuck me in the isolation cell [*shizo*]." "There are thirty-nine of us from Leningrad," someone said. "We were transported here [last spring] in a closed box car for five days like criminals." A fellow patient explained that "you walk through the zone, and they can stop you and strip you down to your underwear."

Others complained of the hybrid medicinal-labor institution that "there is no medical treatment, only work, work, and more work." One patient scoffed, "This is a treatment center? Take a look, how many doctors there are, one expert in substance abuse for 120 to 130 people, no surgeon, no therapist, no inoculator." Yet in response to the journalists' question, Who wants to be cured? only three hands went up. "If the majority of the population drinks," one patient wondered, "why are *we* here?"

But the striking patients did more than complain: they formed the Committee for the Defense of Civil Rights and called for the review of all cases, an end to the use of "chemicals," the removal of guards and special fences, the formation of an independent trade union to check up on the administration, and greater "self-management" of the facility. Incredulous prison authorities, attributing what they called the riot (*bunt*) to the recent transfer to Magnitogorsk of Muscovites and Leningraders, dismissed the patients' grievances.

"They are badly fed?" the chief administrator scoffed. "In their diet they even get buckwheat kasha [a fact confirmed by the patients]. They demand that the store carry sugar, candy, and tea? They get a satisfactory amount of sugar in their diet, and as for candy and tea—try to buy them in a store for people who are 'free.' " Furthermore, the administrator insisted that treatment was conducted according to an established program. Drugs, primarily sensibility ones (called by the patients "insecticide powder"), were used only on those who violated the ban on alcohol and were dispensed strictly in prescribed dosages. As for modern medicines, "We don't even have enough for the children in the city." Admitting that 30 percent of the patients' pay was deducted to help maintain the profilactory, the administrators countered that many of the patients cost the state a fortune. One such "stakhanovite" (norm-buster) compelled the state to spend eighty-two thousand rubles on him.

Neither side seemed willing to give much ground, yet in contrast to elementary journalistic practice, the article failed to provide information on the final outcome of the events: whether formal charges had been brought against either inmates or guards, whether demands had been met and promises kept. Instead, Mozgovoi offered his own resolution to the unprecedented outburst and discussion by focusing on the status and aim of the facility.

"The very structure of the LTP is inhuman and in sharp contradiction to the present attempt to construct a law-based state," he pointed out. But was the LTP a prison or a hospital? It was both, Mozgovoi reasoned, yet it fell under the jurisdiction of the main administration of correctional matters of the Ministry of Internal Affairs, and this fact, he wrote without elaboration, "determines a great deal." An administrator, conceding that the effectiveness of treatment was "not high," made plain that "those who come to the LTP here after having been through a prison colony understand the difference very well."

If an LTP was not quite identical to a labor colony, conditions at LTPs varied, depending not only on management's understanding of their task and choice of methods but on local needs and circumstances. According to Mozgovoi, the physical conditions at LTP 4, a structure the authorities admitted "arose in part because of the labor supply needs of the Magnitogorsk Steel Works," were far worse than in LTP 1, but the "regime" at LTP 4 was not as harsh. Tough cases at LTP 4 were sent to LTP 1 "for reeducation," and almost all patients at LTP 4 worked outside the facility—an option much preferred by patients, although the work was unskilled manual labor.

Having shown the resemblances between the medicinal-labor facility and a prison, Mozgovoi closed the article by reiterating that the problem of alcoholism persisted and had to be confronted, especially in the case of dangerous individuals. But the key issue, he argued, was not to relax or intensify the regime at an LTP but to make such places more effective and, above all, to keep them under public scrutiny and control—in a word, *glasnost*. As Mozgovoi himself suggested, "Zone of Risk" was after more than information for information's sake: the article was conceived and executed as another major advance in the battle for the country's new reform agenda.

Although the ultimate outcome of the extraordinary series of events never became clear, a follow-up of sorts to the story came three weeks later in the form of a review of letters received from the paper's readership. Relying on readers to lend legitimacy to its efforts, the newspaper also sought to rally broad-based public support for change. The selection of letters revealed the newspaper's strategy in handling the matter as well as public opinion.

A few people directed anger at the LTP patients. "They complain they do not like the treatment," one person wrote. "Would they prefer a shot, followed by a piece of chicken as chaser? [Russians snack when they drink.] They complain about their present conditions? What did they do at home to their families? How did their children live?"

Many more letter writers, however, looked beyond the story of individual failing to find social lessons. "It is our disgrace!" wrote one woman. "Inhuman and unlawful exploitation of the labor of essentially sick people, seeing in them cheap labor power. The fact that these people are placed 'outside the law' gives the administration of the LTP and the militia the right to do whatever is convenient for them." She suggested transferring responsibility for the LTP to the Ministry of Health—a suggestion implicit in Mozgovoi's treatment.

In another letter a factory worker echoed the woman's remarks, insisting that the process of incarceration as carried out was unlawful. "There is no law against drinking in public," he pointed out, "only against harming others. If a drunkard scandalizes his family, the wife may leave and collect alimony for her children. If the drunkard does not work, it is possible to enforce the law against work-shy elements. But to take someone's freedom away just like that, without a court, is wrong." Rule of law was to be supreme.

Perhaps the most startling social commentary came from a letter entitled "We Live No Better." It made the point that Soviet life was given expression in the LTP, from which it was possible to judge "free" life. "As it is there," said the letter, "so it is here, with a few exceptions. We live not suffering from a surfeit of food products, comfortable transit, and everyday conveniences, or the protection of law. Changes are a long-term matter. Given all this, those tearful humanists want the 'people behind bars' to live in a human way. Of course, we need comfortable prisons and super treatment centers for alcoholics, but normal people do not live in a human way."

Anyone familiar with the Magnitogorsk newspaper from just a few years ago could not help but be astonished at the comparison between the life of sick individuals and that of ordinary people, yet by 1989 such commentary, far from shocking, had come to seem obviously appropriate. The letter's signature encapsulated the aspirations of the entire city to lead a "normal" life. It was signed "V. Ermolenko, a normal person."

▪   ▪   ▪

At a gathering of local journalists on Press Day, 5 March 1987, Mikhail Lysenko reaffirmed the new policy of *glasnost*. "From now on," he advised, "what only the leadership has known, everyone must know. We need widespread dissemination of information." They did, indeed!

Glasnost, which has come to mean both "openness" and "public criticism," was launched by the Soviet government to win over the country's intelligentsia, to prepare the public for change, and, it was hoped, to involve a newly created, broad-based constituency for change in the process. But *glasnost* seemed to go against deep-rooted cultural traditions, especially the one of ignoring or hiding difficulties and failures. Added to that was the depth of public cynicism. To top it all off, *glasnost* posed momentous political questions, especially about the role of ideology.

Marxism-Leninism, the official ideology of the Soviet state, posited that history was governed by scientific laws and that the existing regime embodied those laws. Thus, it was irrational—even psychopathic—to oppose the regime. Ideology served not merely as a blanket justification for the regime's policies but as an instrument of control, given its ability to disarm potential opposition through the threat of scientifically warranted coercion. And if Marxism-Leninism essentially criminalized nonconformity, rigorous state censorship denied people the very means for opposition. Censors suppressed "negative" information (about pollution, disasters, crimes that were not *supposed* to exist) and reworked statistics and rewrote history to the point of making sensible discussion, let alone informed criticism, virtually impossible.

In addition to their "prophylactic" role, censors encouraged the flow of an inexhaustible stream of information and analysis designed to teach people what and how to think. Media were instruments—in the Leninist phrase, weapons—in the battle to construct a Communist society (rather than instruments in the battle to generate profits). Furthermore, the messages emanating from reading matter, films, radio, and television were reinforced by obligatory courses in Marxism-Leninism in schools, beginning at an early age.

One of the results of such efforts to shape what people knew and how they thought was to make them inordinately skeptical of what they heard and saw from official sources and to promote the proliferation of rumor. Censorship was known to be multilayered, determining what was printed or spoken for the general public and what could be revealed to loyal officials granted varying degrees of privileged access to forbidden matter. This tactic insured that all information was assumed by recipients to be at best only part of a larger whole.

Nevertheless, another result was to make people accept for the most part what they were told. True, everyday experience seemed perpetually at odds with official pronouncements, yet in the absence not simply of alternative information but of alternative ways of reasoning, the official truth could not be definitively disproved. Many people wanted to believe when told of their country's arduous yet victorious rise to greatness. In any case and practically speaking, acceptance of the official truth was a prerequisite for functioning in society. This tendency toward subservience was greatly enhanced by a bewildering maze of ever-shifting bureaucratic rules complete with attendant paperwork and an army of seals, stamps, and signatures. Most everyone became cynical about the nature of laws and regulations and soon learned it was easier not to fight.

Thus, people in effect lived in two different truths: that of their own experience and that of the official propaganda—truths that were not always in conflict, to be sure, but often enough so as to teach individuals at a minimum to be cautious and to train their children in the need for discretion and even prevarication. Even though most people seem to have suspected that there was much they did not know (and a minority understood that much of what they did know was not reliable), few took the time, energy, and personal risk required to find out for sure. When *glasnost* was proclaimed, few people rushed to cast off their armor of skepticism. In their hearts, however, almost all people welcomed the *glasnost* campaign with relief, hope, and, above all, curiosity.

Glasnost arrived in Magnitogorsk later than in Moscow and developed more slowly. The first mild breezes of a new era swept the pages of the *Magnitogorsk Worker* in fall 1986. New rubrics and new kinds of stories appeared, especially those concerned with social problems: articles on the elderly living alone and in poverty, alcoholism, the alienation of youth, the severe shortage of home telephones, poor food supply, and the demoralizing housing crisis. In an interview in 1987, Tatiana Leus, who emerged as the city's leading reporter on social issues, singled out her article "Hotel," which appeared in October 1986, as an illustration of the new attention to social issues.

According to the article, the city was essentially without a hotel. (In fact, there was a hotel, built in 1933, but it belonged to the steel factory, not the city.) Whereas some agencies, such as the city circus, had small buildings in which to house guests, other enterprises were compelled to set aside for visitors apartments designated for family use—a practice that was illegal. Two projects for large city hotels, one drawn up in 1969, the other in 1974, were not realized because the funds from the Ministry of Ferrous Metallurgy never came. Because the city had no hotel, musical, artistic, sports, and other groups did not come. Magnitogorsk was the loser.

The article "Hotel" may seem unexceptional to the foreign reader, but by the Magnitogorsk standards of the time it was an engaged piece of social reportage. Most important, it presented a serious problem *without* concluding on an upbeat note. Back then this was probably the single biggest change in the newspaper. As managing editor Evgenii Vernikov related in an interview in 1987, "Not only do we deal more with social issues; we approach them in the spirit of *perestroika*. In the past, we might have ended such an article with quotations from some official, who invariably would say that, yes, we have a problem here, but we are working on it, and shortly it will be solved. Now we present the social problems just as we see them."

The new approach was selling papers. By late 1987 subscriptions, which had been declining, were up markedly. As one reader wrote, "The paper has become more interesting. It raises urgent issues often and offers sharp critical observations. Moreover, it does not simply criticize but demands concrete answers. For these reasons the newspaper has become more popular, and in every home people look forward to its arrival."

In the conditions of Magnitogorsk, "Hotel" was indeed a big step, but this fact alone indicated how far local journalists had yet to go in freeing the city and themselves from an informational vacuum and ideological straitjacket. Ironically, the paper's previous style and content, by providing a permanently negative comparison for confirming advances, became an invaluable asset.

■   ■   ■

Interest in Magnitogorsk in foreign movies, a large number of which were shown during the Brezhnev era, had always been high—although not necessarily only because of a particular film's reputation. Whatever the subject matter, plot, or quality of the film, there were always the highly valued depictions of Western living standards and life-styles. Yet audiences wondered how typical were the cavernous homes and apartments, sumptuous clothes, fancy cars, extravagant adventures, and beautiful, although enigmatic, people.

Information from the West had also been intermittently available through the "Voices," the popular term for the well-known Russian-language broadcasts of Radio Liberty, Voice of America, and the BBC. Yet while government jamming greatly heightened interest in the broadcasts, it proved no less effective in preventing radio signals from getting through. Since 1985 *glasnost* had brought not only an end to jamming but an acceleration in the amount of information from the West getting through state channels. But for all these advances, the state propaganda machine continued its relentless work. Even more important, Magnitogorsk remained so remote that it was difficult for anyone living there to gain a handle on life in the outside world.

From just after World War II until the early 1980s, Magnitogorsk was "closed" to foreigners. Visitation rights were granted in exceptional cases to representatives of foreign firms invited by the Ministry of Ferrous Metallurgy for consultation work, yet none of these rare visitors had any contact with locals beyond a narrow circle of factory officials. Although the city was "opened" in the early 1980s, few foreigners visited. When I arrived in April 1987, it was beyond doubt that the thirst for knowledge about the West far exceeded the supply. Not merely the sheer number of questions directed to me but their elementary character spoke volumes.

In the summer of 1987, after I had left, my three-part article "Magnitogorsk through American Eyes" caused a sensation. An American had been allowed to speak his mind in the pages of the official "organ of the Magnitogorsk city party committee." Except for some small but significant editorial changes, such as toning down modifiers and reformulating one passage about democracy, the text, a sympathetic and cautious but highly critical appraisal of my two-month visit, was printed in full. Before 1985 this was unthinkable.

In 1987 a living source "from there" constituted an altogether exceptional phenomenon, affording a qualitatively different level of access, but at first the newspaper treated me with the utmost caution. For the duration of my entire trip the editor claimed to be unavailable, and the idea of a publication with me was raised by his deputy only after I had initiated and pursued repeated contact. And if, as seems true, the editors found it useful to publish a critical yet friendly article by me to broaden the reformist thrust of the newspaper, this suggested a certain precariousness in their position. Indeed, at the time there were perceptible limits to the use of the press as an instrument of reform in Magnitogorsk.

In contrast to the coverage of social problems, I found few penetrating discussions of the factory's technological or social problems. As Evgenii Vernikov delicately explained, "The factory doesn't like criticism. They get angry at the smallest hint of criticism, complaining imperiously that the newspaper doesn't understand the complexities of steelmaking and therefore has no right to meddle in the affairs of the factory. Never mind that these 'affairs' concern us all."

In 1987 the most revealing piece of journalism on the problems of the Magnitogorsk Works appeared not in the *Magnitogorsk Worker* but in the central press, namely, *Pravda*. Although the content of the *Pravda* article was subsequently broadcast on the radio several times in Magnitogorsk, the fact that this exposé of the factory's woes came out in the central press and was not even mentioned in the local press strongly indicated how cautious the *Magnitogorsk Worker* was with respect to the giant industrial enterprise.

One singular yet striking exception to the newspaper's subordinate role vis-à-vis the factory was a short article in February 1987 on pollution. The reporter interviewed the factory's chief for pollution control, Iurii Krylov, who admitted that it was not necessary to be an expert to see that the factory adversely affected the environment. "But," Krylov quickly added, "let's be realistic—solving the problem will take years and years. We have already installed some devices, and in the upcoming years we'll install more."

Surprisingly, Krylov's gesture at reassurance, far from being reinforced by the reporter, was challenged. Moreover, the paper reported that the newspaper staff, while carrying out an inspection of the ore-enriching plant, discovered that half the pollution-control devices were not in operation. And it was reported that to boost productivity, factory officials ordered the use in the open-hearth furnaces of acid above permitted norms, thereby substantially increasing emissions from what was already the factory's worst polluter.

By using an issue that had been officially recognized and that had broad public support, the newspaper was able for the first time to stake out a quasi-independent professional position toward an autocratic institution that had been shrouded in mystification. The reporter concluded with two stinging rhetorical questions that cut to the heart of the factory's dominant position in the city: "Don't we in fact live in Magnitogorsk? Don't we consider ourselves the masters of our city?" Even without a full declaration of war, the battle lines had been drawn.

In addition to the factory, other areas of concern remained beyond the newly critical eye of the city newspaper, among them the role of the KGB. Also, information on foreign affairs was not only slight but handed down directly from central press organs, which tediously inculcated regime policy. And even when treating those themes that were considered "safe," the journalists stayed within certain boundaries. Yet the changes as of 1987, although circumscribed, were significant and at times striking. And much more was to follow.

■   ■   ■

In contrast to the as-yet-timid *glasnost* of the newspaper was the booming voice of the Magnitogorsk theater, as expressed in a play entitled *The Redkin Effect,* a 1987 reworking of local productions of various plays from the previous several years, prior to the Gorbachev era.

A worker whose name derives from the word for a bitter plant, Redkin has a suggestion for solving the Soviet economy's productivity problems: everyone should work not for money but for conscience.

Redkin's idea mocks the practice in Soviet industry of worker suggestions for improvement and the notion that enthusiasm alone can serve as a basis for high productivity. The round stage, constructed out of metal scaffolding in such a way that it vividly evokes a Magnitogorsk blast furnace, revolves to reveal various scenes of Magnitogorsk life:

A grocery store that is late to open as the salesclerk slowly files her nails in front; meanwhile, the people in line jostle for position and play all the tricks common in Soviet queues. When the store finally opens, the prima donna salesclerk hands groceries out the back door to a man in uniform.

An old woman carrying huge bundles of goods, who runs from store to store hoarding amid rumors of impending shortages, a victim of the psychology of scarcity.

The boss of a factory shop, who over the telephone shouts commands at his workers, coldly dismissive of their hardships, until a gigantic red phone begins to blink, and the tyrannical shop boss freezes in fright. It is *his* boss, who makes similarly outrageous demands for higher production, to which the now-cowed shop boss can respond only with a meek "da."

Workers triumphantly stealing large quantities of materials from the job in order to work on them at home for private gain.

Pioneers (an organization of young scouts to which virtually all Soviet children belong) marching like robots, barking slogans, and displaying how well they have mastered unthinking discipline and paramilitary behavior.

A hack propagandist with a repertoire of prepared speeches who brings the wrong speech, one on American imperialism, to Redkin's wedding. The propagandist, incapable of spontaneous or independent thought, reads the yellowing text anyway.

The main action of the play involves Redkin's attempt to prevail upon management to implement his proposal. As it turns out, the Japanese find out about Redkin's idea and introduce it, raising productivity by a factor of twenty-one. Redkin's innovation is next introduced in Western Europe with similar, if somewhat less spectacular, results. Finally, Redkin's idea makes its way to the socialist economy closest to the West, Hungary, which the propagandist sees as incontrovertible evidence of the superiority of the socialist economy. At this observation the crowd roared with laughter, and the play was momentarily interrupted.

Do the Soviets introduce their own worker's innovation, which has proven so effective abroad? Not at all. Instead, Redkin is decorated, a gigantic marble statue of him with rippling muscles is ceremoniously unveiled, and his apartment is made into a museum. We are treated to a tour of the new museum, conducted by a typical tour guide. She delivers her well-rehearsed lines in an uninterested, condescending monotone, ignoring all questions. She disingenuously points out that Redkin's black-and-white TV set demonstrates his modesty in personal matters, despite his fame. As an example of his literary tastes, she reaches for the volumes of Alexander Pushkin on the shelves, which elicited a hearty laugh from an audience that knew only too well that Pushkin was standard, required school poetry and therefore reflected no independent exercise of taste at all.

Back in the shop productivity remains unaffected. The play opens and closes with a foreboding white wall, in front of which stands the cast, backs to the audience, unable to move forward. The wall evokes the self-imposed obstacles the Soviets are always struggling to overcome. All the heroic exploits only bring them back to where they started.

The Redkin Effect went beyond anything that appeared in the newspaper through 1987—indeed, it made the newspaper look apologetic—even if the play left the audience to draw the obvious (and not so obvious) conclusions. The theater itself, however, held but a few hundred spectators (most of whom on this particular evening were young). And unlike the newspaper, the theater did not directly feed back into the public domain. However accurate the criticism, no committees would be formed, no investigations carried out.

Moreover, the drama took place in a culture in which access to a photocopier remained a matter of national security, in which ordinary demographic data were state secrets. No more than ten years ago, it was necessary to register the ownership of a typewriter with the police. That was no longer the case, but long after the advent of sophisticated satellite technology, taking photographs from an airplane still required official permission, while accurate and complete city maps remained for official use only. And publishing a journalistic account of the very same problems and in the very same way that the play did at that time risked dismissal and possible arrest and imprisonment for anti-Soviet slander. The Magnitogorsk theater was a privileged cultural space, its special status growing out of the traditions of cultural production in the USSR and the prestige and political clout of the theater's director.

The very sharpness of the play seemed to lead to frustration. Upon leaving the privileged space of the theater and walking out onto the street, the audience was rudely reminded that nothing had really changed. The only thing not criticized in the play was criticism itself. Seeing the play brought home the fact that criticism was a problem: convulsive, shrill criticism, whose positive results were hard to see; criticism for the sake of criticism; criticism so that the government and the people could point to it and reassure themselves that they had criticism.

Perhaps some in the audience went home wondering if it would not be better if criticism ceased to be such an issue, ceased to retain its loud and episodic character, lost its aura. The task seemed to be to remove the special quality of the theater's criticism, not by becoming silent again but by discussing problems and solutions openly and routinely, by being more straightforward, more direct, more honest—in short, by having more regular forms of public expression and debate, which was precisely what the stirrings of *glasnost* seemed to promise.

■   ■   ■

"We could not imagine what it would be like," mused a member of the local intelligentsia, reflecting on what had been a pivotal event in the consciousness of Magnitogorsk's inhabitants. "We read. We watched television. We tried to imagine. As the exhibit drew near, our curiosity reached personally dangerous levels. For us it all looked like science fiction. What kind of civilization could afford personal computers for schoolchildren! I'm a scientist, yet I'm without one.

"Telephones for the deaf. How could that be? Videodisks, facsimile machines, plastic money, bar codes controlling inventories—I have not the words to explain to you what all this looks like to us. Desktop publishing? Do people really have satellite bowls at home? And yet Americans are still human beings, aren't they?"

For five weeks in the summer of 1988, some fifteen months after my first visit, "Information USA," an exhibit sponsored by the U.S. government as part of the Soviet-American cultural exchange agreement, visited Magnitogorsk, the seventh city of an eight-city tour. Managed by the United States Information Agency (USIA), the glossy celebration of American life was accompanied by no less a figure than the U.S. ambassador in Moscow, Jack Matlock, and opened with a speech by the deputy director of the previously jammed Voice of America. Mayor

Mikhail Lysenko, asked by a visiting journalist from the *New York Times* if this was the city's first exhibit from the West, was said to have raised his thick eyebrows and exclaimed, "What do you mean, from the West? From the east, from the north, from the south." The town went berserk.

More than 8,000 people a day descended upon the steeltown's Fiftieth Anniversary of October Track and Field Pavilion to view the high-tech production featuring the role of technology in American life. According to the final report prepared by the USIA, the exhibit in Magnitogorsk drew 244,872 visitors, more than it had in Moscow and in fact "more than in any other city but Kiev, only because for a period of time the [Magnitogorsk] fire marshall restricted attendance." Sixty percent of those attending were younger than thirty.

No one with whom I spoke on my second visit to Magnitogorsk in 1989 failed to remark on the impression the exhibit had made. Upon laying eyes on a formerly forbidden side of American life, many people expressed wonder combined with embarrassment. "It is simply shameful to see how well others live, while Soviet citizens have no access to such technology and conveniences," a number of people lamented. "We have nothing of our own to be proud of," a van driver from the wire factory remarked, slowly shaking his head as we bounced violently over the severely potholed Magnitogorsk roads. Recalling his children's reaction, one steelworker (quoted at length in chapter 1) shook his head, saying, "You should have heard their comments. 'Enough,' they said, 'we're going to America.' This is wrong, but I can't blame them."

Characteristic of its tone, the USIA's own summary report stressed that "most visitors could not figure out why the Americans would bring an exhibit to a place like Magnitogorsk." But that question was easy enough for the local inhabitants; for them, a far more puzzling one was why the authorities in Moscow had invited the Americans at all. "Surely our 'higher-ups' must have been aware of the scandal it would cause and the potential for demoralization?" an incredulous Galina Osolodkova, who had been responsible for hospitality in connection with the presence of some thirty young American guides, asked me. (In 1987 I had given Osolodkova, then approaching her second decade as a French teacher at the Mining Institute, the first copy she had ever seen of the newspaper *Le Monde*, which elicited a similar mixture of embarrassment, defensive patriotism, and disgust at being denied for questionable ideological reasons the very materials necessary to work in her profession.)

Feeling overwhelmed by the images of an apparently superior civilization, the Magnitogorsk newspaper fought back clumsily. American guides were excoriated for nakedly propagandizing the American way of life (as well as for rudeness, a lack of qualifications, a superior and aggressive attitude, and a complete disdain for the Soviet way of life). Under the rubric "One Day with a Guide," a spotlight on a thirty-two-year-old female employee of the Voice of America who worked at the exhibit, the newspaper singled out her supposed acknowledgment that she undertook no preparation for her job of answering questions about computers and her extremely materialistic outlook on life. "Americans simply cannot understand how we can endure such shortages and yet deeply love our motherland," the paper concluded, addressing itself not, of course, to Americans but to the inhabitants of Magnitogorsk.

Meanwhile, people came from hundreds of kilometers away and willingly endured up to five hours outdoors in long lines for a chance not only to see the heralded wonders of American civilization but to engage the young American guides in rare face-to-face conversation. "How much does a car cost? How many hours does a steelworker have to work to buy a kilo of meat? Do workers get to use resort facilities or just bosses? Can everyone go to a hospital when he is sick? Do Americans really think Russians want war?" Previous images of the enemy—unemployment, poverty, homelessness, racism, violent crime, political corruption, foreign interventionism—were swept aside. A new image, one of unbounded technological excellence predicated on the free flow of information, triumphed in its place. Receptivity to that new image was facilitated by the reflexive rejection of anything smacking of the old orthodoxy and by a fascination for things American that had survived all the years of tireless propaganda.

"The exhibit in Magnitogorsk widened the window for us into this interesting and desirable world," the Cheliabinsk provincial newspaper commented. But what, in the end, were the people to make of this brave new world? "What startles me," Aleksandr Chernomyrdin, a local computer expert, told the reporter, "is how widely computers have entered the everyday lives of Americans. They communicate with computers as easily as with television."

■　　■　　■

At its most basic level, *glasnost* meant that the authorities in Magnitogorsk, after being vigorously encouraged in their self-congratulation, collective deception, and false optimism for decades, were all of a sudden directed by Moscow to convince the populace of the need to face the music. "The deeper we involve ourselves in the work of *perestroika,* the clearer its scale becomes," explained Mikhail Lysenko, the public official in Magnitogorsk quickest to embrace the policy of *glasnost*. "Unresolved problems bring in their wake other problems. And all of these are problems of life itself; they are not imagined problems."

But in a radical departure, primary responsibility for realizing the party's new policy of greater openness fell not on party officials but on members of the media. Gorbachev's periodic speeches—including his famous and oft-quoted remark that "we do not even know what kind of society we live in"—conferred on journalists a mandate for vigorous action and an opportunity to augment their influence and power. To the journalists, however, much remained unclear: How far would the openness go? Was everything up for examination? If not, where would the line be drawn, and who would draw it? These ambiguities were further complicated by the confusion at the top about the precise nature of economic and political reform, a confusion reflected in the differing views expressed by certain leaders.

Then there was the matter of censorship, which, far from being an afterthought or vestige of a more repressive past that had been overcome, remained integral to the legitimacy of the ideology and thus of the regime. Censors enforced the sacred concept of *partiinost,* or "party-mindedness," the guiding principle in all intellectual matters according to which everything (especially truth) had to be subordinated to the party's interests (as defined by the rulers of the moment). In the hands of the authorities, party-mindedness functioned as an every-ready technique for manipulation and, above all, as an unquestionable justification of Communist party authority. As *glasnost* continued to develop, an inevitable showdown loomed between the party-mindedness enforced by censors and the independent reporting practiced by journalists.

Meanwhile, with censors on the retreat, the parameters of *glasnost* were essentially left to journalists to establish, and a bold new style of investigative reporting soon emerged in newly authoritative national weeklies such as *Ogonek* and *Moscow News,* monthlies such as *Novy mir* and *Yunost,* and television programs, especially the wildly popular radical news and variety show "Vzgliad." But because *glasnost* impinged upon the ideological foundations of the regime, the determination of its limits remained a hotly contested and explosive issue (although one framed in terms of freedom from censorship rather than the legitimacy of Communist party rule).

Pushing the assumed, although unspecified, "boundaries" ever farther, Moscow journalists pounded the drumbeat of criticism incessantly and pursued the next sensational revelation, thereby providing a model for the provinces to emulate. The standard set by "leading" publications and programs demonstrated, however, that even if there were no ambiguity in the leadership's elaboration of the concept of *glasnost,* the effective use of *glasnost* presumed not merely the regime's acknowledged sanction but the existence of the user's courage, critical thinking, and imagination. On this score the Magnitogorsk newspaper showed itself up to the task. Halting steps in 1987 toward "taboo" subjects gave way in 1988 to sophisticated in-depth treatments on institutions whose existence was previously unacknowledged or denied. By 1989 no aspect of city life had escaped the newspaper's searing spotlight—not even the very rationale of Soviet society: social security.

In a series of articles, Tatiana Leus explored the sacred cows of retirement benefits and medical care, with shocking results. "After a lifetime of work," Leus wrote, "the inhabitants of Magnitogorsk can look forward to support from the state." Indeed, of Magnitogorsk's population of 438,000, almost 20 percent received some kind of pension.* But what kind? Most pensions, it turned out, were sixty rubles or less per month—hardly enough to survive. A typical daily diet for those pensioners not receiving assistance from family members consisted of boiled eggs, toast, jam, and, when available, tea. And basic medicines, although generally not outrageously expensive, were hard to come by all the same.

Most elderly people lived with relatives, but for pensioners without family, the state provided nursing homes (where approximately 330,000 elderly people across the USSR lived). Yet of the elderly lodged in Magnitogorsk nursing homes, 80 percent had living relatives. Some of them had been told they were being taken to the hospital by relatives eager to assert possession of the older person's apartment. (Older people do not have any money that relatives and others scheme to acquire, however.) A trip by Leus to investigate the living conditions at one home revealed that instead of the fifty people specified by government regulations, residents were served by a meager staff of twelve and lived in squalor. In other words, far from a comfortable retirement in reward for a job well done, old age might mean poverty at home or in an institution. And if Leus's portrait of old age was bleak, her sketch of

---

* Normal retirement age for women is fifty-five; for men, sixty. Some people retire even earlier, such as those working in steelmaking shops, who may retire with full benefits at age fifty. About one-third of all retirees continue to work. There is a ceiling on how much they can earn in combination with pension benefits.

the city's health system would frighten anyone into staying healthy forever.

"How Much Does 'Free' Medical Care Cost?" she asked in yet another groundbreaking article. "For a long time free medical care has been an object of pride in our society," she wrote. "It was considered one of our chief accomplishments. It was not customary to talk about the conditions in which our doctors worked. Who looks a 'gift horse' in the mouth?" But "we are paying for free medical care with our health; the gift horse has rotten teeth."

"How much longer are we going to pronounce with pride the words 'free medical care'?" she asked, estimating the annual cost of a hospital bed in the city hospital at about five thousand rubles. Leus was less interested in conveying the specific figure than in bringing home the substantial monetary costs of that care and, more important, the even more costly health effects. To that end, she recounted an excursion to city hospital no. 1, "the best known, the one with the best specialists, the best equipment, and in the worst shape."

"In the summer water had to be carried into the hospital in buckets, like before the war. And now, in winter, there are constant interruptions" in the supply of water. "It is twelve degrees Celsius in some parts of the hospital, to say nothing of the lack of elementary supplies. Those compelled to stay in the hospital survive on food packages brought in by relatives. All the city's hospitals and clinics are served by a single laundry service, making for very poor results. There are beds in the hallways, beds in bathrooms. It's not an inn. You can't hang a sign that says, 'No vacancy.' "

"The material and technical base of the city's medical facilities are in an extremely difficult situation," N. E. Kulikov, chief of the city's Health Department, explained. "Most of the hospital is housed in buildings not up to the task; some of them are collapsing. Only a misfortune could force a person to check in and remain in hospitals such as ours." On the door of the only bath in the cancer ward hung the sign "Closed. Potential Danger." The entire wing had only two toilets, both of which were described as "exceedingly morbid." Some rooms contained up to fourteen patients. "We are a hundred years behind developed countries of the West," the reporter quoted the chief of the oncology dispensary as stating.

In such conditions, Leus wrote, doctors "routinely work miracles" to save people's lives. But, according to Kulikov, instead of the 2,190 doctors specified by official norms the city had 1,205, including 68 of 109 surgeons, 99 of 137 gynecologists, and 171 of 364 pediatricians. And the shortfall was growing. In 1988, 38 doctors left Magnitogorsk, primarily for lack of housing.

Although she hinted in the title to her article that privatization might be the answer to the city hospital's woes, Leus ultimately blamed government policy. "Money is allocated first and foremost to the factory's needs, housing is a distant second, medical care and other services get the meager leftovers," she wrote. Thus, to the implication of the superiority of capitalism was added an indictment of the Soviet government. *Glasnost* in the Magnitogorsk newspaper seemed to have a logic of its own based on alternately explicit and implicit comparisons, sometimes despite a journalist's intentions.

■   ■   ■

"We're afraid of the KGB, the Ministry of Internal Affairs, the Procuracy, bosses, colleagues at work, the city party committee—we're afraid of ourselves. Who are we, people or slaves?" asked Viktor Shraiman, director of both the Magnitogorsk city theater and the local puppet theater, in a *cri de coeur,* "For All That, I Still Believe," which appeared in the *Magnitogorsk Worker* in February 1989. Shraiman's article opened with colorful reminiscences of the absurdities of the Brezhnev era encapsulated by two incidents.

The first involved a touring Polish theater group that came to do a children's play, entitled *The Duck-Activist*. But the authorities deemed it to be "ideologically harmful, even diversionary." "A member of the cultural administration, who was a university teacher and a philologist, explained that for Soviet children the word *duck* [*utka*] would be associated with the 'ducks' [decoys] of Western radio programs. . . . I was so bold as to assure them that for the Soviet kids who would see the show, the title *Duck* would be associated only with a zoological duck and nothing more." On the verge of cancellation, *Duck* was saved only by Shraiman's dogged efforts.

The second incident involved an attempt to perform a play for adolescents called *Five Gold Coins* (*Piat' zolotykh*), in which the five coins "represented reason, courage, trustworthiness, and other wonderful human qualities." But "just about the same time, the fifth gold star appeared on the jacket of Leonid Il'ich [Brezhnev]. Such an association arose in some authority's mind." As with *Duck,* much frustrating and senseless wrangling was necessary so that the play could be staged, although under a different name.

In presenting these bitter and sad recollections, Shraiman himself complained that they nonetheless failed to convey the depth of despair brought on by Brezhnevism. He proposed to elaborate by relating the travails of the city's celebrated puppet theater, Buratino, founded by him in 1973, and he reserved his severest invective for the struggle over the theater's facility. "The theater," he wrote, "was designed by well-thinking people with unfortunately no concept of a theater: freezing in winter, stifling in summer, it was equipped with a stage without pockets to conceal and reveal scenery and had but twenty square meters of space to store all scenery in between productions.

"In this diabolical box called a theater, we have lived for sixteen years! And, my dear God, how many times during these years did we see bosses and commissions who would come, 'study the problem,' promise help, and then do nothing." It even happened that the authorities tried to evict the theater so that they could install a prepared-food retail outlet in the space. A compromise was reached, and the theater lost half the building. Later, city officials, mindful of the theater's public following, profusely apologized, but the food store stayed.

"Finally, they agreed to build a new theater. A competent architect drew up a plan, which was accepted by the theater company. In the process, however, it underwent revisions, was reduced in size, lost some features, and suffered delays. All the while it was being built as a 'service facility' [*khozblok*] to 'fool' financial authorities." For many years all across the country new buildings for cultural institutions were pro-scribed because housing and "other" needs (primarily industrial ones) were accorded priority—a slap in the face few people involved in culture took lightly, especially because there continued to be precious little housing for actors and artists.

"We were not sure it was just a ruse," wrote Shraiman. "Maybe it would be a *khozblok* and not a theater." In any case, to this day the new theater remains unfinished, while Shraiman no longer looks forward to its completion: the design had been so altered that it had become un-suitable for a theater. "Sixteen years, seventy productions seen by mil-lions of patrons around the USSR and abroad to great critical acclaim, but no decent building" was the sad conclusion to the story of what those involved in the theater understood as their tragic effort to bring culture to an industrial wasteland.

After unburdening himself of the saga of the theater's turbulent ex-istence at the mercy of the culture bureaucrats, Shraiman took up what he called Magnitogorsk's "sensory famine." "I will tell you why I love to travel abroad," he wrote, fully aware that although more than 95 percent of his audience would not have had the opportunity to share such an experience, most had seen the previous summer's American exhibit. "I can endure calmly the shocking abundance in the stores, I can survive the service that is otherworldly for the Soviet person, the kindness unfamiliar for the Soviet person encountered in hotels, offices, and restaurants, *but* I cannot avoid taking pleasure in the superlative urban design. I can stroll for hours through the streets of Tokyo, Paris, or New York, thirstily taking in the colorful creations that give rise to a feeling of eternal holiday.

"On Western city streets there is no senseless information of the variety that adorns our streets as the physical realization of administrative idiotism—all the calls to fly the planes of Aeroflot (as if we prefer to fly to Riazan on the planes of American Airlines), to put money in 'the' savings bank, to insure property. The information on Western streets is always meaningful and useful, and at the same time they are little masterpieces of urban design. . . . In the end, I do not bother about what they are advertising. I take pleasure in the composition, the plasticity, the color." To the indictment of bureaucratism rampant in the Soviet Union Shraiman added an encomium of an idealized West, long a reference point and source of inspiration for the Magnitogorsk theater director, conveyed by him to the public over the years through his plays and now through the newspaper.

■   ■   ■

Tatiana Saraeva had worked in the dreaded passport office at Magnitogorsk internal affairs headquarters for a number of years. There were two kinds of passports in the USSR: one for everyday identification, which contained information about one's place of work, residence, nationality, and marital status; another for traveling abroad. While everyone age sixteen or older had to possess the former, few people ever hoped to obtain the latter. Moreover, every Soviet citizen was required to register his or her place of residence with the militia, who placed an official stamp in the internal passport granting permission to reside there. Far from conferring the right to foreign travel, the word *passport* in Russian had come to symbolize the state's thirst for control over its own citizens. With *glasnost* that was beginning to change.

Officer Saraeva, visibly surprised by the presence of an American citizen, scoffed when asked whether she had ever spoken with an American before. "At my desk! Inside the local internal affairs office, one floor below the offices of the local KGB branch!" "And one above the former KGB interrogation cellars where so many people were shot," I added, pointing down, but she showed absolutely no concern, responding helpfully to all my questions. "Like everyone else, I read your article two years ago and was deeply impressed," she said with a smile.

Saraeva directed my attention to a backlog of applications for external passports, which were still not available to anyone as a matter of course but were being granted to everyone who presented an invitation from someone living abroad. "The rules have become looser and the number of applications has multiplied, but the size of the staff remains the same," she sighed. In addition, her office processed the temporary living permits of all foreigners residing in Magnitogorsk, of which there were several thousand and more arriving each day. Saraeva saw perhaps better than anyone else the process whereby the former isolation of the city's inhabitants was being eroded.

There still remained the business of "internal passports." As Saraeva explained it, however, much of her time was taken up with the many domestic scandals and battles over housing occupancy rights after divorce and death. Without hesitation she praised the easing of restrictions for external passports and underscored the need to abolish the internal passport system, although she suggested no alternative for regulating the allocation and occupancy of state-owned housing.

Saraeva welcomed the reforms but like most of her compatriots felt unsure about exactly what they would entail. "We are all worried," Saraeva admitted, speaking volubly. "Before we lived quietly; we didn't know. Now everything we read alarms us. We don't even know exactly why we are alarmed. But everyone feels it, this tremendous daily anxiety. Such are the times, very unsettling. This, for us, is the biggest change."

■   ■   ■

In early 1989 the director of the steel plant, concerned about the presence on factory grounds of an inquisitive reporter, in effect "arrested" him. This awkward moment demonstrated perhaps more than any single event the break that had taken place between the formerly hegemonic steel plant and the city's main source of printed information. The great factory could no longer expect the newspaper to be its cowed, compliant servant. Indeed, the factory director, sensitive to the arrival of a new era, apologized to the paper's editor after releasing the reporter. It would, he said, never happen again. A partial, although significant, realignment of power had taken place.

Institutionalization of the newspaper's considerable power did not come about as the result of a decree. Nor could that preeminence be attributed to the absence of an alternative daily. The authority of the *Magnitogorsk Worker* stemmed from its content, seen in the light of the importance of information in any contemporary society and of the boost provided by the contrast between the *glasnost*-era newspaper and its Brezhnevian incarnation. As breakthrough followed breakthrough, the readers became thirsty for more, wondering, What will be next? By 1989, there appeared to be no limits.

In retrospect, the unfolding of *glasnost* in Magnitogorsk came to seem more than a haphazard series of breakthroughs. It appeared to many as a directed process involving the continued widening of the boundaries of the examinable. Everyone intimately involved with the newspaper over the last several years agreed that its startling transformation was effected, whether wholly or only partially according to design, by Valerii Kucher, the editor since 1983.

"In order to judge all matters consciously," Kucher wrote in an editorial in 1989, "it is necessary to know everything about them. . . . There are still those who wonder if people are understanding 'correctly.' Should they know? Won't this information 'damage' their thinking? This will not do. We are creating an open, democratic society. . . . Our city like no other has been under the influence of stereotypes and dogma. And it seems to me that the task of the newspaper consists in the destruction of tired conceptions, to show readers that it is necessary to guard not pretty words but the human interest."

Kucher's tactics for implementing this program were closely attuned to the Soviet milieu: disarm the power of rumor by disclosing fact; establish and encourage public opinion and involvement through polls, solicitations of the opinions of leading experts in a variety of fields, and debate; preempt opposition by those unaccustomed and disinclined to such openness by self-consciously addressing the possible limits to *glasnost*, showing there can be none; and affix responsibility and encourage more responsible management by demanding and receiving responses from officials. Everyone acknowledged the impressive results, especially Kucher's newfound enemies in the local party hierarchy.

Journalists at the newspaper agreed that Kucher's greatest dexterity was exhibited in his battle with the bureau of the city party committee, on which Kucher sat, and which theoretically acted as the ultimate editorial board. "The paradox of our journalistic existence," Kucher pointedly explained, "consists in the fact that 120,000 readers support the *Magnitogorsk Worker,* but our work is evaluated by only a few people. And their evaluation at times does not correspond with the feelings of the city's inhabitants." But the weight of the readership's backing, expressed in hundreds of supportive letters skillfully used by Kucher, proved decisive. In this case at least, the public emerged stronger than the apparatchiks—if only because the public had a loyal and astute representative in the apparat.

And having won the trust of the ever-growing readership and wrested de facto control from the city party committee of what nominally remained its official organ, Kucher also insulated the content of the *Magnitogorsk Worker* from shifts in the ideological wind coming out of Moscow. The paper ceased waiting for signals from the Kremlin and followed its own course of action geared to local issues and the complexity of local politics. Cautious and indirect intimations about problems caused by the steel plant were replaced by debates between experts offering opposing points of view on whether the plant should be fully revamped—and if so, how—or perhaps partially, if not fully, retired. Similarly, discussions were published on private property, a multiparty system, and human rights. By 1989 the *Magnitogorsk Worker* had become unrecognizable, even by 1987 standards.

No less remarkable than the radical transformation of the newspaper was that of Kucher himself, a longtime party member who before becoming editor did a stint as a functionary in the apparat. When queried face to face Kucher remained inordinately circumspect, clearly having learned the art of sidestepping questions and the importance of keeping private his innermost thoughts. But he evinced a profound commitment to professional journalism and freedom of information.

Conceding that behind-the-scenes censorship, although monumentally decreased, still existed, Kucher vowed to eliminate it completely. "It is essential that all citizens of our country know what is permitted and what is forbidden. It is necessary seriously to fight for the rights of the citizens of our country and the rights of journalists to information. This right must be buttressed legally." Even in these times, Kucher's words were unusual for someone who was at least technically still an apparatchik and a member of the *nomenklatura* (those on the secret appointment list).

Part of the explanation for Kucher's intellectual development must lie in the brief but formative experience of the Khrushchev period. Yet many party members of Kucher's generation (those in their early and middle fifties) with high positions in Magnitogorsk did not share anything remotely like his vision or willingness to embrace the Gorbachev reform program. For Kucher the experience of a career as a journalist inculcated in him a sense of professionalism in that craft, while the course of events beginning in 1985 pushed him farther along in that direction than he ever imagined he would go. Yet even as he battered the system daily, Kucher continued to see himself as loyally serving the party in his work, struggling to blend the two sides of his hybrid status as party functionary cum *glasnost* journalist.

In the newspaper's rise Kucher provided indispensable leadership and clout, but he did not create the necessary staff out of thin air. The group of a dozen or so journalists working under him, having originally pursued their calling out of interest, had been able to develop their careers chiefly on merit, even if most (although not all) joined the party. In the new possibilities opened by *glasnost,* they responded by combining, as Kucher did, a fierce pride in professionalism and an abiding sense of social commitment.

.   .   .

Such was the progress of *glasnost* in Magnitogorsk by 1989 that even my request to spend several hours inside the infamous city hospital no. 1 was granted despite deep misgivings by the director, Dr. Anfisa Andreeva. "Medicine is part of the social sphere, which is not on the highest level," she cautioned, trying to prepare me for what lay in store. She regretted that "only 4 percent of the state budget goes for medicine. This is a pittance."

Andreeva singled out overcrowding and the lack of modern technology as the two biggest problems. She was then interrupted by an urgent phone call. "What's going on there with the water? The pressure is falling?" Returning to the conversation, she emphasized that Magnitogorsk hospitals were, "of course, far behind the West, but, with the exception of certain special medical centers, not really behind Moscow.

"Construction on the present building complex of city hospital no. 1 began in 1942. The first patient was admitted in 1947. In forty years, more than one million patients have been treated. This does not include patients visited on regular rounds made to the countryside. Each patient is entitled to seven square meters of space. The actual amount is closer to four." But a walk through the hospital revealed that in many wards cots lined the narrow hallways, virtually blocking all traffic; the rooms, cluttered with fifteen or more beds, resembled refugee centers.

Since 1987 the hospital's physical plant had been undergoing its first major overhaul. Most departments were being expanded and rebuilt; some newer equipment was being added. The hospital had no computers. The most advanced equipment, primarily of East German make, dated from the late 1970s but would have been unrecognizable to anyone who had been a patient in a Western hospital since well before then.

Andreeva stressed that the staff members under her direction were "sufficiently skilled; they work hard." Her remarks were echoed by the hospital's chief lung specialist, who claimed that "by Soviet standards, our department is not bad. Our hands are no worse; we just don't have enough of them. Of course, the equipment is old and we lack many things. There are not enough sterilizers or gloves. We hope for improvements." Most physicians accepted their lot stoically. One volunteered the comment that her work was "no different from that in any wartime hospital."

A scheduled operation that was to be made accessible for observation had to be canceled. There was no water. Andreeva disclosed that as part of its reconstruction the hospital was building its own water pumping system. When I asked how in the meantime a hospital could function without a regular supply of water, she reiterated construction plans and cited recent party decisions on the social sphere. An accompanying surgeon sighed deeply.

"Patients don't complain," Andreeva asserted. "They understand our conditions; they know we do our best." When I asked a room full of patients—who were told they were in the presence of an American—if they were satisfied, one of them, after a look of disbelief and a moment's hesitation, came forward and instead of answering began to describe her ailments in detail. She was visibly disappointed to learn that I was not a medical doctor, but a historian.

Each day the morgue received an average of four bodies. The staff was required to perform an autopsy on every one, regardless of the wishes of the deceased's relatives, as a check on doctors' diagnoses. Refrigerators were collective, not individualized, and overcrowded. Some bodies were lying on tables packed in ice. The stench was overwhelming. Andreeva was obviously aware of the impression such a scene would make. Yet as reluctant as she was to display the full extent of the hospital's woes, Andreeva complied with all my requests, even more keen to avoid seeming out of step with the new openness.

■　　■　　■

An ordinary room with rows of pewlike benches containing the plaintiff and her family; a few tables for the attorneys, judge, and court staff; and a boxlike enclosure containing two defendants and flanked by three uniformed militiamen were the scene for the first Magnitogorsk trial witnessed by a foreigner. The charge was rape.

In 1987 four boys, the oldest born in 1967, got together, got drunk, and by their own admission had sex with four girls, the youngest born in 1973, in various parts of an apartment: the kitchen, bathroom, a living room couch, and a sofabed. A year later, in December 1988, the father of one of the girls found out about the incident and turned to the courts for redress. Two of the four boys were arrested. Five months later, their case was being heard before Judge Valentina Khazieva of the city court.

Heads shaven, the defendants had already spent several months in pretrial detention. Characteristically, individuals accused of crimes in the Soviet Union serve up to six months in jail before trial; some may be behind bars awaiting trial for years. A previous criminal record is the first piece of information introduced at trial, regardless of the charge. Acquittals number between five and six per one thousand cases.

In the Soviet legal system, as in the Japanese, there are no juries. All cases are decided by a judge, who is assisted by two "people's assessors." Attorneys for the defense are not mandatory. The accused can request an attorney but does not automatically receive one; often defendants do without representation. (If the defendant is a minor, however, then counsel is mandatory.) In this case, an attorney for the defense and the prosecutor, who had prepared the case, were present but said little. The judge did almost all of the questioning.

People's assessors are "elected" at their place of work. Each enterprise receives a request to send people to the court every so often to serve for fifteen-day periods, with their wages paid by the court. Having served, assessors often return. "It's very rare to get active ones, those who ask questions," Judge Khazieva lamented. "Even when I ask them if they have any questions, they usually shake their heads. They prefer to listen. Most are women. Of course, they are not judicial experts. But with time they do learn the law."

Cases originate with the militia, so named to distinguish them from their Western counterparts, the police, supposed servants of the bourgeoisie. "The militia are permitted two months for an investigation," Khazieva explained. "They can get more time only with the permission of the procurator. An investigator draws up an indictment, which is shown to the court. If we think there is sufficient reason, we accept the case. We ourselves cannot increase the charges, although we can lower them or ask for further investigation. Later, there can be appeals, reviewed by a three-judge board. Some cases may even be appealed higher than that."

During the second day of the trial, Judge Khazieva questioned one of the girls in whose name charges were being brought; two years after the alleged rape, she was sixteen. After establishing that sexual intercourse had taken place in the apartment, the judge asked a series of questions: "How did you end up alone with the defendant in the apartment? Who saw you together? Did you ask them for help? Did you resist? Did you got to the hospital afterward or seek help?"

The girl replied, "I did not resist. I did not seek help." "You were afraid," the judge interrupted. "Yes," came the barely audible reply. The girl added that after the original unreported incident, she had further intercourse with the accused in the woods and in dirt-floor basements beneath apartment buildings. The judge was troubled by what she considered to be the girl's uncanny lack of sense in how to avoid dangerous situations and how to seek help. The judge spent considerable time trying to establish why the girl at no point appealed for help, why she "endured" it.

The girl admitted that the boys who allegedly gang-raped her on several occasions never threatened her to keep quiet, which, Khazieva reasoned, suggested that they must have known she would not tell anyone. Even later she continued to meet with them in public and private. And one after another, boys began approaching her for sex. "It never occurred to you, why they were hitting on you?" the judge asked, dumbfounded. "Of course it did. They must have told the whole neighborhood it was possible to screw me," the girl said through tears. Not only did the girl make no effort to escape from dangerous situations, the judge ascertained; one time she managed to leave, only to return voluntarily a short while later.

Judge Khazieva appeared incredulous. "Why didn't you seek help?" "It would have been useless, useless," the girl shouted. At this point, she broke down in sobs, and her body began convulsing. An ambulance was summoned. Looking away from the quivering girl, a male attorney remarked to no one in particular, "They can really act, when they need to." A recess was declared, and the judge invited me to her chambers.

When in 1987 I had expressed a desire to my hosts at the Mining Institute to witness a court case of their choosing, they flatly refused. For these educators this request confirmed even more than all the others that I had come to Magnitogorsk mainly "to dig up dirt," which they evidently thought abounded and had to be concealed. In 1989 it was no longer necessary to secure the permission of a host institution; the judge agreed without hesitation. "To tell you the truth," she stated, "no one had ever before expressed an interest in talking to me about my work."

In the case before her the judge explained that the two boys were being charged under article 117.3 (forced gang rape) of the Russian Federation Criminal Code. If convicted, they faced a sentence of five to fifteen years. A lesser charge, such as article 119 (voluntary sex with a minor) carried less severe but still substantial penalties. The decision was entirely up to Khazieva.

Noticeably disturbed by the events in question, the judge seemed torn about what to rule because of how the girl had acted in the circumstances. Because the boys admitted that intercourse had taken place, claiming it was consensual, the judge thought it necessary in determining the validity of their assertion to focus on the girl's actions—this despite the legal stipulation that sex with a minor could never be consensual. In evaluating the girl's testimony, the judge seemed incapable of acknowledging that anyone could regard appeal to the authorities as futile.

"I don't understand her behavior," the judge said, shaking her head for emphasis. "She did not turn to anyone for help. Fourteen years old. I just don't know." The judge revealed that she had her own teenage daughter. "No one has ever dragged her off to a basement." Meanwhile, emergency medical personnel finally came. The young girl was taken out on a stretcher, crying and still shaking violently.

"Every day it's like this for me," the judge continued. "Insanity. They scream, often abuse me, and then refuse to leave the room. They try to prove that I'm not following the rules or that our system is wrong. It's gotten very difficult to work. The stress is extreme." In Judge Khazieva's ward, there were six judges, three men and three women. She was the only woman who handled criminal cases. "We can't always take it," she remarked. "We're not made of stone. Yet we're not supposed to show any emotion."

The judge, who was forty, talked about her new apartment, for which she and her husband had waited more than a decade. "The building is so poorly built, no satirist could describe it. I tell you the plain truth. We can't buy furniture. We have the money. There's just none to buy." She talked about the lack of a telephone at home. "Actually, it's a blessing. My husband is a shop chief at the steel plant. If we had a phone, the few hours he's able to get away from the plant there would be no peace." Her salary was 241 rubles a month. Her husband made three times that. They had no car, but they did possess a color television set. Her biggest wish was for a vacuum cleaner. "There's a mountain of dust every day when I get home. But where can we find one?

"I'm very, very busy. Too busy. The judicial calendar is full for several months. I must read all my cases thoroughly, which I often end up doing at home. I get twenty-eight days to finish a case, and I have several going on simultaneously. I'm responsible for any delays, such as if this girl is not able to resume testifying tomorrow. I feel pressured to hurry to meet the deadlines, but I can't. It's not right. Then they yell at me. There is no respect for judges or for the law. We do not even have a law to prevent people from insulting and threatening judges right in the court. I am poorly paid. Our quarters are cramped. Let's face it—we're not a priority.

"Nevertheless, I like the fact that I don't depend on anyone. I am completely independent. I run the case. I make sure it goes properly. I take pleasure in the law and in having responsibility. It's hard. I work and work but don't see any results. In fact, crime just rises. I don't know what more I can do." In the case before her, the judge returned a verdict of guilty to the lesser charge of sex with a minor and gave as the sentence three years in a labor colony.

■   ■   ■

As *glasnost* advanced, all manner of information about and explicit comparisons with the West became frequent in the *Magnitogorsk Worker*. Like the American exhibit, such comparisons showed the Soviet Union in an extremely unfavorable light. For instance, it was reported by TASS and carried in the Magnitogorsk paper that between 25 and 33 percent of all produce grown in the Soviet Union was wasted. Forty percent of all potatoes harvested were wasted—an astonishing figure that did not even include those that had not been gathered during the harvest but had been left to rot in the fields. By contrast, TASS reported that Holland, a highly urbanized country far smaller than even a single province of the Russian republic, lost about 1 percent of its harvested potato crop.

If scandals in agriculture stirred little controversy in a population long used to food shortages, no reportage conveyed the impression of Soviet inferiority in the face of Western superiority better than that of L. D. Sak, a leading Magnitogorsk neurosurgeon invited to visit an Australian hospital who returned with a glowing report. Sak's commentary, delivered in a nonsensational but passionate tone, followed and built upon Leus's pathbreaking indictment of Soviet medicine. In this way, health care, one of the principal bases upon which supposed Soviet superiority had always been asserted, turned out to provide one of the chief vehicles for undermining those cherished beliefs.

Dr. Sak discovered that despite widespread rumors about the unaffordably high costs for individuals of Western medical care, 87 percent of the population was insured, paying between 1 and 4 percent of their salaries for the privilege of being treated by the most up-to-date equipment in the world. "Those who pay 1 percent of their salary for insurance lay in rooms with two to three people and a color television," he wrote. "Those who pay 4 percent get private rooms—with a telephone, color television, VCR, and refrigerator." Sak did not ask, but his readers could not help but wonder, how many Magnitogorsk households, forgetting about hospital rooms, could claim ownership of such inventory.

"Those 13 percent of the population who do not pay insurance are treated in state hospitals," he continued, "also without charge. . . . The concept of 'food packages' does not exist. A patient may order any meal (in keeping with the doctor's recommendation). Visitors bring flowers, videos, and books.

"In every hospital a visitor may drink a cup of coffee with a biscuit— without charge. A nurse who has been rude to a patient or visitor is fired in such a way that she cannot find work as a nurse anymore. She has no choice but to change her profession or leave the country. . . . Life expectancy is seventy-six to seventy-seven for men, seventy-nine for women (second in the world, after Japan). Infant mortality is very low.

"The hospital where a doctor works subscribes to all the medical journals he needs free of charge. Specialists receive extra pay for knowledge of a foreign language. . . . If a patient wants to thank a doctor and pay him or her extra, it is not considered a bribe. . . . If a doctor has worked for the same company for ten years, he is entitled to three months' paid vacation.

"As far as diagnostic equipment is concerned, in Australia it is computerized, even in hospitals for dogs. The problem of somehow 'getting hold of medicine' does not exist. If the prescribed medicine is not available in Australia, the pharmacist simply obtains it from abroad. In a word," concluded Doctor Sak, echoing a familiar slogan, "everything is done for the benefit of the people."

An editorial note placed after the interview urged the reader not to view the interview "tendentiously: how great things are 'over there,' how bad they are 'over here.'" Instead, the note identified a different goal: to demonstrate how much could be achieved when serious attention was devoted to social issues. All the same, scores of readers voiced precisely the conclusions the editor's note sought to dispel.

■   ■   ■

At the Magnitogorsk theater, *glasnost,* having initially boosted morale and imparted a renewed sense of purpose, underwent a profound transformation between 1987 and 1989, by which time the new freedom became problematic and even unwelcome.

Voices, the hit of 1989, was composed entirely of quotations from previously forbidden works by selectively published novelists and poets: Osip Mandelshtam, Boris Pasternak, Aleksandr Solzhenitsyn, Mikhail Bulgakov, Anna Akhmatova, Marina Tsvetaeva, Vladimir Vysotsky, Aleksandr Galich, Joseph Brodsky. "Absolutely nothing was added, not a single word, to their 'voices,'" declared Evgenii Terletskii, the theater's principal performer and the person behind the compendium, his eyes intense with pride and emotion. "It became public just this year, but we lived it many years already. This was our intellectual food. Poetry was always close to our hearts. We breathed in its air; it made us whole and free."

Voices grew out of better than ten years' worth of conversations on bare, uneven wooden stools around a makeshift kitchen table—a kind of intellectual emigration of intimate friends exchanging gossip and forbidden literature, all of it eventually confiscated by the KGB. "It was very quiet here during the Brezhnev period," Terletskii admitted while we were seated around that very kitchen table, he reciting satirical poems and singing unofficial songs from the camps and the war. "We had no 'dissidents.' Everyone barked, like a dog, 'Hurrah!' 'Long live . . .' The organs [KGB] interfered on occasion with our productions at the theater, but usually not directly. A few people, myself included, every now and then managed to bring back from our trips to the big cities a forbidden book or samizdat. These would make the rounds, until word inevitably got out and the materials were confiscated. Although no one I know was sent away, our circle remained very small."

In the play, while Terletskii and others perform the songs and read the poems and excerpted stories of the Russian language's most prominent cultural figures in the twentieth century, two *chekisty,* or members of the security police, go about their business of tormenting, arresting, interrogating, and punishing the creators of Russian high culture. Scene after scene brings forth the power of exquisite poetry and the drama of senseless persecution.

Osip Mandelshtam's biting 1933 epigram about Stalin, whom the poet called the "cockroach-mustached" Kremlin mountaineer, "murderer and slayer of peasants," with "thick wormlike fingers." Word of the existence of the epigram led to the poet's arrest, followed by a police request, with which Mandelshtam complied, to write out the poem for the police archives.

The intervention by Pasternak on Mandelshtam's behalf in the form of a letter to Stalin, who then telephoned Pasternak and offered reassurances. Stalin's voice is joined by those of other cultural policemen, such as Brezhnev's ideology chief, Mikhail Suslov, whose stentorian comment upon reading Vasily Grossman's novella, *Everything Flows*—"it cannot be published in this country for at least 200 years"—turned out to be wrong by more than 170 years.

The long poem "Requiem" by Anna Akhmatova describing her seventeen months in prison queues in Leningrad with other women, desperately hoping for some information about their disappeared loved ones, in which she speaks of "the hour of remembrance" and wants "to remember each one by her name, / But they took the list, and no one remains."

Yevgenia Ginzburg's *Journey into the Whirlwind,* a memoir of her arrest and experiences in labor camps among women, especially of one woman accused of being a Trotskyite (*trotskistka*) who muttered that she had never in her life ridden a tractor and therefore had no idea why they had arrested her for being a tractor driver (*traktoristka*).

Perhaps the quintessential moment in the play that captures the conflict between cultural heroes and villains is the 1966 "trial" of Joseph

Brodsky for parasitism, an event that took place during the lives of the cast. Scenes from the interrogation and trial are calculated to shock:

Judge: What is your occupation?

Brodsky: I write poems. I translate. I suppose . . .

Judge: Never mind what you "suppose." Stand properly. Do not lean against the wall. Look at the court properly. Have you a regular job?

Brodsky: I wrote poems. I thought they would be printed. . . .

Judge: That doesn't interest us. We're interested in what institution you were connected with.

Brodsky: I had contracts with a publishing house.

Judge: Then answer. Did you have enough contracts to live on? Give us a list of them with dates and the sums they were for.

Brodsky: I don't remember exactly. . . .

Judge: What is your real trade?

Brodsky: I'm a poet. And a translator of poetry.

Judge: Who has recognized you as a poet? Who has given you a place among the poets?

Brodsky: No one. And who gave me a place among the human race?

Several witnesses testify on Brodsky's behalf, supporting his contention that he has indeed worked very hard, although he has not been paid very much. Defense counsel contends that Brodsky did not write some of the poems of which he stands "accused." A psychiatric report ordered by the court deems Brodsky fit to perform hard labor.

"Witnesses" for the prosecution also appear. One Smirnov remarks, "I am not personally acquainted with Brodsky, but I wish to say that if all citizens adopted the same attitude as Brodsky toward the accumulation of material values, Communism would not be built for a long time." Nikolaev, also careful to dissociate himself from Brodsky while nevertheless providing "testimony," concurs: "I am not personally acquainted with Brodsky. . . . Brodsky isn't only a work-shy element. He is a militant work-shy element. Brodsky must be treated ruthlessly." The last remark evokes applause from the "spectators" in the courtroom.

Requests by the defense that the prosecution's "witnesses" produce evidence are rebuffed. Instead, a plumber, speaking "as a citizen and a representative of the public," is permitted to declare that Brodsky's "activities don't satisfy me as a worker," although the plumber has to admit that he had not read Brodsky for the simple reason that none of his books could be found in a library.

In its summation the prosecution proceeds by slandering Brodsky, quoting calumnies published in the official press and adding choice words of its own. "Brodsky isn't a poet, but a man who writes puny verses. . . . We must compel Brodsky to do forced labor. We must banish him from our heroic city [Leningrad]. He is a work-shy element, a lout, a man who is spiritually foul." The judges return a "verdict" of five years' forced labor.*

The public reenactment in *Voices* of previously private conversations amounted to much more than a performance; it was the culmination of the moral and intellectual odyssey of a small group of self-styled intelligentsia, despairing of their fate yet making the most out of it intellectually and emotionally. For the overwhelming majority of Magnitogorsk inhabitants the only luxuries are emotional—zones of feeling and cultivated gardens of personal relationships. Among writers and artists this situation is further heightened by their burning sense of mission and quest for moral purity, which pervade their art.

Ironically, the removal of the cultural police from the life of the theater left these artists in a void. Gone was the tension, the constant pressure against which they defined themselves. Deprived of the obstacles that paradoxically provided them with their capacity to create, they suffered not simply from the anguish of not knowing what to do; they also felt robbed of a rationale for doing anything at all. After more than a decade together, the group disbanded. Terletskii, a Jew, decided to emigrate to Israel. Shraiman, also Jewish, was not sure.

•   ■   ■

Someday the theater in Magnitogorsk may rise again to become a beacon of truth through the unique power of the word in Russian culture. For the time being, however, such a distinction belongs to the city newspaper. For decades an unprincipled mouthpiece of Stalinist and then Brezhnevite propaganda, the *Magnitogorsk Worker* in a brief time has made itself into an increasingly professional and politically committed source of enlightenment and justice.

Utterly free of accounts of fires, murders, and plane crashes; devoid of descriptions of celebrities' affairs; and without photographs of women in lingerie, the *Magnitogorsk Worker* is lively, fair, and concerned above all with analyzing and improving life in Magnitogorsk and with

---

* Later pardoned and released, Brodsky incurred repeated harassment until his emigration in 1972. In 1987 he joined Solzhenitsyn as the second Soviet writer living and publishing in exile to receive a Nobel Prize for literature.

providing absolute support for Mikhail Gorbachev. In 1989 *Pravda* singled out the *Magnitogorsk Worker* as one of the country's two best provincial newspapers, judging from letters sent by readers.

In Magnitogorsk, as in the Soviet Union generally, *glasnost* has been
propelled forward by an immense appetite for knowledge of the outside
world. If in seeking to account for the receptivity of Western examples
one would be wrong to exaggerate their inherent appeal, one would be
no less incorrect to underestimate their attraction, especially in the form
that they became available to Magnitogorsk inhabitants. We must also
keep in mind the evolution of Soviet society in the years since Stalin's
death, particularly the formation of a substantial group of educated and
aspiring technicians and professionals and the attainment of near-uni-
versal literacy. Whereas under Khrushchev, circulation for the literary
monthlies in which such authors as Solzhenitsyn were first published
never exceeded several hundred thousand, under Gorbachev circulation
for those same monthlies soared to several million and would have
climbed far higher had not paper shortages necessitated imposing limits
on them.

Even during the Brezhnev era, information about Western life leaked
through little by little. Under Gorbachev the dam was allowed to burst,
letting in a flood whose impact was compounded by the earlier efforts
to hold it back. *Glasnost*—whether through television, the movies, newspaper reports, exhibitions, travel abroad, or direct contact with foreigners at home—has enabled Magnitogorsk inhabitants to learn immeasur-
ably more than ever before about the West. But in the process they have
had to confront the challenge to their system posed by a fuller vision of
the West, however inaccurate or one-sided.

"Many Soviet citizens," explained Vladimir Ishimov, a local sociologist, "have long suspected that their living standards were far below
those of the West, but it is another thing to have this suspicion confirmed with graphic reporting. Readers share a deep anger at having
been deemed unworthy of knowing basic facts about their own lives and
country and having been systematically lied to." True enough, yet most
people at the same time have expressed gratitude for finally being
deemed worthy of the truth and for the possibility at long last of living
in it.

Just as significant, although not immediately obvious from a day-to-
day perspective, with the aid of the newspaper Magnitogorsk society has
opened up to itself. In just a short time it has become "normal" to acknowledge social problems, to speak about them, and to allow outsiders

to see. The shame is still there, but it is tempered by the strong desire for contact and the quiet pride of having such contact sought by sympathetic visiters. Magnitogorsk inhabitants have learned many unflattering and painful facts about their lives. Nevertheless, most people have come to believe that knowing the truth, even when harsh, is preferable to hiding behind comforting, but ultimately self-defeating, half-truths.

But if *glasnost* in Magnitogorsk has brought about a far-reaching, if not readily visible, moral healing, this has come about less in the service and more at the expense of the Communist system. No less profound than the discovery of having been systematically lied to and the satisfaction from finally being able to know the truth has been the explosion of the widely shared belief that the Soviet Union possesses a more humane system than capitalism does.

In apparent confirmation of the effects of ideology and censorship, the people of Magnitogorsk have been shocked to learn—from a barrage of stories about comparative living standards, social services (health care, pensions, housing, poverty), and political and legal systems (past and present)—not that their way of life was maybe inferior to the West's but just *how* inferior it seemed to be, materially *and* morally, despite all the struggle and sacrifice. *Glasnost,* which was intended to energize the population and rally it around the reforms by exposing society's ills, has by the logic of its own development evolved into an officially promoted debunking of the Soviet order. But by itself *glasnost* does not constitute an alternative.

CHAPTER THREE

Squaring the Circle
Reform of and by the Communist Party

"Looking back over my sixteen and a half years in the party," confided Aleksandr Baryshnikov in a long letter to the Magnitogorsk newspaper published in January 1989, "I come ever more frequently to the conclusion that there is much I cannot understand . . . that maybe I really am a Communist of the 'stagnation period,' and that now I'm behind the times, although I'm only forty-two years old."

But evaluating the Brezhnev years, now derisively known as the "period of stagnation," in the light of *perestroika*, Baryshnikov recalled that "back then we did not know it was stagnation. . . . [Today] many say that in the textile industry people used to get credit for work they did not do. Let's even say it happened, but stores were flooded with shirts, pants, suits, and overcoats! Where are they now? Refrigerators, televisions, washing machines—they were all freely available. Where are they now? Where? Who will answer me? I do not overly praise that era, but neither do I raise my hand against it."

As for *perestroika*, Baryshnikov pointedly noted that since 1985 prices had been rising slowly but surely—not officially, he recognized, yet all the same, "we're being prepared for a big price increase." The advent of cooperatives was no less ominous. He asserted that "90 percent of the people know that the coops are fleecers, as the majority of Communists

say, but only in whispers. In public they say, 'Sure, they're necessary.'
. . . In villages these coops will become kulaks; in cities, capitalists," Baryshnikov warned. "It is necessary, very necessary that people live better,
but not in such a way that some live better at the expense of others. In
this matter, I'm sorry, I'm no helper for the party."

Baryshnikov expressed concern for the young. "Where are we leading
them?" he asked, fiercely objecting to the recent film *Little Vera,* an in-
dulgent but stark portrayal of Soviet life in a grim industrial town
resembling Magnitogorsk (it was actually shot in Mariupol, formerly
Zhdanov). There are no recognizable heroes in the film, whose one re-
deeming character, the spunky Vera, is driven by the perfectly conven-
tional circumstances of her life to attempt suicide.

New party slogans irritated him. " 'All power to the soviets!' What's
this slogan for?" he wrote. "Soviets already have power." "Democracy!"
he continued. "A beautiful word. But what do we need it for without
discipline? The pluralism of opinions will become a pluralism of actions.
Let's recall Armenia, Azerbaijan. Why are our soldiers dying there?
They don't have the right to defend themselves. Enough of that vandal-
ism.

"How can one live? Just accept the cooperatives—the fleecers, the
private taxis, the extortionists, the *Little Vera*s, cooperative meat at
four or five rubles a kilo, meat pies at 'negotiated prices' of thirty-four
kopecks, pants for one hundred rubles, and other products of 'energetic
people'—no, I cannot," he concluded. To make matters worse, "the
clergy are interviewed in the newspaper; they even show them on television. On the 1000th anniversary of the conversion to Christianity of
Rus, they let them into the Bolshoi Theater, even into the Kremlin!"

But wherever Baryshnikov turned to vent his frustration, his complaints were met with the same words: "It's the policy of the party! So
I figured that since I do not understand the policy of our party, and I
will never agree with it, it's better if I left the party. Let private taxi
drivers, coop members, shish-kebab stand operators, whomever this
policy helps and whoever with both hands is for it, let them enter the
party. Once the time of those who are solely out for themselves has
passed, I'll rejoin. But for now I cannot be in the party; my conscience
won't allow it. Therefore I'm leaving. I don't want to be ballast."

Within a week the newspaper received 120 responses to Baryshnikov's confused but sincere outpouring of frustration and doubt. A. Kurnosov, deputy party secretary at the railroad yard where Baryshnikov
worked, responded in some anger. "He seems to think that *perestroika* is

directed *against* the people," Kurnosov wrote. "By whom? The party? His position amounts to, 'There's no need to think; they do the thinking for us.' He blames the film *Little Vera*—but it is actually real life being shown." Kurnosov pointed out that "only Gorbachev allowed Baryshnikov to speak out, yet using *perestroika*, Baryshnikov claims he doesn't like it."

Some people thought Baryshnikov was an invention; others felt someone named Baryshnikov probably existed but that the journalists composed the letter. The newspaper insisted that Baryshnikov wrote the letter, although it reported that he had not yet formally submitted his request to leave the party. Only a few of the published letters defended Baryshnikov, but even those that attacked him nevertheless showed that he was not the only one who was alarmed.

"Baryshnikov's letter," wrote V. Starkov, a nonparty teacher at the Mining Institute, "is the fruit of sixty years of political and economic disinformation, of illiteracy, especially economic illiteracy, and of despotism." Was this, in fact, what the decades-long leadership of the Communist party had wrought? To be sure, in publishing Baryshnikov's letter and readers' responses, the newspaper, far from seeking to discredit the party, wanted to demonstrate how the party was being transformed and, above all, to push it farther down the path of reform. But the location and direction of that path were becoming murkier and murkier. Starkov accused Baryshnikov of "running like a rat from a sinking ship."

■   ■   ■

As of 1989 there were about twenty-five thousand Communist party members (one out of every thirteen people) in Magnitogorsk. All members were affiliated with a primary party organization (PPO), often called a party cell, at their place of work (or at a neighboring one, if theirs was too small to have a PPO). At the time, Magnitogorsk had several hundred such PPOs, thereby giving the party a ubiquitous presence throughout the city and qualifying the autonomy of any organization or institution. Enterprises, courts, hospitals, and schools had to obtain the approval of their respective party organizations before firing, promoting, or just shuffling around party members on their staff. Party cells could in turn make their own recommendations to management on personnel and other matters affecting their institutions.

Magnitogorsk's PPOs were directly responsible to one of the city's three district committees (*raikom*), which corresponded to urban administrative divisions. The sheer size of the steel plant's PPO—nine thousand members—meant that the party committee there was really its own *raikom,* as was the party at the large wire factory. Members of the *raikom,* along with secretaries of the largest PPOs, were not expected to hold other jobs. Party work was their sole occupation. They were, in other words, apparatchiks.

Above the *raikom* was the city party committee (*gorkom*), which had ninety-five full and eighteen candidate members and was nominally the highest authority in the city. Nevertheless, most *gorkom* members held regular jobs outside the party, while day-to-day administration was carried out by a separate *gorkom* apparat. *Gorkom* members who were not part of the apparat gained clout back at their enterprises from their membership but had little say in running city affairs. Conversely, only the most highly placed among the seventy-odd full-time employees of the apparat were even members of the *gorkom* itself. The apparat, in effect the real power in the city, included the *raikom* staff and the party secretaries of the largest PPOs.

Moreover, within the *gorkom* there was a bureau of twelve to thirteen members, all but a few of whom were the highest ranking members of the *gorkom* apparat. A ruling group within the ruling group, these apparatchiks linked Magnitogorsk with the next tier up in the party pyramid: all members of the bureau sat on the provincial party committee (*obkom*) in Cheliabinsk, which in turn answered to the all-union Central Committee in Moscow (until 1990 the Russian republic was the only one without a republic-level party organization; see figure 1).*

As reflected in its structure, the Communist party was an administrative machine with a hierarchical chain of command. It also functioned as a huge personnel department, either placing Communists from its notorious *nomenklatura* in key positions of responsibility in industry and government or requiring those already in such positions to join. In this capacity, the party served as a mechanism for extracting loyalty through career advancement and privileged access to scarce goods and services.

Communists at every level of the party pyramid were expected to work for the people in carrying out the party's program, but this was

* Parallel to the party pyramid there is a state apparatus, with the Supreme Soviet in Moscow, a republican soviet in Moscow (since 1990), a provincial soviet in Cheliabinsk, and a city soviet and three district soviets in Magnitogorsk composed of deputies who are formally elected. But as Gorbachev has readily admitted, the soviets, without the power to tax and thus without financial resources of their own, have no effective power. The reverberations in Magnitogorsk of efforts to reform the state administration beginning with the Supreme Soviet are dealt with in chapter 5.

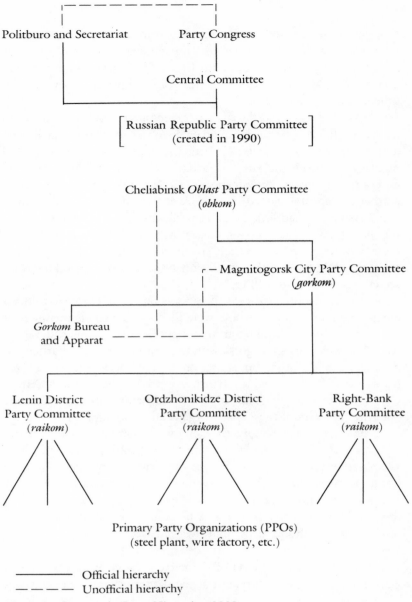

Primary Party Organizations (PPOs)
(steel plant, wire factory, etc.)

———— Official hierarchy
– – – – Unofficial hierarchy

Figure 1. Communist Party Hierarchy (1989)

Note: The Politburo (i.e., political bureau) and Secretariat theoretically served the Central Committee but actually stood above it. Similarly, the *gorkom* bureau and apparat (i.e., local secretariat), although technically subordinated to the *gorkom*, operated above it. The *gorkom* apparat, not all of whose members were on the *gorkom* itself, included every functionary of the *raikom*s and the top layer of officials in the largest PPOs.

especially true of those engaged in party work as their full-time occupation. Elena Karelina, the Magnitogorsk newspaper's correspondent for party affairs, had the latter consideration in mind when she posed the question of party reform, asking, "For whom does the apparat work?" In response she put forth a reform agenda: make party life "more interesting" for party workers and "connect" the work of the apparatchik to the lives of the people.

In voicing this aspiration Karelina recalled a vision of the party that had sparked calls for reform under every Soviet leader since (and including) Lenin: totally dedicated, superhumanly active members working utterly unselfishly for and in the closest contact with the people to carry out the party's platform unquestionably. But if, as Baryshnikov's *cri de coeur* showed, the party's latest summons to remake itself and get behind the new policy was not met with universal approval by the rank-and-file faithful in Magnitogorsk, responses by those outside the ranks of the party, judging by hundreds of conversations in the spring of 1989, were characterized by extreme skepticism laced with contempt. "The Eternal Hurrah, our avant-garde," one nonparty manager laughed, scoffing at the notion of party reform. "The game is over. Everyone knows that the party has shit all over itself."

Was the party in Magnitogorsk capable of reforming itself and becoming the spearhead of the "new line" introduced by the Moscow leadership? Was the local leadership in Magnitogorsk even interested in finding out? Notwithstanding the tradition of "party discipline" whereby instructions from above were received as firm marching orders down below, by early 1989 the results of attempted party "renewal" in Magnitogorsk had raised doubts in the minds of the initially enthusiastic reform-minded local party cadres.

■   ■   ■

In 1987 there was absolutely no visible sign in Magnitogorsk of party reform. By 1989 party reform, variously called "renewal" and "democratization," was one of the dominant issues in the city. The turning point had come in the spring of 1988 when, citing the need to overhaul the basic structure of the party, the Communist leadership in Moscow announced a party conference for late June, the nineteenth such gathering but the first since 1941.

Perestroika was first unveiled as the party's program at the Twenty-seventh Congress in February 1986. The next national meeting of Communists—theoretically where ultimate party authority resides and which convenes roughly every five years—was scheduled for 1990. A sense of impatience with the pace of reform led to the revival in the interval between congresses of the lapsed tradition of the party conference. Because it was extraordinary, the conference was expected to inject momentum into the essentially stalled reform process still described as *perestroika*.

For the party in Magnitogorsk the first order of business was the "election" of delegates to the conference. According to newspaper reports, in the city's Ordzhonikidze *raikom*, where there were six candidates for two positions, a hand vote was taken. Ivan Romazan (factory director and Central Committee member) and Iurii Sychev (the party secretary for the mechanical shops) emerged victorious. Meanwhile, in the city's right-bank *raikom*, Bal (a brigadier) was selected from two candidates, and in the Lenin *raikom*, from among four candidates, Vitalii Riabkov, a member of the *gorkom* bureau, was chosen. "It is not worth concealing that not everyone at the meetings of the party active [expanded *gorkom*] agreed with the suggested election procedure," the newspaper wrote, apparently in reference to the open balloting.

Next the *gorkom* met to endorse the four "elected" candidates. But it also "added" two workers, N. Vertoletskii and Odetova, to the list, both of whom had been defeated at the lower level meetings. The matter then passed to the *obkom*, where the election of Bal, Vertoletskii, Romazan, and Riabkov was "confirmed" but that of Sychev and Odetova (neither being members of the *gorkom*) was overturned. Stobbe (first secretary of the city committee) was added to the Magnitogorsk list out of the blue.

The "final" results of the Magnitogorsk elections to the conference were there for all to see: not all of those elected became delegates; not all of the actual delegates had been elected. In addition, it emerged that Ivan Romazan had been absent on vacation when his candidacy was put forward and endorsed at a factory party meeting. "He's the boss. One decides for all, and all vote for one," explained one seasoned party veteran, disgusted by the results, in subsequent conversation with me.

Elena Karelina approached the chief of the Magnitogorsk party's organizational bureau, Anatolii Klishin, one of the thirteen members of the *gorkom* bureau, and asked him to explain why Vertoletskii, also a member of the bureau, could be chosen by the *obkom* when he had failed to get elected at the *raikom* party meeting. She was told that the *obkom* had taken into account the "social composition" of the Magnitogorsk party organization: Vertoletskii was a steelworker.

"One way or another, then," Karelina pressed him, "it happens that democracy has only begun to develop, and conditions for its violation are already being created. Everyone wants to look like a democrat, but objectively they act differently. How often is it possible to fall back on the excuse, 'We're still learning'?"

"I remind you," Klishin responded, "that alongside the deployed processes of democratization, internal party structure continues as before. We [the *gorkom*] are not the final authority. The *obkom* may correct us at any time. Democracy exists at the level of discussion, but at the level of implementation, democratic centralism takes over."

■   ■   ■

In March 1988 the newspaper disclosed the formation of a "group" calling itself Counter Movement and led by Valerii Timofeev, a construction worker, and Vladimir Sidorov, a music teacher. The group's reasons for forming were not given, but the newspaper slammed it for lacking a concrete program. "How easy it is to criticize, to point fingers," the editorial scolded the group, admonishing its members: "Don't hurry to make noise." Only when the paper accused the group of appealing to emotions with such slogans as "Get rid of all open-hearth ovens at once" did it emerge what Counter Movement might be about.

Similarly, the newspaper faulted the group for failing to obtain official sanction for a public demonstration held the previous November—the first (albeit indirect) disclosure of a very newsworthy event. The paper added in passing that since that time no group had been granted permission for a demonstration, as no "deserving requests" had been submitted.

A meeting between representatives of Counter Movement and city authorities was finally arranged. Upon arrival, those attending discovered that the appointed place was suddenly closed for "emergency renovations." Far from singling out such behavior for censure, the paper excused it as reflecting a "lack of experience living in conditions of democracy." In any case, the meeting was rescheduled and took place on the "renovated" premises.

At the meeting, Shamraev, a teacher at the Mining Institute, characterized the proceedings pejoratively as a "polemic." He made a point of mentioning how closely Counter Movement's "program"—which he gave as "solve all the social problems of the city, develop the city's culture, pay more attention to the city's ecology, and reestablish the city's history"—resembled the existing party program. "Why then," wondered Shamraev, "is this organization necessary?" In other words, thanks but no thanks; the party neither needed nor wanted helpers.

But soon the authorities reversed themselves, giving Counter Movement—colloquially known as an "informal" (*neformal,* from the English word)—the formal status of an "amateur [*liubitelskaia*] organization attached to the Leninist Komsomol palace of culture," a recreational facility owned and managed by the steel plant for its employees. That the group needed official recognition, attachment to a state institution, and a reason to exist other than its members' own desire to do so seemed to be taken for granted.

Similarly, subsequent treatments of Counter Movement by the newspaper, although still hostile, were also less clumsy. "What kind of *neformals* could form in Magnitogorsk?" asked Vladimir Mozgovoi in a long and carefully crafted article later that summer. "There are no old buildings; therefore, there is no problem with preserving our architectural heritage and national culture. That leaves ecology." Mozgovoi implied that preservation of national culture and ecology were the only possible vehicles for launching oneself into politics from outside the party apparat. Unfortunately, he neglected to discuss the strong reaction of the apparat, clearly taken aback by the new phenomenon thrusting itself into the apparat's previously monopolized domain. Instead, he focused on the group's formation.

According to Mozgovoi, "Counter Movement was first formed in the fall of 1987 as a 'group of general social direction.' Only later did they discover the ecology theme." He suggested but did not state that there might be an element of opportunism involved. Mozgovoi pointed out that Counter Movement called itself a "patriotic organization" but was careful not to associate openly with a "discredited movement." No specific movements were mentioned, but the Moscow-based Russian chauvinist and avowedly anti-Semitic Pamyat (Memory) came easily to a Magnitogorsk reader's mind. In keeping with the article's style, however, Mozgovoi left open the question of why Counter Movement, the first sanctioned "unofficial" political organization in Magnitogorsk, might desire such affiliation.

■   ■   ■

In connection with the special party conference, a campaign of party certification (*attestatsiia*) was undertaken across the country. Formerly, such examinations of party members were called by the technical term *chistka,* which originally signified a purge or cleansing of the ranks but under Stalin came to mean their wholesale slaughter. Such unpleasant Stalinist connotations dictated use of a different expression for the current cleansing effort.

"Certification of specialists, engineers, workplaces, and shops are conducted regularly in accordance with various demands," the Magnitogorsk newspaper pointed out, "but Communists are being certified for the first time in many decades. To what end?" No clear answer was provided. Yet as even low-level party members were aware, inside the upper reaches of the party an internecine struggle over the course of the reforms was taking place. Although the fate of the country was thought to hang in the balance, party discipline dictated that such a conflict remain behind closed doors.

Explaining none of this to its readership, the newspaper instead asserted, perhaps disingenuously, that the central leadership "did not expect that the certification would arouse and worry Communists so much." Evidently, anticipated or not, this was exactly what happened. The article itself was an obvious effort to calm the ranks.

"The conversation at a certification takes place in an extremely friendly, comradely tone," the paper reassured its readers. "The person being certified is invited to sit at the table with the members of the commission, so as not to have to answer questions standing up." How comforting such contrasts with previous practice could have been is hard to gauge. In any case, notwithstanding these precautions there was evidently some friction.

"There have been instances," the paper reported, "when certain party members, not infrequently distinguished people in the past, categorically opposed certification. Some even said so at party meetings: 'Who has the nerve to doubt my party-mindedness?' " Defying the rules, some members did not wait for the certification and simply turned in their party cards. Yet reciting party regulations, the paper pointed out that "a member of the CPSU [Communist Party of the Soviet Union] is obliged to observe party and state discipline, which applies equally to all party members."

Of the 20,829 Communists who had passed through the certification by 1 September 1988, almost half, 9,127 members, had received some kind of admonishment, but only 76 had been expelled. It was hard to know what to make of these figures, and no one from the leadership indicated whether it was good news or bad. Nevertheless, First Secretary Stobbe did conclude his assessment of the purge on a self-critical

note, conceding that "unfortunately, the main goal of the party certification—the raising of the leading role of Communists in *perestroika* and
in the whole life of working collectives—was not attained everywhere."

Summaries of the certification in particular primary party organizations revolved around the same themes. "The certification of Communists is a new form of work," Valerii Mikhailov, party secretary for the
factory's huge rolling shops, was quoted as saying. "It justifies itself.
Activeness has risen perceptibly; more people are speaking at party
meetings." Mikhailov admitted, however, that some Communists were
saying, "A month will go by, then two, a year, and won't things return
to the way they were?"

According to Mikhailov, in his shop twelve Communists were expelled, and seventy-eight received admonishments and therefore had to
go through the process again. A few voluntarily quit, despite the necessity involved in such an action of having to get up and formally explain
one's exit in front of the entire party committee. "Some people," Mikhailov acknowledged, "may be wondering what will happen to a person expelled from the party." Indeed, but he did not say. Instead Mikhailov summarized the reactions of those expelled: "Some take it badly;
others try to make it seem as if nothing has happened. A few just wave
their hands and say, 'I'll survive without the party.' " As for those who
had resigned, none was quoted, but this scarcely mattered; their decisions to give up their party cards already indicated that they had drawn
the same conclusion.

At the top the purge formed part of what would be an unsuccessful
effort by reform-minded Communists at the party conference to gain
control of the national organization; in Magnitogorsk the purge served
as a kind of loudspeaker for broadcasting the party's ills, delivering what
amounted to a self-administered blow to the party's prestige and confidence. Maybe the letter writer Aleksandr Baryshnikov was not so confused after all when he concluded that despite the rhetoric, the reform
program meant the destruction of the party and that the duty of all true
believing Communists was to resign or, as he implied, to hunker down
and resist *perestroika*. With substantial material privileges threatened as
well, *perestroika* just did not seem to make that much sense for the very
organization charged with leading the way at the local level.

■   ■   ■

Counter Movement met every Sunday morning at the palace of culture. On 16 April, there were nineteen people, more than half of them

women and all but three older than forty. Well past the announced starting time, it seemed no meeting would take place. One woman asked,
"Who will lead us?" There was no response. Then a man got up, went
to the front of the room, announced his name as Gai, and stated that he
would give a report on the legal subgroup's activities, which consisted
of a campaign against the Magnitogorsk newspaper.

"They don't publish our letters or answer our complaints," Gai asserted. "They're not interested in addressing serious questions. Yet
there's nowhere else to go: the trade unions, the party, the Procuracy,
they're all connected. All they care about is getting hold of oranges and
fashionable clothing so they can live well and speculate." When Gai
asked the small group if anyone had written a letter to the newspaper
that had gone unanswered, several hands shot into the air. But upon
closer questioning, it turned out that these people either had not mailed
their letters or had received answers, just not ones that satisfied them.
Gai wrote down their names anyway. "Let *them* prove they answered
your letters," he remarked.

One woman who had been glaring at me for more than an hour suddenly asked who I was. At first neither she nor anyone else believed my
answer. But one person who recognized me convinced the others that
it was so, at which point the woman apologized. "I thought you were
'from there,' " she said, referring to the KGB. "I'm sorry if I offended
you, but you see we hear that 'over there' they know everything about
us."

As the meeting wore on the discussion touched on everything from
Soviet power—"it died with Lenin"—to the April 1989 events in
Tblisi—"a disgrace" (not an injustice)—where an unknown number of
people, including women and children, were killed during a demonstration by soldiers wielding shovels. Someone asked where new letters
ought to be sent: to local deputies, to the central press, to the Central
Committee? Aside from the writing of angry letters, the group did not
appear to have a function.

According to one man at the meeting who appointed himself spokes-
person but refused to give his name, the movement had no formal membership. "Whoever shows up, shows up," he said. "I am not a leader.
Our leaders have not been coming to the meetings for more than a
month already. There are seven of them in the council. At first we
fought for ecology; now we're combating alcoholism." When he began
to fudge an answer to my question about the larger goals of the movement, one of the women interrupted, "Yes, why do we exist? Maybe we

should close down." A man made a proposal to "assemble the council and settle once and for all why we exist," but someone else objected that our leadership doesn't need us, that's why they don't come." On that note, the meeting petered out.

In the fourth issue of *Breathing*, an independent, typewritten literary monthly, an anonymous writer published a well-informed exposé of Counter Movement. The author pointed out that the group's leaders, Timofeev and Sidorov, "begged the city authorities to register their group while conducting essentially no organizational work among the populace in order to achieve public recognition, which is higher than any official acknowledgment." Not surprisingly, the writer concluded, "they are used like a puppet by the apparat."

Indeed, the registration of Counter Movement in Magnitogorsk would be cited again and again by the city party committee as proof that "reform" was proceeding nicely. Never mind that registration was granted only after the *obkom*, recipient of a barrage of letters mailed by leaders of Counter Movement to the Central Committee, sought to show its own reform bona fides and reprimanded the Magnitogorsk city committee for its "antiquated attitude toward dialogue with the people." After some prodding, the Magnitogorsk apparat reevaluated the emergence of Counter Movement, discovering just how valuable the existence of an informal political group could be.

■   ■   ■

Throughout 1988 the *Magnitogorsk Worker* continued to press for the "cleansing" of the party, airing even the most damning criticisms with the aim of fostering the party's rebirth. In addition to its attacks on the ossified bureaucratism of the apparat, the paper took aim at the issue of cynical careerism.

In a letter printed in the newspaper V. Bazylev, a nonparty teacher at the Mining Institute, wrote that people joined the party purely out of calculation. " 'Get into the party while you're in school,' they say. 'It's easier to earn a diploma that way.' " According to Bazylev, such thoughts often emanated from above. He offered the example of a person being groomed for a leadership position in any Soviet institution. "When they discover he has no party card, they quickly assemble the necessary recommendations, he becomes a 'candidate' member for the minimum period, and so on." Perhaps frustrated by his own status, Bazylev wrote that "one can rise to a certain level without party membership, but higher, no way."

Obviously disgruntled, Bazylev noted that "to try cleansing the party of such members is useless. You have to get at the roots. If membership were not associated with privileges and prestige, then it wouldn't be necessary to determine who doesn't [really] belong." But curiously, instead of advocating the removal of all privileges, as his letter seemed to suggest, Bazylev limited himself to recommending a reduction of the ranks by elimination of all those who were using their membership for their own good. "Who needs nineteen million anyway?" he asked rhetorically. But who would be left if all the "opportunists" had to leave? And how was the party to replenish its ranks in the future? Why would anyone become a member, if not to obtain privileges?

        ■   ■   ■

On 28 July 1988 the newspaper published what it called "answers by the chief of the city KGB, Viktor Grigorevich Lavrishchev, to questions from the editor." It was a shocking publication, not least because the mysterious organization came out into the open for the first time yet did so without either apology or explanation, simply identifying itself (and its head) as if it were any normal government institution.

Lavrishchev asserted that he was responding to letters received by the newspaper on the "leaflet" (?) distributed in the city and signed GIMN (?). "The city KGB branch is also getting such letters requesting us to take action," he revealed, without specifying the content of the leaflets. "L. G. Cheshev, a driver, sent in a leaflet with a note appended to the back: 'Respected comrades of the KGB! In July those leaflets appeared in mailboxes. I heard that such trash is being posted around the city. Can it be that you are not able to apprehend the "authors"? This is real propaganda against Soviet power and the state. It is impermissible.' " Here in a request from the "people" was Lavrishchev's mandate.

"The numerous letters of citizens prompted the city KGB, together with the Procuracy, to evaluate the facts as described in the letters," Lavrishchev continued. "We came to the conclusion that the activity of the group GIMN falls under the jurisdiction of the KGB." By way of explanation, he asserted that the content of the leaflet (still unspecified) "touches on the political basis of our state" and that GIMN "acted in a secret underground manner."

Lavrishchev's "responses" to the editor's questions were followed by two long quotations from the rectors of the Teachers College, Valentin Romanov, and the Mining Institute, Vitalii Riabkov. Each scholar set out to demonstrate why the theories put forth by GIMN were not true

Marxism-Leninism, which these theories evidently claimed to be. (Only here do we get any sense of the content of the leaflets.) Their exegeses resembled the familiar heresy-hunting of Stalinist and Brezhnevite vintage, complete with appropriate citations from Lenin's *Collected Works*. In refuting the arguments of GIMN without presenting them, Lavrishchev himself could not claim to be an expert on Marxism-Leninism. But with the cooperation of the city's two "highest authorities" on scientific truth, Romanov and Riabkov, he did not have to.

In conclusion, Lavrishchev lauded the driver Cheshev and all those who performed their civic duty by informing the KGB whenever they came across something suspicious. Yet despite the seriousness of its transgressions, GIMN was merely admonished. To a question about how the newspaper's readership was demanding "severe punishment" for the conspirators, Lavrishchev replied with magnanimity. "Of course, in the present conditions of democracy and *glasnost* the opinion of the people is decisive," he allowed. "But we can take into account that during our discussion with the members of GIMN it became clear that they are not irreversibly lost people. It must be said that from the first days of their birth the organs, following the traditions laid down by Feliks Dzierżyński, have been concerned not to punish people but to help them get on the right track."

By highlighting this "lenient" treatment of the supposedly dangerous GIMN, Lavrishchev sought to make maximum political capital for the KGB out of the appearance of the city's first "dissidents." The advent of a group consisting of no more than half a dozen devoted "Marxists," by an irony of history, provided convenient justification for the continued existence of the repressive organs even in the new era of *perestroika*. Yet in the end Lavrishchev's attempt to fashion a new public image for the KGB as an agency devoted to and working within the law yielded a bizarre amalgam of Stalinism and *glasnost*.

■   ■   ■

As low as the reputation of the Communist party had fallen, that of its preparatory organization, the Communist Youth League, or Komsomol, had fallen lower still. Membership in the Komsomol for all students of high school age was technically voluntary but in effect mandatory, if only because nonmembership invited unsolicited scrutiny (to say nothing of the potential damage to one's career). Only a small percentage of Komsomol members were accepted into the ranks of the party, although people often remained Komsomol members until the age of thirty and beyond. Like the party, the Komsomol had its own apparat, which disposed of a great many resources, from concert tickets to vacations abroad.

My discussions with scores of young people revealed almost universal alienation and an extreme, almost rabid contempt for the Komsomol. Even the more thoughtful among the youth had nothing positive to say about life in Magnitogorsk and only loathing for the Komsomol. "We have nowhere to go, nothing to do," one young woman lamented. "There's not a single café or watering hole. Earlier we went to discos held at schools and other places, but now they're packed with twelve- and thirteen-year-olds, so us older kids no longer go. You just can't imagine what it's like for us.

"We can't get books. Even the library doesn't have anything decent. If I showed you our collection of foreign literature in translation you'd be moved to tears. And there is absolutely no opportunity to practice a foreign language—why bother to learn one? Indeed, how could you learn one? Travel is out of the question for all except the ordained.

"As a Young Pioneer, I can remember being so proud and happy to wear the uniform, the red scarf. We thought we were special and that we could do anything. We sang songs together. No sooner did I enter the Komsomol than cynicism set in, just like that. It's hard to explain but everyone goes through it. You can pick out the kids in your group who are going to become the next generation of apparatchiks.

"At first there was massive enthusiasm among youth for *perestroika*. We went out of our heads. Now we're fed up. How long can you go on hoping in the absence of *any* results? Just the same lack of opportunities, the same restrictions, the same bureaucratic types wielding power. They said Komsomol membership would finally be voluntary, but we don't trust them. Who among us is going to be the first to leave and assume the risk, and for what?"

That question was put to Aleksandr Anikhin, first secretary of Magnitogorsk's Komsomol, by a reporter from the wire factory newspaper in 1989. "Today the Komsomol must wash itself clean," he conceded. "But I think we made a mistake in 1986 when we opened the floodgates and began to criticize the Komsomol without grounds. I'm not against criticism as such; I'm against unconstructive criticism." Anikhin described his own situation as that of a person under siege, but he indicated that he was fighting back.

"People, even some of the older generation, are saying all kinds of things. They say that previously the Komsomol gave out medals for

God knows what. But let's take Stalin's time, Brezhnev's time. Who helped aviation? The Komsomol. Who helped the navy? The Komsomol. An emergency arose, who liquidated it? The Komsomol. And the fields were plowed—by the Komsomol. In Afghanistan the youth fought. Today on every important construction site in the country there are youth."

Asked to comment on the desirability of other youth organizations, Anikhin was dismissive: "I don't see any real alternative youth organizations in Magnitogorsk. There are groups of an unofficial character, but I'm certain that none of them can offer the kinds of opportunities that the Komsomol can." Indeed, aside from references to past heroics, I combed the interview in vain to find a justification for the continued existence of the Komsomol other than that of maintaining control over scarce resources.

■   ■   ■

Vladimir Zerkin, one of the leaders of GIMN, agreed to meet with me at his home. When I arrived, he took me underneath the building to a dirt-floor cellar, where he had set up a small workshop. "There are no bugs here," he commented as we sat on concrete blocks.

"I left the army in 1978 and joined the Magnitogorsk militia," he began, intensity in his eyes. "In 1985 I was fired. They were knee-deep in corruption, and I wouldn't look the other way. They were afraid I was going to blow the whistle.

"In May 1988 GIMN, which stands for Group for the Study of the Marxist Heritage, was formed by the union of two groups: the original GIMN, which I began in January 1988, and another group, without a name, begun in the fall of 1987 by Borodin, my cousin. We shared a serious commitment to the classics [of Marxism].

"Toward the end of June 1988, we distributed several leaflets exposing the present system for what it is. The first and second one in four hundred copies; the third, eight hundred. We chose the residential districts with the highest concentration of workers and slipped them into mailboxes under the cover of darkness.

"On 9 July people were called in for a 'conversation' [with the KGB]. Some people wrote up 'explanations' [confessions], which they then signed. How were the organs able to discover who we were so fast? This was when it became clear that Borodin was a secret KGB informer, something I should have suspected.

"Lavrishchev's article in the newspaper appeared that same month. At work they fired me the next day. I wrote a response to Lavrishchev's slander but received no answer from him. But I did meet with Kucher, the editor of the newspaper. He lectured me on party-mindedness and the fact that the newspaper was the organ of the city party committee. It was clear he was not interested in fundamental change either.

"For the rest of the summer we did nothing, out of fear. At the end of August we were given a warning by the chief procurator that our activities were anti-Soviet and unconstitutional. 'You should consider yourselves warned,' he repeated sternly. In July, August, and September 1988 I was under constant surveillance, twenty-four hours a day. I was accompanied wherever I went, my phone was tapped, my neighbors were 'recruited' to assist. I know they didn't plant a bug directly in the apartment because it takes time to install the devices (I've seen them) and neither my wife nor I was ever away from the apartment for more than two hours. So they enlisted the upstairs neighbor to listen in and watch us.

"In October within our group we had an argument about whether to issue another leaflet. This forced a split back into the original groups. The group originally without a name continued to call itself GIMN. We—the forerunner GIMN—decided to adopt the name Workers Group. Then the members of the splinter Workers Group accused me of being an employee of the KGB, so I'm on my own now. I don't need them anyway. The real constituency for a new movement is the working class.

"*Perestroika* is not a revolution; it is the ideology of the bureaucracy. Our system is not socialist; it is not based on Marxism. If you go back and read Marx, you'll see that he intended nothing like what we have.

"They're preparing another 1937. You can see by the decrees that are being issued to ready the repressive machinery. There'll be an edict soon ending *glasnost*. *Perestroika* is a double game. Meanwhile workers are ready for a real revolution. Our task is to get in touch with other true Marxists. There are many around the country. Because of the state's repressive apparatus we are forced into a conspiratorial mode, which is how we work best anyway.

"How big was the Bolshevik conspiracy when they began? And look how they overturned all Russia before the revolution was stolen by the bureaucrats. Only a new workers movement, an iron dictatorship of the proletariat, can save the situation. It will not be possible to avoid blood-shed."

■   ■   ■

One of the decisions reached by the special party conference had been to schedule new elections to party posts in the locales. In Magni-togorsk there were far fewer nominations than expected, especially given the goal of raising rank-and-file "activism." It was freely acknowl-edged that many Communists were afraid to assume responsibility in the aftermath of the certification, during which a large number of those in such posts had been rebuked for being too "passive." Moreover, the elaborate procedures drawn up for the nominating process, ostensibly to prevent the unwieldy proliferation of candidates, aroused great skep-ticism.

The newspaper frankly reported that people suspected "all these sessions for nominating the discussion are nothing other than a grand charade, a show of democracy, growing out of a desire to appear innovative and thereby earn political capital. And at the dis-trictwide meeting, everything will be fixed so that those desired by the top will be elected." That the behavior of "certain individuals" had served only to confirm these suspicions was noted with re-gret.

Repeated assurances of alternative candidates and a secret ballot did little to dispel the sense of orchestration. In a familiar ploy, turnover in the leadership of party cells was "permitted," but all positions in the *raikom*s were assigned from above according to the secret list. When the results were announced, the newspaper revealed that three representa-tives of the *obkom,* including the first secretary, had taken part—as spec-ified in party regulations. To the extent that there was a surge of activism from below, it took the time-honored form of venting long-held griev-ances against local higher-ups under the cover of even bigger higher-ups from outside.

Not long after the party conference, a meeting took place between the city's five returning delegates and the party "active," a select group of comrades thought to be the most loyal and active. Yet in a newspaper account Elena Karelina admitted that the mood in the auditorium was tense and that "the party rank and file were not always in agreement with the delegates." When Vitalii Riabkov claimed the conference was distinguished by its "modesty" (no "mementos" were distributed to the delegates), he was challenged from the floor. "Why then were six separate Volgas needed to pick up the [six] delegates upon their return at the Magnitogorsk airport?" someone called out. Riabkov's response, if he made one, went unreported.

•   ■   ■

Vadim Borodin, a twenty-nine-year-old schoolteacher who co-founded GIMN, claimed during an interview at his apartment to have spent his entire life studying Marxism. "In Marxism I see, above all, a formidable methodology," he explained. "The group GIMN was formed precisely to study that method seriously." Whereas his counter-part Zerkin saw in Marxism a tool for making another revolution, Borodin took pleasure in the analysis. The conversation soon turned to his relations with Zerkin.

"I know what he says about me, that I'm a KGB informant," Borodin acknowledged. "People say the same about him. He thinks he knows everything about how the KGB works; he thinks they follow his every move. Zerkin is a classic paranoiac. As for his accusations, I can only tell you what happened that July.

"While I was away for a few days in Moscow and my parents were at work, my wife was visited by the KGB. They asked if she objected to their looking around a bit. Stunned, she reflexively answered that she did not [object]. They made a thorough search, took a number of documents, all of which they later returned (no doubt having copied them).

"Over the phone I spoke with the city procurator, who advised me to make a formal complaint. I considered this useless because my wife had not asked them their names, and anyway she had agreed to let them 'look around.' Had she said no, their action would have been illegal. You see we have laws, but they are flexible.

"As soon as I returned from Moscow, the KGB called for me, as I expected. They picked me up, drove me to their offices, and we had a friendly conversation. After that, they came around to talk with me a few more times. That August the procurator hinted that we might get into trouble if we continued our actions."

Borodin produced a pile of typewritten papers, articles he had writ-ten on topics ranging from divisions within the party to beauty contests that served as the vehicles for discussion among the group. Without visibly tiring he went on for hours about the undiminished fecundity of Marxism, brushing off the objections I raised on the basis of the ex-perience of Eastern Europe and his own country.

■　　■　　■

"In our country, *perestroika* was begun on the initiative of the party," Lev Stobbe told the newspaper in a 1988 "interview" in which no questions were asked. "The people supported the party. Now it's necessary to go further. This is possible only under conditions of the growth of the democratic basis of life in the party itself. And this leads to the problem of elevating the avant-garde role of the party in the renewal of the country by means of the democratization of the party's inner life. In this consists one of the guarantees of the irreversibility of *perestroika*."

Around the time of these remarks, in the fall of 1988, the Magnitogorsk apparat was reorganized with great fanfare. Some departments were abolished (industrial transport, construction, trade and finance), new ones were formed (socioeconomic development), and old ones were reorganized (agitprop becoming ideology). In explaining the new demands and style of party work, Stobbe emphasized that the reorganization would free the party from a concentration on economic matters and enable it to attend to political and ideological matters. Moreover, "less paper meant more face-to-face contact for the apparat with primary party organizations." But when asked by the newspaper whether the new names for the various departments would involve little more than the need to order new business cards, Stobbe conceded that "such a danger exists."

In conjunction with the reforms of the apparat, Elena Karelina interviewed Anatolii Makeev, first secretary of the Lenin district party committee (*raikom*), in the spring of 1989. Around the time of the special Nineteenth Party Conference in 1988, there had been talk of eliminating the *raikom*s as part of an effort to reduce the bloated party bureaucracy. But it was decided to retain them, a decision popular with few people. Karelina's interview was an attempt to face this dissatisfaction. Makeev's district, which included the Mining Institute and the wire factory, was considered the most "progressive" of the three in the city, yet he could not help but be on the defensive when, for example, he was asked to address the issue of the *raikom*'s budget.

Makeev claimed that revenues, which amounted to 496,000 rubles, consisted entirely of members' dues payments. Expenditures were 225,000, with the balance being sent to Moscow. Out of its budget the *raikom*, according to Makeev, paid the salaries of twenty party workers and two drivers as well as typists, technical clerical workers, and cleaning people; the salaries of secretaries of the largest primary party organizations within the *raikom*'s jurisdiction; subscriptions to newspapers, journals, and agitprop materials; and trips by the staff. "It would be beneficial if the entire financial activity of the party became accessible to a wide circle of people," Makeev remarked. "If everyone knew how miserly were the funds disposed of by the apparat, it would kill the rumors and gossip." So much for sucking the blood of the people. But he said nothing (nor was he asked) about the many apartments at the *raikom*'s disposal. Except for the top bosses at the steel plant, no one obtained apartments faster than the apparatchiks did.

Karelina pointed out that it was not her first conversation with party workers, none of whom had ever expressed satisfaction with his or her material position. "Why do the people have a slightly different impression, to put it mildly, about the circumstances of a party worker?" she asked.

"Everything is relative," Makeev responded. "A first secretary gets 330 rubles, 375 with the additional allowance for living in the Urals. When I was a shop boss, of course I earned more." Makeev added that earlier, apparat staff could vacation in factory-owned resorts. "Now it's hard to get reservations even at our own party resorts." He made no mention of the fact that there were *no* resorts set aside for teachers, food-service employees, homemakers, and many, many others.

"My next question," Karelina continued, "is perhaps not completely appropriate, and I ask your pardon. But I learned that soon after our meeting you will be in Cheliabinsk to take care of your health, at the *obkom* hospital. What, in our city there are no decent specialists?"

"I had an operation in Cheliabinsk," Makeev replied, "and it is perfectly natural that the doctor who performed the operation should continue to monitor my condition." Why he initially went to the *obkom* hospital in Cheliabinsk, however, was left unexplained.

■   ■   ■

At the end of a lecture delivered by invitation in a large auditorium filled to capacity at the Teachers College, I announced that I had brought a copy of the program of the Democratic Union, a self-styled but unrecognized political party based in Moscow that advocated "capitalism and bourgeois democracy." At the suggestion that all those interested come to the podium and that one volunteer step forward to read my one copy aloud, a large crowd of students gathered around me, one of whom began reading. Another standing nearby seemed to be intently observing those present; I later learned she was a student at the college and the daughter of the local KGB chief.

The Magnitogorsk KGB recruited locally, chiefly in the language departments of the Teachers College and the Mining Institute. Naturally everything was done with the utmost discretion, but it happened that other students learned who among them signed up. Both men and women were sought. Those combining superior intellectual abilities with physical prowess were most highly prized.

By no means did everyone living in Magnitogorsk come in contact with the KGB. In fact, some people claimed to have discovered the existence of a local branch office only after having made my acquaintance. People employed in key industrial shops, including the construction of the new steelmaking converter, whose work was subject to independent KGB monitoring, were among those most likely to come in contact with KGB personnel

Glasnost notwithstanding, neither the size nor the current budget of the KGB in Magnitogorsk had been publicly disclosed. Vladilen Moshkovtsev, a longtime party propagandist and writer, claimed he was invited to give a lecture as part of the KGB's cultural training. He asserted that more than twenty young people in uniform were in attendance, although he conceded that an undisclosed number of others were on duty somewhere else at the time of the lecture.

One young man who used to work for the militia pegged the number of KGB operative staff, including those working in surrounding villages, at around fifty. Another, who claimed his friend worked for them, insisted there were no fewer than seventy-five full-time employees. "That's not counting their use of informants everywhere," he noted, adding, "none of whom is paid. Informing is strictly 'voluntary.' "

In 1987 it was possible to be permitted into the reception and office area of the KGB, still located in the same building in whose cellars the forerunner NKVD had shot hundreds of people. Inside a young man and an athletic young woman, both in civilian clothes, were engaged in a competitive game of table tennis. Pictures of Dzierżyński, the organization's founder, hung on the wall.

The duty officer, on whose desk were nine phones, many of them different colors, was extremely polite although perhaps a bit taken aback that I had rung the bell. Ignoring for a moment the ringing phones, he escorted me to a conference room and closed the door behind me. After a long interval he returned with the suggestion that I come back the next day for an interview with his chief. But the next morning, the day prior to my departure, the chief was not to be found. Similar requests in 1989, made on the steps outside the offices—entrance to the facility was now barred owing, in the words of the duty officer, to "repair work"—were refused.

■   ■   ■

"It's been a difficult last three years: a new organizational structure, new style and methods of work, and radical electoral reform," First Secretary Stobbe confided to the delegates to the Thirty-third Magnitogorsk Party Conference, which convened in November 1988. "But," he added reassuringly, "problems and contradictions are to be expected. Mistakes are not excluded when one changes on the move." Whose mistakes he had in mind, however, went unmentioned.

Stobbe revealed that in comparison with 1987, entrances into the party in 1988 had declined by half. "Those leaving," Stobbe reported, "now exceed those entering." For the first time since 1938, the party was shrinking. No explanation was offered, however; nor was any mention made of the fact, discussed throughout the city, that a majority of those quitting were workers, in whose name the party ruled.

In the version of his summary report printed in the newspaper, the first secretary quickly passed over the city's problems (pollution, housing, provisions, health care, and "informal" political groups). He offered a backhanded compliment to the newspaper and then expressed confidence that "it will not forget the principle of party-mindedness in its work." (Later at the *obkom* conference he was more direct, calling on the apparat "not to hide behind closed doors but to defend the beleaguered 'foremen' of *perestroika* from the newspaper's attacks.") Stobbe's absurdly inept report could not have provoked much satisfaction even among the upper levels of the embattled Magnitogorsk apparat.

Discussion was evidently lively, judging by the account given in the newspaper (later confirmed in many conversations with those who attended). "I respect first secretary Stobbe," G. A. Chukharev delicately began, broaching a previously taboo subject. "But do you know, Lev Georgevich, that behind your back people call you 'the city director'? I understand this as an expression of the desire to participate in the solution of the city's social problems." The party, however, was by no means ready to "surrender."

"The party began *perestroika,* and now, as we have moved from talk to concrete deeds, the opinion has arisen that the party is not capable of finishing what it began," one of the first speakers, B. A. Piksaev, a worker who sat on the *gorkom* bureau, was quoted as saying. He disclosed with alarm that "there are discussions about the necessity of a multiparty system." But all was not lost. "The party is cleansing itself," Piksaev averred, "by raising the awareness of its members. 'Learn to direct' [*pravit*], to be the master and not an outside observer, to be active in the struggle for discipline, quality, to be responsible for one's assignment," he exhorted. Others were not so sure.

A. M. Artemov complained that "in its attitude toward the informal group Counter Movement, the city party committee showed its fear of open discussion with the people." He divulged that after the group announced its formation, secretaries of PPOs were sent instructions with the heading "secret" that warned functionaries about the dangers posed by the informal group. Yet, he continued, soon "the city newspaper informed us that a meeting had taken place between the party committee and the leaders of Counter Movement, about how fruitful their discussion was, and, it turned out, about how Counter Movement was raising vital issues." The leadership, he suggested, was disorganized. Moreover, according to Artemov, local preparation for the special party conference in Moscow, begun six months in advance, "was carried out like a military operation: in secret. . . . The report for the city committee was kept under an army of official seals. So much for *glasnost* in party work."

One of the senior party officials in attendance, V. S. Fedoseev, then second secretary of the *obkom*, tried to dismiss rumors of the party's apparent disintegration in a long, rambling speech filled with generalities and evincing a definite smugness. "Entrances into the party have declined a bit, and everybody's panicking," Fedoseev remarked. "Today there are more than twenty million [*sic*] party members. It's no big deal if the number of new recruits declines a little." Complacency, however, did not seem the order of the day.

Less than universal approval was voiced about the party's current program. For example, all those who spoke about cooperatives did so only to vilify them. "Coops are a fine thing, but who regulates their prices?" asked N. V. Drogovoz, a brigadier at the mine. "They engage in open speculation. . . . In fact, when they scoop up goods made at state enterprises [for resale], they create shortages."

V. V. Kameneva, a schoolteacher, sounded a related concern. "Youth evaluate socialism and our reality by which cooperative they're going to work for and where they can earn more. What's left of the spiritual? Nothing. They equate Marxism with fascism." Why this might be so was left unexplained, but Kameneva bemoaned the influence of the press, especially its concentration on the negative. "Children don't believe in the Komsomol anymore, or the party. Egregious offenses are being committed not only in the press but in families. Have mercy, comrades, on children's souls!"

Such was the alarming state of disorientation at what should have been a triumphal gathering of Magnitogorsk Communists in the new era. The apparat, however, seemed to be riding out the storm. In a ballot without alternative candidates, Stobbe was unanimously reelected first secretary.

■   ■   ■

In September 1988 Karelina published what she called "an open dialogue with the leaders of GIMN, Igor Zimin, Vadim Borodin, and Vladimir Zerkin," that was really an account of a public meeting. Writing that "I just don't feel like doing a stenographic report of a three-hour discussion," Karelina was free to give the material the accent she desired.

"They keep referring to Marxist theory. Who knows it? Who remembers it?" Karelina asked. "Zimin claimed that we don't have socialism. 'Correct, we don't,' agreed one worker sitting with him. 'What kind of socialism could it be if meat and sugar are rationed?' " Karelina boomed back that "it was the party that first pointed this out! Not GIMN members." Who caused such a mess in the first place, however, she did not say.

Karelina professed sympathy for her interlocutors, regretting that both Borodin and Zerkin were fired from their jobs the day after the KGB revealed their identities in the press. "We must work with them to convince them, not fire them," she wrote condescendingly. But she flatly rejected their propositions. "To a working person," wrote Karelina, "it is not altogether clear how the conclusion of GIMN's leaders that our *perestroika* is nothing but a bourgeois-democratic reform, how such a conclusion will in a practical sense aid in the solution of concrete social problems that have accumulated in our life. Think, argue, disagree sharply—who's against that? But who will follow the calls to take power through an armed uprising? Who needs reflections on the possibilities of terror?

"Yes, it's true, our economy is very sick. Yes, it's true, there were serious retreats from socialism. But we see the guarantees of improvement in the conception of *perestroika,* in the political reforms of the Nineteenth Party Conference. But the members of the group GIMN want to discredit the entire path traversed by our country; they think that a better method of curing would be to change the system through revolution, peaceful or unpeaceful. The new system they envision is an iron dictatorship of the proletariat. What separates us from them is the belief or nonbelief in *perestroika*."

Little was said of the mood in the hall during the confrontation. But Karelina did relate at length the comments of one woman who suggested that the problem was less in the system itself than in those running it. "These fellows are partly right, although as far as strikes go, I'm not in agreement with them," the unidentified woman was quoted as saying. "I'm so sick of the little princes, but I don't have the strength [to fight]. You look, how small an enterprise is, yet the bosses always ride around in state-owned cars; they can't take a step on foot. Where are those party members who think about the people and not about themselves?"

.   .   .

If anyone in Magnitogorsk could be said to represent a young generation of new thinkers in the party, it was Sergei Shchetnikov, party secretary at the wire factory. Modest, although not without ambition, soft-spoken, although firm in his convictions, Shchetnikov headed the city's second largest PPO. "For a long time we have been accustomed to thinking that only persons fifty years or older ought to be in leadership positions," the thirty-two-year-old Communist protested in a spotlight on him in the wire factory's newspaper. "We need to recognize that in many countries people in their thirties are not considered too young to lead. This should become the norm for us, too."

"I consider myself among the 'left forces,' " he told me from behind his desk. "But I do not think the left are extremists; I'm against extremism. Left forces are those that acknowledge that today there must be a variety of opinions, a many-sidedness of the party.

"We need to learn how to disagree. For so long we took the view that there was only one answer to every question. If you had a different answer, either you kept your mouth shut or you opened it and you were finished. Finally we're moving away from such rigidity.

"It's difficult for us to learn the new ways. The first time I came up for election as factory party secretary there were several candidates. The vote was very, very close. I won, but because it was a special election (the previous secretary had left his post early), the regular election date came soon thereafter. But at the second election I was the only one on the ballot.

"The same thing happened at the city party conference in the vote for first secretary. First they included the incumbent Stobbe on the ballot. Then when we were asked if anyone had other recommendations, no one said a word. We must continue to make forward steps, whatever else we do, continually forward. Now there are fewer party members, but the ones who stay are better. We must work for the people and for production."

Shchetnikov gave his blessing and party approval to the formation of a group at the wire factory called Businesslike Interaction. Composed of engineers, managers, and party functionaries, the group—essentially the factory party committee without its worker members—met regularly to discuss a wide range of current topics. "Whereas previously the work of the factory's intellectual cadres was taken up with what was called agitation and propaganda, now we are concerned with the experience of such advanced countries as Japan and the United States," said the group's resident sociologist, Vladimir Ishimov. "We prefer a sociological approach to an ideological one."

By "sociological" Ishimov meant "scientific inquiry into the most advanced forms of social organization possible. We are looking for ways to adopt what we consider best in, say, Japanese and American practice and to refine and perfect this experience further." "As a start," added Oleg Pashin, second secretary of the factory party committee, "we took down all the stupid agitational posters around the factory."

When asked why the factory, which produced wire, needed to support a party committee of functionaries and sociologists who met to discuss world affairs, neither Pashin nor Ishimov could provide an answer. "It doesn't," said Shchetnikov, interrupting the silence. He acknowledged that the factory's workers had begun to use the word *parasite* openly to characterize the factory's party committee, whose leadership was widely considered as reformed as any in all of Magnitogorsk.

One afternoon several weeks later, as I prepared to be interviewed for the wire factory newspaper, Shchetnikov and Pashin engaged me in conversation about my "party affiliation." He wanted to know to which party I belonged (Democratic), what my membership entailed, and how my party's organization differed from that of the Soviet Communist party. When did I join? Were the dues steep? Could I leave the party at any time without unduly affecting my career? Did the party maintain district committees in addition to city ones? As I answered his questions, Shchetnikov, looking puzzled, remarked, "but that means that the Soviet Communist party is not really a political party at all."

■   ■   ■

In September 1988 the newspaper of the Cheliabinsk *obkom* published an article entitled "The KGB and *Perestroika*." The piece was presented as an interview with Major General Iurii Poliakov, chief of the *oblast* KGB (and Lavrishchev's immediate superior). Poliakov, we learn, was born in 1931. His father, a collective farm chairman, was a beneficiary of Stalin's new order in the villages. In 1953 Poliakov was graduated from the prestigious Moscow Railroad Institute and posted to the southern Urals. In August 1956—in the wake of the Twentieth Party Congress and Khrushchev's "secret speech" on the crimes of the Stalin era—Poliakov claimed he was recruited into the KGB. Thirty years later, he became KGB chief in Cheliabinsk.

Poliakov's theme in the "interview" was that there was a new KGB. "Around 60 percent of our leadership and operative staff are younger than forty years old," Poliakov revealed. "All have higher education and experience in party and Komsomol work, and each has shouldered the responsibility of military service. . . . Those who drink or are not modest [in their personal lives] are soon asked to leave. . . . There is the strictest observance of socialist legality. We work within our jurisdiction, as determined by the constitution and laws of the USSR." Exactly what they did, however, was not specified.

The open-ended activities of the KGB's notorious Fifth Department, charged with snuffing out "political crimes," were supposedly delimited to comply with new legislation more narrowly defining such transgressions, but it was hard to determine what these formal changes meant in practice. In any case, the KGB's acknowledged domestic responsibilities—which ranged from counterespionage, combating organized crime, and detecting malfeasance to monitoring construction sites, industry, and transport—seemed to exclude nothing.

"My workday begins at 8 A.M. and ends, as a rule, between 8 and 10 P.M.," Poliakov explained matter-of-factly. "I work on Saturdays and often on Sundays, as do, by the way, my co-workers." No doubt they did.

■   ■   ■

PPOs scheduled meetings perhaps once a month, sometimes every other month, depending on the flow of business. On 25 April 1989 a meeting of the party cell at the Mining Institute took place. A presidium for the meeting, nominated from the floor and elected by acclamation, took its place on the dais flanked by gigantic portraits of Marx on the left wall and Lenin on the right.

As was customary, Anatolii Makeev, first secretary of the district party committee, attended. Unusually, however, the auditorium was packed with nonmembers, and a large number of people signed up to speak. Normally such a gathering of the institute's Communists generated little notice or enthusiasm. But on this occasion emotions were running high, owing to the controversy following the publication of an article in the institute paper by the chairman of the philosophy department, Aleksandr Arzamastsev, called "Political Pluralism." Mikhail Kaiukov, first secretary of the institute's party committee, was the first to speak. He attacked Arzamastsev's article as a betrayal of Leninist principles. The article was a retreat, the institute's head Communist argued, and reflected a defeatist attitude.

Arzamastsev spoke next, defending himself and speaking ardently of the need for some "new thinking." Reiterating the stance he took in his article, he called for a multiparty system and the introduction of private property. Although he insisted that his proposals were consonant with Marx's basic teaching, Arzamastsev, a longtime member of the Communist party, was consciously advocating the party's dissolution. In the confrontation between Kaiukov and Arzamastsev one could see the radically different visions of two reform-minded Communists, both of whom considered themselves solidly in favor of *perestroika*.

Next up was Chistota, a representative of the generation that fought in the war, who in sounding the themes of discipline, order, and patriotism emerged as the common enemy of the divided "progressive forces." Groans and murmurs of "Stalinist" could be heard in the audience, but Chistota pressed on, declaring, "I am for *perestroika*. It's just that we, the old guard, are treated like second-class citizens, as if we had committed some monstrous crime instead of devoting our whole lives to the construction of socialism."

Like Arzamastsev, Chistota confronted Kaiukov and the policy of party reform with a serious challenge, this one from the "right." Of the two sets of choices—reform through the party versus an end to the party's monopoly, or reform through the party versus neo-Stalinist retrenchment—the latter battle eclipsed the former.

Suslin, the next speaker, changed the topic, calling for the resignation of the rector, Vitalii Riabkov. Visibly nervous, Suslin cited a number of dubious occurrences that he attributed to Riabkov's leadership. The crowd was stunned, many people wondering if Suslin had lost his head, taking on the institute's power structure in public. At this point the presiding chair asked the audience to respond to several written requests by Communists who desired to leave the meeting early, usually because of a child's illness. (Attendance at party meetings was mandatory.) All such requests to leave early were approved right away.

Mnukhin then got up and attacked the meeting itself, which drew the first and only applause of the day. "Nothing ever gets decided at party meetings," he declared. "Even if a decision is taken, it is not implemented. The whole history of the party shows how difficult it is to work with this structure. We need a multiparty system." Having gotten it off his chest, Mnukhin sat down contentedly. But the Arzamastsev forces were determined to do more than score rhetorical points; they wanted a resolution approving his "theses" to be adopted by the meeting.

Dozens of speakers on the list had yet to speak, but the votes had been reckoned beforehand, and Arzamastsev, now joined by Kaiukov, was confident of "victory." In the face of the "threat" from Chistota, the gulf between the positions of the reformers Kaiukov and Arzamastsev was temporarily breached through the use of the open-ended word *pluralism*. Who but a Stalinist would vote against the need for "pluralism"? Put another way, a vote against pluralism could be seen as a statement of one's own sympathy for Stalinism.

For the next two hours, the only suspense was provided by the wait to see who would get up to defend the besmirched reputation of Riabkov. It turned out to be the rector himself, who displayed uncharacteristic impatience and unease. When the discussion was finally closed, the Arzamastsev resolution recommending "political pluralism" passed, with publication to follow in the institute newspaper. A date for the next party meeting was announced. People filed out of the hall, the two huge icons of Marx and Lenin looming over the emptying room. "The Stalinists," someone said, "have been dealt a blow."

■   ■   ■

"GIMN was called in and warned," said Konstantin Anikin, chief procurator of the city's large Ordzhonikidze district, a jurisdiction that included the steel plant and several other large industrial enterprises. "One article in their charter calls for the overthrow of society by means of violence. This is a violation of the constitution. We told them to work to change the law if they were not satisfied but in the meantime to comply with it. They did not make a formal complaint with the Procuracy about any illegal search. This is the first I've heard of it."

After sixteen years in the Procuracy, Anikin expressed general satisfaction during an interview in his office. "I like my job very much. It's more interesting and challenging than work in the courts. I am responsible for overseeing the functioning of the whole society, from economic activities to policing and investigative work.

"With *perestroika* things have definitely changed. Formerly we were 'expediters,' constantly urging people to do what they were supposed to, and quicker. Now we can actually pay attention to our real function: the observance of the laws. New laws are being passed with great frequency: the law on state enterprises, the one on cooperatives. We are responsible for seeing these laws enacted.

"As for criminal issues, there have been few changes. Murders are still few (six in the first three months of 1989). All but one were knifings, guns still being a rarity here. But what is new is that local crime statistics were published for the first time this May in the newspaper."

Although his office gave public lectures and organized other exchanges with the public, Anikin admitted that people did not know the laws. "We get a surprising array of questions during our informational visits to working collectives. People are often confused or misinformed about the laws. They go to the newspaper instead of the Procuracy with questions and complaints. It frustrates us, especially because the public doesn't seem that interested in learning the laws.

"Complaints are made on the basis of emotion or personal interpretations of the law. Few people can vouch that a law has been violated. When shown otherwise, they continue to complain, going elsewhere in the hope of obtaining a more sympathetic reception.

"We are overwhelmed with work. Our district is gigantic, but our office is small (we're eight: the chief procurator, a deputy, four senior staff, and two investigators). Just covering the steel plant alone is an enormous task. I have one staff person responsible for all industrial enterprises in the district. Complaints, all of which have to be investigated, pile up.

"We have great difficulties in our dealings with the militia. Their pay and working conditions leave something to be desired. We have two to three foot patrolmen for every ten thousand people. This is obviously inadequate. They should be models for our youth, into sports, clean, educated, but not all measure up. I know they're under increasing pressure, but they lack professional skills. Although they're supposed to know the laws, few have any legal training, so they often come up with peculiar interpretations. I must follow their work closely.

"We also keep an eye on the city's lockups. In Magnitogorsk there are medicinal-labor facilities for alcoholics, an investigation detention center, and a strict regime colony for those convicted of serious crimes. There is also a program for people who have been convicted but are allowed to live in dormitories. Such people must work and must sign back in the dorm by 10 P.M. They may not leave the city without permission. There are three to four hundred people in this category.

"We have relations with the local department of the KGB. There are instances of cooperation in crimes involving state security. Pretty much, however, they go about their business. To be honest, I am not familiar with all of the cases they are working on."

■   ■   ■

Aleksandr Savitskii had patiently worked his way up through the party apparat, becoming by 1989 second secretary in the Ordzhonikidze district party committee. Unusual for an apparatchik, he was writing a history of Magnitogorsk in verse, focusing on what he viewed as the human drama of ordinary people.

"Capitalism borrowed a great deal from socialism, from our example," Savitskii remarked over dinner in his apartment with his family. "This was right and helped capitalism survive and prosper. We failed to do this, to borrow from capitalism, and we are paying the consequences for our rigidity.

"Socialism is now going through a grave crisis, just as capitalism many times did, particularly during the 1930s. I do not doubt that our crisis, too, will pass, although we will perforce transform our system, just as you did yours. I foresee a new big crisis for capitalism on the horizon, arising out of debt problems, especially those of the Third World. Anyway, it won't do to divide the world into capitalism and socialism. We live in one world. Human values are universal.

"The last two years we have experienced an ideological revolution. The old way of seeing things has been completely smashed, which produced great confusion, of course. Only now are we beginning to sort things out and finally anchoring ourselves firmly in the new way of thinking."

Like most apparatchiks, Savitskii had been abroad, spending time in Cuba, West Germany, and Syria. He had read up on other countries, in part with the help of materials distributed to the apparat but otherwise unavailable. Characterizations of him had tended to be more positive than those I had heard of most other Magnitogorsk functionaries, but his position as an apparatchik remained uppermost in people's minds.

"Sure, he's bright, " remarked a person who knew Savitskii and many other apparatchiks well, "but he has been deformed by the system. There's no getting around it; one cannot become someone in the bureaucratic apparatus without being shaped by it. Unconsciously one learns modes of behavior and thinking that, try as one might, are impossible to unlearn. Membership in the apparat is forever." It is almost impossible to find someone inside or even outside the apparat who would disagree with this formulation.

Lately Savitskii had become extremely active, spearheading a local push for "people's diplomacy," efforts below the level of the national governments to have individuals from the United States and the Soviet Union get better acquainted. As a result of his contacts, among other things, several dozen Magnitogorsk teenagers were included in a national group of Soviet youth able to spend the summer of 1989 in the United States. (Magnitogorsk in turn hosted American teenagers.)

Needless to say, great interest surrounded the selection of students (and chaperones) for the unprecedented trip to America. A series of intellectual contests was publicly held. Yet despite the apparently open and meritocratic process, suspicions were deep that connections had played a role, especially after word got out that Savitskii's daughter was among the elect. (It was taken for granted that Savitskii himself would be able to make many trips to America.)

Elena Karelina was directed by Kucher, the newspaper's editor and a member of the ruling party bureau, to conduct an investigation. Her article brought to light the possibility of nepotism but never directly took a position. In Karelina's treatment, several other issues—such as whether the type of examinations given could be expected to produce the well-rounded, outgoing students who would best represent the USSR abroad—took up far more space than the question of Savitskii's influence in the selection process. Many people read Karelina's long article as an apology for Savitskii. Certainly the potential damage to his career was minimized by the article's tone and content.

Savitskii was also the head of a new organization called Interclub, a multinational group that included Bashkirs and Tatars as well as Russians. Expressly nonpolitical, members saw themselves as promoting the culture of the Tatar and Bashkir national minorities, which composed a small but significant percentage of the city's population.* Interclub had

* According to the 1979 population census, there were twenty-nine thousand Tatars and nine thousand Bashkirs living in Magnitogorsk. Data from the 1989 census on the national composition of the population were still unavailable by the summer of 1989, but it was widely believed that in the intervening decade Magnitogorsk had experienced an

the status of an amateur organization registered at the steel plant's Ordzhonikidze palace of culture, which was located in the same district where Savitskii was a district committee secretary.

After a meeting of Interclub, one young woman took me aside and explained that she and another person came up with the idea and began to meet informally with a small group of people. "Then the apparat found out, and they immediately moved in," she recounted. "They gobbled us up. I guess they chose Savitskii for the job because he's 'culturally' inclined. But he plans these big events like caravans of camels trekking here from Central Asia in a reenactment of something that supposedly happened in the 1930s. We had a different idea of what we wanted."

■   ■   ■

In "A Window of *Glasnost*," the typescript publication of Counter Movement, it is possible to get a clearer idea of the views of the leadership. For example, Vladimir Sidorov wrote an article complaining that the city newspaper refused to publish his response to Mozgovoi's article. "The newspaper people know full well," Sidorov wrote, "that the fate of *perestroika* depends on whom the workers go for: for the patriots or for the internationalists," a code word for Jews. Another article, "Zionism without the Mask," was an openly anti-Semitic tirade. Several times the publication drew attention to the ties between Counter Movement and other "patriotic" organizations, such as Fatherland in Sverdlovsk and Motherland in Cheliabinsk.

Curiously, later issues contained articles by two members of the postschism GIMN, Igor Zimin and Vadim Borodin. "The programs of GIMN and Counter Movement differ from each other rather strongly," Borodin wrote. "Nevertheless, the possibility for cooperation between the two groups is greater than with any other." He added that their common goal was "education" and that they had discussed the question of terror, both sides concluding that it was "harmful." By rejecting the

---

influx of Bashkirs from surrounding villages. On the basis of passport registrations the city's Statistical Bureau estimated the Bashkir population in 1989 at thirty thousand (6 percent of the city total) and the Tatars at sixty-five thousand (15 percent). At the time of my second visit to the city, interest in national minority issues had been awakened. Discussions focused on retaining cultural identities, especially languages. In the 1970s a group of distinguished retired Tatars succeeded in their efforts to press the authorities for construction of the city's first mosque, built on the road linking Magnitogorsk to neighboring Bashkiria. Magnitogorsk also has a Russian Orthodox church, built around the same time. (The city's first orthodox church opened in 1946 but was later closed.) During the Easter celebration in 1989, church attendance was comparatively low, with older women predominating.

use of violence and associating itself with the officially sanctioned Counter Movement, the new GIMN distanced itself from the publicly rebuked original GIMN and sought to insure the new organization's continued existence.

■　　■　　■

Rumors of an impending public split in the party became widespread during the national party conference in the summer of 1988, but no such schism occurred then. All the same, many people felt that appearances notwithstanding, the party was badly divided into two camps, and it was only a matter of time before the split became public. When in the spring of 1989, a small group of Communists announced the formation of the Group for Assistance to *Perestroika,* people thought, here at long last was the Magnitogorsk party's "*perestroika* wing."

This association of proreform Communists described itself as a "voluntary, independent social movement acting in agreement with the Soviet constitution and supporting the party's course for the rebirth of the Leninist conception of socialism, for the fundamental transformation of all spheres of the life of Soviet society." By failing to offer an explanation for the apparent duplication, the group of Communists implied that the party as then constituted might not be up to the task. Otherwise, why was it necessary to form a separate movement to act alongside the party?

In any case, among its goals the group listed the following: to eradicate all the consequences of Stalinism and the period of stagnation; to fight for human rights, national cultures, and "progressive" forms of economic activity (only cooperatives were named); and to bring about socialist pluralism and all power to the soviets. The group claimed to be open to the possibility of federation with other, like-minded groups, although none was named. The group's organizational structure, including the designation of a general conference as the highest organ and, between conferences, a coordinating council, bore a striking resemblance to that of the existing Communist party.

Fewer than a dozen names appeared after the text published in the city newspaper, of which the most prominent were Vilii Bogun, the former city architect; Iurii Polev, the chair of party history at the Teachers College; and Aleksandr Arzamastsev. None of the names corresponded to key members of the party hierarchy. Only one, that of Nikolai Agafonkin, was associated with the apparat. In fact, Agafonkin was best known as the rumored *gorkom* "plant" in Counter Movement.

"Our country has experienced many difficult hours, but the situation has gotten much better," Polev related in an interview. "With the establishment of a law-based state we will create the possibility for realizing all rights. But we must still complete the transition from capitalism to socialism, which was interrupted by Stalin."

Arzamastsev, in contrast to Polev, evinced little enthusiasm for the project and dismissed the dramatic gesture involved in the announcement. "They asked me to join; I did not object," he remarked in his office. "Polev wrote the program. He took most of it from the literature that circulates out of the Baltic countries. I looked it over; it seemed okay.

"Basically, people are not satisfied with the tempo of *perestroika*. They're looking for new ways to become active. This is in fact what they have been told to do. You can't blame them for trying, but what will become of it, I cannot say."

■   ■   ■

Subsumed under the Ministry of Internal Affairs, the Magnitogorsk militia shared a building with the KGB, whose status, that of a state committee, was roughly equivalent to a ministry. The two "ministries" in fact were closely connected. In Magnitogorsk, one could often see Fedor Bulatov, the city's chief of militia, together with Lavrishchev, the local KGB chief.

Bulatov was particularly sensitive to complaints about the officers in his charge. "Few people understand the strain of militia work, the low-lifes we come in contact with, and the kind of inhuman deeds they perpetrate," he stated during a meeting in his office. "Nor do people properly appreciate the difficulties imposed on us. At long last we acknowledged that crime is a normal social phenomenon. It's no longer embarrassing to have crime, to speak and write about it. This is a step forward. But lately our work has become even more complicated.

"We decided to have a look at the West and maybe to borrow some things. And what did we borrow? Demonstrations. Why couldn't we have borrowed the West's ability to work? Then even I would have accepted demonstrations in the bargain."

At one such demonstration in the late summer of 1988 Bulatov felt compelled to respond publicly to charges made by Zerkin that he was fired from the militia because he would not keep quiet in the face of embezzlement and corruption. "In fact," Bulatov calmly retorted, "he falsified and hid crimes. He was caught, given a second chance, did it again, and was fired." Bulatov dismissed accusations of chronic abuses by the militia but in the same breath assured that he was on top of the situation. In 1987 and the first eight months of 1988, he claimed, fifty-one people had been fired from the "organs."

■　　■　　■

When asked to name the outstanding young Magnitogorsk Communist, several knowledgeable people in the city recommended Nikolai Kuklinov, first secretary of the Ordzhonikidze district committee. Kuklinov together with his wife extended me the hospitality of an evening of tea and conversation in their spacious and well-appointed apartment. (We met at his suggestion, related through an intermediary.) They were shocked when I turned down an offer of exceptionally scarce Brazilian coffee, numerous large cans of which were visible in the cluttered pantry.

Smooth and collected, Kuklinov recited his biography without prompting, although in a version that was later contradicted by others who knew him. Unlike all other party officials I met, he was not taken aback by direct and forceful questioning. Nor did Kuklinov blink when mention was made of his being installed in Magnitogorsk by the *obkom*'s second secretary, V. Fedoseev, who had just been removed in disgrace, although this clearly could turn out badly for Kuklinov as well.*

"It's not always easy to figure out what he's cooking up," Kuklinov remarked about Gorbachev. "Often the implications of his actions do not become clear until a while later. This naturally dictates a cautious and long-range view." At one point late in the evening Kuklinov let slip that at first he had worried about the consequences of meeting with me but then changed his mind. "I saw that if Savitskii had done it, I could meet the American, too," he said. When pressed further, Kuklinov allowed that "in our present situation it did not seem like an entirely disadvantageous thing to do."

■　　■　　■

"Why," asked a popular joke that made the rounds in Magnitogorsk, "is there no soap or laundry powder? Answer: because the party is try-

---

* In late 1988 a scandal broke out, nicknamed "flying geese," about several *obkom* officials who used their authority to gain entrance to a state hunting reserve without proper passes and were denied access by incorruptible gatekeepers who then reported the incident. Pressure from the Cheliabinsk correspondent of *Izvestiia* led to an investigation by central authorities. "This year the *obkom* has not found it useful to respond to a single publication about Cheliabinsk in *Izvestiia*," the journalist complained in a report of the incident. After much foot-dragging, Fedoseev finally resigned from the *obkom*. He soon resurfaced as a deputy minister of ferrous metallurgy, but all those previously associated with him remained under a cloud.

ing to wash itself clean." That it was, and with the results fitting to the paradoxical assignment. The goal of the party reforms was to make the party more responsive to the people and at the same time to give its rule legitimacy. In the process party politics was supposed to have been reinvigorated. But in Magnitogorsk many people began openly to question if the party was capable of reforming itself and, ultimately, if even a reformed Communist party was compatible with democracy.

Indeed, in Magnitogorsk party forums, instead of being strategy sessions on how best to carry out the new program of *perestroika,* became acrimonious occasions for complaining and finger-pointing. Beholden to party discipline, top Magnitogorsk Communists did not openly advocate an end to *perestroika,* but neither were they dancing in the streets at the thought of submitting to angry public scrutiny and being battered for the country's accumulated ills.

Nevertheless, responsibility for the failure of party reform in Magnitogorsk could not be said to consist in a confrontation pitting reformers against conservatives, which owing to the intransigence of the latter resulted in a deadlock. Opposition to reform there certainly was, but as was demonstrated by the Magnitogorsk elections to the special party conference, which were summarily, although legally, overturned by the higher level *obkom,* the overriding problem lay in the profoundly undemocratic structure of the party. Moreover, even if the party were somehow to achieve a measure of "democratization" in its operation, it would remain in large measure a parasitic body, as reform Communists at the wire factory came to realize.

The party's raison d'être was ideological, not technical or professional. During the civil-war era "political commissars"—people trusted for their ideological purity—were introduced alongside army officers who had served under the tsar but who after the revolution fought for the Reds. By extending this practice to other realms, the party's watchdog role was institutionalized not just in the army and militarized security police, but in the judiciary, schools, industry, and government, thereby allowing the party to supervise all institutions from behind the scenes. With such "commissars" able to monitor anything that went on in society, the party in turn was unaccountable not only to the population at large but even to its own rank and file. Monopolizing all political activity, the party for the most part excluded all nonmembers from politics while offering members participation without power.

Until recently the party even maintained a monopoly on the evaluation of its own performance and on what people could read or view.

The party owned, ran, or supervised all newspapers, television and radio stations, lecture halls, movie houses, and billboards. But as we saw in chapter 2, the major Magnitogorsk daily managed to win for itself a measure of independence from the *gorkom* ideologues. This remarkable accomplishment was achieved only because of the skillful efforts of one man, Valerii Kucher, whose principled commitment to freedom of the press was refracted through his total support for Gorbachev's reforms. But Kucher's lead was not followed by anyone else in the local party hierarchy, some of whom contemplated ways of removing him only to shrink from the prospect of doing so and risking being publicly identified as antireform.

In an important sense Kucher *was* the reformed wing of the party in Magnitogorsk. Other self-styled reformers, such as Polev and Arzamastsev, remained too far outside the power structure (not surprisingly, because Arzamastsev essentially advocated the end of party). Their project of a redundant "*perestroika* group" alongside the party proved itself capable of momentarily attracting publicity or "winning" debates at meetings of primary party organizations, but little else. Meanwhile, the effects of Kucher's commitment to using the newspaper for promoting party reform were other than those intended. True, the party's misrule was exposed, but in the bargain the question of the party's incompatibility with democracy was let out of the bottle.

With the workings of the party having been partially pried open to quasi-independent journalistic investigation, the party in Magnitogorsk was forced to become somewhat accountable for its rule. But this did not mean the democratization of the party so much as the public acknowledgment of the party's alienation from the people whose interests it could no longer pretend to represent. To an extent unimaginable even in 1988, by 1989 fear had passed from the people to party members and, above all, to the apparatchiks, who were suffering from very low morale and experiencing an unfamiliar feeling of being under siege. Members of the local party elite, however, their fingers to the wind, showed themselves to be more adaptable to the difficult new circumstances than many would have predicted.

With the party elite backpedaling, some of the rank and file, including workers, began voting with their feet and bolting the party. Their reasons varied. According to the newspaper, some admitted to being shocked at the revelations about the party's past. Others claimed that their spouses forced them to quit. There were those who felt they could not carry out the increased demands made of party members and even those who reckoned that, given their high salaries, it would have been a shame to continue paying party dues, calculated as a fixed percentage of salary. If most of those leaving the party did so less out of political protest and more because of a feeling that too much was being required of them or that they were not getting anything for their dues, maybe this was why former Communists were not inclined to form new political organizations. As a result, their exit from the party amounted to a significant, although one-time, statement.

Defections from the party ranks seemed likely to continue, thereby compounding the effects of the drop-off in the number of new applicants. In the meantime, Magnitogorsk still had a large number of Communists. The best among them, such as Sergei Shchetnikov, stubbornly clung to the program of reform through the party, recognizing that the party's role in society had to fundamentally change, although unsure of what a fully reformed party would look like. Others, such as Aleksandr Savitskii, were busy using their positions to take advantage of the new possibilities that *perestroika* opened up, hoping that their efforts would at the same time serve as sufficient evidence of their reformed status. And then there were those without illusions, such as Nikolai Kuklinov, who, foreseeing deepening troubles for party cadres, were carefully, craftily biding their time, waiting to get a clearer sense of the best way to salvage their careers. Yet although the long-term outlook was grim, for the time being the apparatchiks' fortunes, all things considered, could have been worse.

Even though the myth of unshakeable party supremacy was forever destroyed, no substantial challenge to the hegemony of the Communist party apparat in Magnitogorsk arose. While Aleksandr Arzamastsev publicly called for amending the infamous clause in the Soviet constitution that provided for the Communist party's monopoly on power, he conceded that such a turn of events could have little more than a symbolic effect on the structure of power and authority in Magnitogorsk. "Real political parties able to compete for power cannot," he agreed, "be conjured up out of the air."

Neither of the new "unofficial" political groups, Counter Movement and GIMN, resembled anything remotely like a political force, let alone a political party. Counter Movement, Russian chauvinist, brashly admitted to having no permanent membership; GIMN, Marxist, acknowledged it could count its members on one hand. One could sense the potential public support in Magnitogorsk for a successful grass-roots political movement outside the Communist party, but the leadership for such a movement was sorely lacking.

Meanwhile, an acrimonious schism developed within GIMN, which was followed by a bizarre "alliance" of one splinter faction with the officially sanctioned Counter Movement, a turn of events that involved more than endemic sectarianism or an affinity between "Marxists" and Russian chauvinists (united in their opposition to "bourgeois liberalism and private property"). These developments underscored the fact that in order to survive, the sadly inept "unofficials" had to play the game according to the official rules.

Unlike examples elsewhere in the country, particularly in the larger cities of Russia and throughout the national republics, in Magnitogorsk "unofficial" was not quite the proper term for these new political groupings. In the case of Counter Movement, their unofficial status was belied by their registration by and close association with the party apparat. By contrast, the reformed GIMN, although still technically "unregistered," was officially permitted to exist, and therefore no longer under the constant threat of legal action. And if at first they were severely harassed by local authorities, both Counter Movement and GIMN came to play critical roles in legitimizing the alleged "reformed" spirit and practice of the city party committee and the KGB. In that sense, the unofficials were very much an extension of the official power structure.

As for the official power structure itself, to the foregoing comments I need only add that the new emphasis on the rule of law, however sincere, was called into question by the continued existence of the KGB, a repressive apparatus whose activities remained beyond both public scrutiny and the purview of the district procurator, by his own admission. Until reliable civil control could be established over the workings of the KGB, it seemed best to remain wary of assurances that the security police had been permanently transformed.

Afternoon shift change at the main factory gate. (Photograph by Anatolii Kniazev)

Consumer goods produced at the steel mill. (Photograph by Anatolii Kniazev)

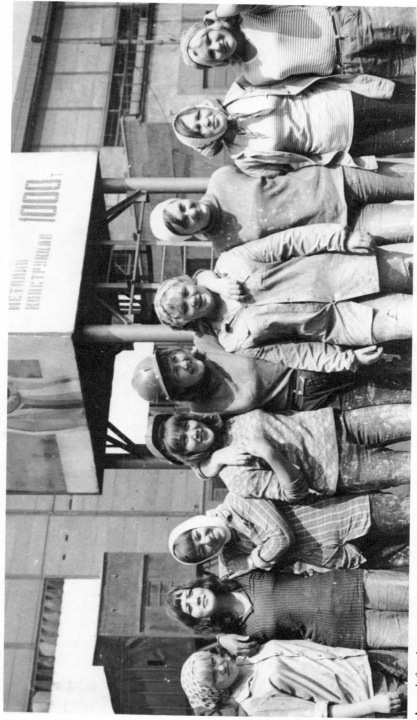

A crack female construction brigade posing at the new steelmaking shop they are building. (Photograph by Anatolii Kniazev)

Blast furnaces at the Magnitogorsk Works. (Photograph by Anatolii Kniazev)

Top of page: Blast furnace operator directing the flow of molten pig iron. *Above:* Posing for photographer immediately after his shift. Temperatures in the furnace reach sixteen hundred degrees Celsius. (Photographs by Anatolii Kniazev)

"Worker-heroes" with their medals. (Photograph by Anatolii Kniazev)

Electrically operated ladle carries molten pig iron, the primary ingredient for making steel, from blast furnace to open-hearth oven. (Photograph by Anatolii Kniazev)

Cathedrals of the modern age: the inner expanse of the gargantuan open-hearth shop no. 1. (Photograph by Anatolii Kniazev)

Automated conveyor in the rolling mill pushes white-hot steel slabs toward scissors for cutting into rails and structural shapes. (Photograph by Anatolii Kniazev)

Magnitogorsk's ruling elite posing for the annual May Day photograph, 1989. *First row, far right,* Valerii Kucher, newspaper editor; *first row, fifth from right,* Mayor Mikhail Lysenko; *first row, seventh from right,* first secretary Lev Stobbe; *first row, eighth from right,* factory director Ivan Romazan; *first row, ninth from right,* Deputy Mayor Aleksandr Leislia; *first row, tenth from right,* Mining Institute rector Vitalii Riabkov; *second row, in uniform,* police chief Fedor Bulatov; *dead center, black hat,* local KGB chief Viktor Lavrishchev. Bulatov and Lavrishchev are watching the author as he runs up and snaps the shot. (Photograph by Stephen Kotkin)

A new center of power: the *Magnitogorsk Worker. Left to right,* editor Valerii Kucher, managing editor Evgenii Vernikov, political columnist Vladimir Mozgovoi, social reporter Tatiana Leus. (Photograph by Stephen Kotkin)

"Information USA" exhibit, July 1988. *Opposite:* Pre–opening day review for local VIPs at the Fiftieth Anniversary of the October Revolution Sports Pavilion. *Top of page:* People waiting up to five hours for a glimpse of American technology. *Above:* U.S. ambassador to the USSR Jack Matlock (*left*), his wife, Rebecca Matlock, and factory director Ivan Romazan on a tour of the steel plant's nearby lakeside resort. (Photographs by Anatolii Kniazev)

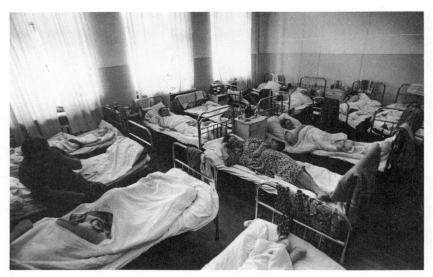

City Hospital No. 1. *Above:* Patients resting in a typical room designed to accommodate half as many. *Opposite:* A washroom down the hall. (Photographs by Vladimir Dumbrovskii)

View from an upstairs window of the Mining and Metallurgical Institute.
Several kilometers off in the distance, the steel plant defines the city.
(Photograph by Anatolii Kniazev)

Women clearing tram tracks on a Magnitogorsk thoroughfare. (Photograph by
Anatolii Kniazev)

Sausage, margarine, lard, butter, and honey on sale at low state prices.
(Photograph by Stephen Kotkin)

АПРЕЛЬ
1989 г.
САХАР

МАРТ
1989 г.
ВОДКА

АПРЕЛЬ
1989 г.
КОЛБАСА

State-made goods delivered directly to the street and sold off the back of a
truck. Piqued pedestrians approach to find out what is for sale. (Photograph
by Stephen Kotkin)

ФЕВРАЛЬ
1989 г.

МАСЛО

Monthly ration coupons limiting purchases of
sugar, vodka, sausage, and butter.

Homegrown harvest for sale at a streetcar stop. (Photograph by Stephen Kotkin)

Secondhand automobiles for sale at the city's open-air "peasant" market.
(Photograph by Stephen Kotkin)

Site of the original Old Magnitka settlement, now covered with bungalows and overtaken by superblocks of prefabricated apartments. (Photograph by Gennadii Gubanov)

One of a dozen cottages built in the 1930s for the new Soviet elite in the former settlement for American engineers and consultants. The author stayed in the cottage, now maintained as a guest house, during his first visit in 1987. (Photograph by Stephen Kotkin)

A lecture given by the author at the Teachers College. (Photographer unknown)

After the lecture the author holds the platform, about to be read aloud, of the Democratic Union, an unrecognized political party based in Moscow that was the first to advocate private property and parliamentary democracy. (Photographer unknown)

Looking much as they always have, voting booths for marking ballots before they are dropped into the urn at back. In 1989, for the first time ever, voters were given a choice of more than one candidate. (Photograph by Stephen Kotkin)

March 1989 meeting organized by Counter Movement, one of two new "informal" political groups, one day before the vote for seats to the Congress of People's Deputies. *Speaking,* Anatolii Makeev; *behind him,* Counter Movement co-leader Valerii Timofeev. (Photograph by Stephen Kotkin)

Victory Day, 9 May 1989. *Opposite:* A widow at the grave of her husband.
Above: Veterans of the war in Afghanistan. (Photographs by Iurii Popov)

One of a series of 1932 publicity photographs of "new man" Viktor
Kalmykov, former peasant turned literate skilled worker, and his wife, Emilia
Bakke. Kalmykov was arrested and shot in 1937. (Photographer unknown)

Front page of the *Magnitogorsk Worker*, 1 January 1938, with the greeting "Happy New Year, Comrades!" Against a background depicting technological achievement and smiling people, the banner exhorts, "Forward to New Victories!" The omniscient father bestows his approval. (Photograph by Stephen Kotkin)

"From the Home Front to the War Front." World War II memorial depicting the contribution of Magnitogorsk to the victory over the German invaders, as a steelworker facing west passes the eastern-forged sword to a Soviet soldier ready to turn and slay the enemy. Shown during the local Festival of Song. (Photograph by Anatolii Kniazev)

Magnetic Mountain, the site of iron-ore deposits that were the original impetus to construct Magnitogorsk. The deposits are now entirely used up. (Photograph by Gennadii Gubanov)

Statue of Stalin that was once astride the main factory gate. It was replaced by
a statue of Lenin in 1961. (Photographer unknown)

Cable accumulated in a warehouse awaiting shipment to anxious customers.
(Photograph by Anatolii Kniazev)

"Is Life Going to Go on like This Forever?"

Hopes Raised, Then Lowered

At a shop selling toothpaste that a reporter from the Magnitogorsk city newspaper visited in the fall of 1987, there was a gigantic queue. A salesclerk was approached and queried. "They've been buying ten tubes apiece," she gasped, "first Bulgarian, then domestic. The next day we sold out of tooth-cleaning powder, which is normally not very popular."

During the conversation, another salesclerk brought out laundry powder. The crowd surged forward. People began shouting and trying to cram their "catch" by the fives and tens into their shopping nets.

"Others hoard, I'm hoarding."
"We're afraid that soon there won't be any."
"My friend advised me, get what you can, soon there won't be any."
"Why am I buying so much? Because there's none."

One woman stated that she was just trying to stay ahead of the game: "I read in the newspaper *Trud* that there were interruptions of toothpaste. So I hurried to stock up. I saw that there's no soap. I decided to buy at least some of the coarser variety. So I stood in line for twenty bars."

Another concurred: "I learned from my neighbors that in Sverdlovsk laundry powder has not been on sale for a month already. Our trade operates unrhythmically, so it's necessary to make reserves." A skeptic, however, disagreed: "They put out these rumors on purpose in order to fulfill the plan, to move the stuff sitting in warehouses." Two years of *perestroika* had done little in Magnitogorsk to alter the absurd nature of daily life.

An announcement in the spring of 1989, the fourth year of *perestroika* and the seventy-second of the revolution, that laundry powder and soap would be rationed was greeted with a sigh of relief. In the face of the long absence of these items from the shelves, many people, especially those with small children, feared they would never see such necessities again. Now there was hope. "If the authorities issued the coupons, logically that meant there would be something to redeem them for," one woman reasoned, trying to suppress her doubts.

While the introduction of rationing was welcomed, the disclosure of the quantities to be made available caused shock and disgust: two hundred grams of hand soap (equivalent to one normal-sized bar), two hundred of coarse soap, and seven hundred of laundry detergent per person every *three* months. Was this, many scoffed, what *perestroika* had wrought? A rumor began to circulate to the effect that in Leningrad at the nadir of its history, during the wartime blockade by the Germans that lasted nine hundred days and in which perhaps as many as one million people died, each inhabitant could obtain the equivalent of one bar of soap per *month*—three times what was being sold under *perestroika*.

The proposed day for the introduction of the coupons for soap and detergent came and went. Another month passed: no coupons, no explanation. The suspicion arose that supplies had not come in or, if they had, that they had been siphoned off by those with privileged access to them. The real explanation was much simpler: the city had no paper to print the coupons. "Is life going to go on like this forever?" a young housewife asked me and then put a finger across her lips to discourage a response.

■   ■   ■

Advertisements urging people to "use taxis" could be found in several places in Magnitogorsk. One journalist decided to take the advice. He approached fifteen drivers of state taxi cabs, asked to be driven to what he called an "unprestigious address," and made clear that he was willing to pay the fare. All fifteen refused. "I'm out of gas," one told him. "I don't have the time," another shrugged. A third advised the reporter to take the bus, even suggesting which one, by number. Another simply said, "I'm going in the other direction," before driving off. Nothing new here.

In Magnitogorsk there were approximately thirty thousand cars (only slightly fewer than there were telephones) for the city's 438,000 inhabitants, who composed about 135,000 households. A little more than twenty-two thousand cars were in private hands. The rest were state owned. Not infrequently, those with ready access to a chauffeur-driven state car also owned a private one.

A private car, depending on the model, cost between eight thousand and twenty thousand rubles (roughly, three to seven years' wages at the average pay level). For those with the money (limited credit was available), the wait to purchase a car exceeded ten years. Used cars could be purchased without delay, but rarely for less than fifteen thousand cash. Brand-new models bought for fifteen thousand could be resold on the spot for thirty thousand or more.

Private cars did not enter into the city planners' calculations, and as a result, none of the apartment complexes had a parking facility. Instead, garage parks with rows of attached jerry-built structures had sprung up at various points outside the city limits. For car owners the distance between home and garage rarely amounted to less than five kilometers and often exceeded fifteen.

On any given day, at least half of the cars moving through the city were black Volgas ferrying officials and bosses at high speed. Most owners of private cars limited usage to the occasional trip out of town, especially during the summer, but a number worked the streets as gypsy cabs. A wave of the hand by the side of the road stopped almost any private car. "Hitching" a ride cost anywhere from one to five rubles, depending on the distance. Night "rates" were considerably higher. In general, the cost of a ride of a few miles in a "private" taxi usually exceeded that of a state taxi by a factor of five. Nevertheless, refusals by "privateers," even for an "unprestigious" address, were rare. Just as before *perestroika*, services, in this case taxicabs, were more readily available outside the official state economy.

■   ■   ■

Clusters of widely spaced prefabricated boxes, consisting of apartments with standard designs (in both left and right versions), fanned out from the central arteries of Magnitogorsk. An occasional splash of color on the concrete exteriors did little to dispel the look of instant decay. "Whose soul does not ache upon seeing the raw, greenless, mournful new residential clusters, the neglected roads, the deformed five-story apartment buildings, the lack of recreational areas, the ugly posted agitation," wrote Vilii Bogun, until 1989 the city's chief architect and a man intimately involved in the design of Magnitogorsk for more than thirty years. "How many years have we been building the city, and we still can't get it the way we want it?"

So few were the apartment types that apartment dwellers, when queried, could refer to their units by the planners' technical designation, and everyone would instantly know the layout and dimensions. Bogun stressed that such architecture could not but have a deleterious effect on people's consciousness. "The city," Bogun reflected, "is viewed like a warehouse for storing manufactured goods—just so many square meters of space. . . . From an early age, a child unwillingly becomes accustomed to standardization. At age three, he goes to a standardized nursery school; at age six, a standardized elementary school. He lives in a standardized apartment building, plays in a standardized courtyard. Each day he passes a standardized store, cinema, and so on."

As measured by city planners, each resident of Magnitogorsk possessed an average of 8.8 square meters of living space (compared with 16.6 in Bulgaria, 35 in Sweden, and more than 42 in the absurdly wasteful United States; 9 square meters is the equivalent of a 9 by 9 foot room). These averages, however, concealed significant inequalities. Fifteen percent of all Magnitogorsk families had less than 5 square meters per person. Another 20 percent had between 5 and 7. On the other hand, 2.5 percent possessed more than 20 square meters per person—a bounty of space few people in Magnitogorsk had ever seen.

To understand an individual's housing situation, however, it was not enough to know how many precious square meters that person had; one also had to know the nature of that space. In Magnitogorsk 20 percent of all apartments were "communal"—that is, each bedroom was occupied by a separate household, with all residents using a common kitchen, bathroom, toilet, and entranceway. Furthermore, almost nineteen thousand people, most but not all of them unmarried, lived in what were called dormitories, where space was very restricted and communal facilities were spread even more thinly.

Nor was overcrowdedness limited to those in communal living situations. Not only were apartments with their own kitchens and bathrooms small, but about 36 percent of the people with such accommodations also had in-laws or other relatives living with them. All told, fewer than 50 percent of Magnitogorsk residents had their own self-contained apartments *and* lived as single families without relatives (a figure that exceeds even the doubling-up rate in New York City).

To qualify for new housing, a family had to possess less than 9 square meters of space per person. As of 1 April 1988, 28,430 families were on the housing lists of Magnitogorsk enterprises. Another 2,005 families were on the city soviet's list. A separate list kept for invalids and participants of the Great Patriotic War had 207 names. In all, 30,637 households, out of approximately 135,000, or roughly 20 percent, were awaiting housing.*

Despite the continual construction of housing, the waiting lists were expanding. For example, in 1985 the list of the Metallurgical Works—the enterprise that builds the most housing in the city—had 14,673 families. By 1988, after furious construction, the number stood at 14,836. Those employed at the steel plant waited on average fifteen years for an apartment, according to official sources. Those on the city soviet list (schoolteachers, doctors at city hospitals, police) waited on average twenty years. *Perestroika,* the authorities were chanting. Meanwhile, people had to live.

Upon the marriage of their children, almost all families had to accept the arrival of a son- or daughter-in-law into the home, knowing that the new bride and groom could remain their entire adult lives (hoping to inherit the space). It was common to find three generations, and sometimes even four, living under one roof. Households had little choice but to devise a rotating schedule for use of the apartment. Older members were often banished to the kitchen or to a movie for the entire evening while younger ones entertained guests. At the same time, the grandmothers, conveniently, were always around to baby-sit, and often they did much of the standing in line and cooking for the whole household.

In such conditions the very notion of a room changed. All rooms became multipurpose: living rooms were also dining rooms and at night became bedrooms. The conversions were often remarkable to behold. Sometimes, in the rare instance that someone, usually a widow, had an extra room, she might try to rent it out privately to a boarder. It could

* All adult members of a qualifying household were legally entitled to request housing at their place of employment. Some households had two to five members on lists. When lists were cross-checked, the authorities discovered that around one-fourth of those waiting "disappeared"—that is, they were members of one household looking for one apartment. Thus, the "actual" number of families in line for housing was thought to be around 22,500.

happen, however, that the city considered a vacant room in an apartment "communal" and offered it to someone on the housing list.

．   ．   ．

"All violent crimes," explained Mayor Mikhail Lysenko in 1987, "without exception are alcohol related, and even many nonviolent ones can be traced to . . ."—at which point he tilted his head back and flicked his index finger against his throat, making the familiar Russian gesture signifying drinking. *Perestroika* or no *perestroika,* I was told by passersby on the street, people drank; this was Russia.

An antialcohol campaign was one of the first measures announced by Mikhail Gorbachev when he became general secretary in the spring of 1985. The availability of beer was severely curtailed, while vodka was rationed: one liter per adult family member per month. But in the face of a tidal wave of opposition from Magnitogorsk workers, the rationing of vodka was repealed locally in January 1987.

Not only workers expressed dissatisfaction. Some housewives had complained that rationing actually encouraged drinking, as their husbands reasoned it would be a shame to let the cards go to waste. Speculation with ration cards had been rampant. In February 1987 one woman wrote to the local newspaper, "I have no more patience to endure further media coverage of the campaign against alcoholism. In my view, nothing at all has changed, despite the punishments and preventive measures." She explained that she had two children, her husband drank, she called the militia, he was fined, and she paid his fine from the household budget. Always "the children lose out." She asked poignantly, "Where does he get the alcohol? Is it possible the authorities don't know where the speculation is going on and who's behind it?"

Sergei Kotelnikov, deputy rector of the Mining Institute and at the time chair of the city's sobriety society, conceded in early 1987 that "although quite a bit has been done, we have yet to see fundamental changes" in the problem of alcoholism. Rationing of vodka was soon restored, and local authorities also shortened the hours for the sale of alcoholic beverages, essentially to four afternoon hours per day. Long lines resulted. Curiously, although heavy drinkers were overwhelmingly men, a considerable number of adult women could be seen in the queues. Bottles bought for twelve rubles by those with time to wait in queues could be resold for twenty—not exactly evidence of the oft-remarked sloth of an indifferent population.

Rumors spread of the proliferation of moonshine. During the first four months of 1985 in the city's Ordzhonikidze district, 853 tons of sugar and 18 tons of tomato paste, two ingredients for home brew, were sold. In the same district during the first four months of 1987 (with roughly the same population), 1,136 tons of sugar and 38 tons of tomato paste were sold. Relying on tips, the authorities stepped up raids on still operators. In 1985, 163 cases of alleged moonshining were heard; in 1986, 359; and in the first two months of 1987, more than 100—a yearly average of more than 600. After one raid, a person's apartment was described as "if not a wine cellar, then probably the warehouse for a gigantic wedding in merchant's style." Sixty percent of those caught were women; as a rule, they were older than forty.

Drunks encountered on Magnitogorsk streets were liable to be taken to one of three sobering-up stations (*vytrezvitel'*). Those hauled in were seen by a doctor, had their pictures and blood samples taken, and were given showers. They had to stay until they were sober (in any case, not less than three hours). A report was filled out, and a bill, for thirty rubles, was sent to the person's place of employment, where it was deducted from the next paycheck. An additional fine—up to fifty rubles—could be levied. During the last year before the onset of the antialcohol campaign (1984), sobering-up stations in Magnitogorsk recorded 27,000 "visits." Of that number, 140 were by women.

An excursion to one sobering-up station revealed a stark, spotless, yet dark converted cellar with little furniture beyond thirty-one hard cots spread throughout a half dozen rooms. A map on the wall resembled a battle plan, red pins designating each store in the city where alcohol was on sale. According to the staff, some individuals had been brought in two, three, and even four times.

After a while, repeat offenders were taken directly to the city's drying-out prison, technically known as a medicinal-labor profilactory (*lechebno-trudovoi profilaktorii*). Sentences were relatively short, typically six months, although one could get as long as three years. All "patients" were required to work, either on the premises or outside under guard, in the hope that they would be reformed.

One taxi driver, boasting of his time at the facility, proudly drew attention to a huge scar on his arm, which he attributed to the normal "hooliganism" there. "It's rough inside, but not too rough," he remarked, with a wave of the hand. "Many get out only to return, like my brother-in-law, the shark. Some 'graduate' to higher levels of incarceration. I drive a cab, keep out of trouble. I'm going to buy a bungalow soon—twenty thousand rubles."

If he fulfilled his quota, the cab driver took home about two hundred rubles a month. His wife's income and mother-in-law's pension amounted to another ninety rubles, making a combined yearly income of about thirty-five hundred rubles. When I asked how he could afford to buy a bungalow, the cab driver conceded that he made his "real money" nights and weekends as a "private" mechanic, using spare parts and tools from the central taxi garage. Although he would not say, it was even possible that his technically illegal side activity was organized by the taxi garage itself, for a percentage.

•   •   •

By 1989 *perestroika* had brought no apparent improvement to Magnitogorsk's grocery stores; as before, one could find milk, eggs, bread, low-quality frozen fish, animal fats, some canned goods, and various grains. Yogurt, a primary children's food, was still less plentiful. More popular scarce items such as sugar, meat, butter, and sausages were still being "rationed," meaning that purchases were allowed in limited quantities and only with the presentation of coupons distributed at residences in accord with the number of people in the household. For other "luxuries," such as cheese, the city did not bother to issue coupons: there was little to be had. Vegetables, even cabbage, were still not regularly available in stores, and fresh fruit was rarer still. Yet despite the perennially bare shelves, the average Soviet citizen was said to consume approximately thirty-four hundred calories a day, more than his or her counterpart in Sweden or Japan but less than in the United States.

Amid the relentless talk about shortages, it was revealed that the Magnitogorsk population consumed bread, potatoes, and sugar well above nutritional norms. By contrast, consumption of milk and dairy products, vegetables, fruit, eggs, fish, and meat fell well below what Soviet experts considered optimal. In 1989 the city newspaper reported that buckwheat kasha, a favorite of the Russian kitchen and one of the healthier varieties of food, was being distributed only to the sick by prescription. Fifty percent of Soviet women and 25 percent of men were thought to be overweight.

Few issues commanded more of the populace's attention than that of meat availability. In the summer of 1988, during the hoopla surrounding the special party conference, the newspaper reported that "lately it has been possible to buy fatty pork, less often beef. There are chickens, liver sausage, and two other varieties [known by their prices, R 2.90 and R 2.20, rather than by brand names]. Once in a while you can obtain frozen *pelmeni* [ravioli]. Fancier sausage, smoked sausage, and hot dogs are in effect unavailable."

Magnitogorsk had a single large meat factory producing sausage. In the pages of the newspaper one day in February 1989 an angry letter writer expressed the widely held suspicion that "every day every employee of the meat factory takes home a minimum of two kilos of the best grade meat." To avoid detection during spot inspections for theft, according to the letter writer, female employees hid in showers. Others passed meat through the fence to avoid the guard at the gate. Moreover, guards were known to be less vigilant during lunchtime than at the end of a shift. There was plenty of meat, the letter writer implied, but it was being pilfered.

The problem seemed simple enough: there were thieves; catch them. On 19 February 1987 an electrician, B. L. Shaparov, was reported to have been detained while attempting to crawl under the meat factory's perimeter fence. Thirteen rubles, 68 kopecks' worth of meat products were found on his person. Shaparov was fined 150 rubles. On 2 September of the same year he was apprehended in the same place with the same "baggage." Shaparov, the newspaper report implied, should have been fired after the first incident and denied an opportunity to repeat his crime.

Yet although some insider meat thieves were being caught (during the first eight months of 1987, for example, fifty employees were detained attempting to carry inventory home), firing them was another matter: there was no one to replace them with. In fact, according to A. M. Geller, director of the meat factory, the plant was compelled to take on former and *present* convicts. Geller also bemoaned the fact that there were not enough refrigerated trucks to transport meat and that no trucks had hooks inside; the meat was simply piled on the floor. But far from eliciting sympathy, newspaper interviews allowing besieged supply officials to vent their frustrations incited the reiteration of criminal allegations.

In truth, Geller's problems were greater than many would have liked to admit. The meat factory, as the newspaper explained, was located in a remote part of town, and the daily round-trip commute exceeded three hours for most workers. A month's wages at the plant, as specified by national planners, averaged 130 rubles, about 90 rubles less than the city average. According to the secretary of the plant's party committee, no one working at the meat factory had received an apartment in the previous twenty years.

For disgruntled consumers, rampant theft was but one perennial bugbear; declining sausage quality was another. According to Geller, who conceded the point, there was a simple explanation for the decline: out of 100 grams of meat products the plant has been required by instructions to produce 108, then 111, 113, and finally 116 grams of sausage. The plant accomplished this task by diluting the sausage with soy, pig skins, and paste made from unspecified substances.

Hot dogs had always been a popular, although generally unavailable, snack food in city eateries. After many years the meat factory finally succeeded in purchasing its own hot-dog maker, but despite expending all possible effort, workers could not get the brand-new machine to function. Geller reported that he was trying to locate a different supplier to obtain another model, so far unsuccessfully. Planners preferred when possible to concentrate production of an item in one firm, rather than to spread production out and encourage state firms to compete against each other.

Faced with no other choice, a large number of townspeople grew their own food—potatoes, radishes, onions, cucumbers, tomatoes—on little plots outside of town in a kind of return to a subsistence economy, but for urbanites. An apartment balcony stocked with jars of pickled homegrown tomatoes took some of the hard edge off the long winters without fresh vegetables. For those who wanted to supplement their own efforts, fruits of the private "harvest" were made available for sale beginning in the spring by diligent grandmothers at bus and tram stops around town; these women punctuated otherwise drab street scenes by giving various places in the city the look of small informal farmers markets. Prices for homegrown vegetables were higher than those in state stores, but vigorous competition within the ranks of small growers kept the indispensable private crop affordable.

■   ■   ■

The total area of Magnitogorsk, almost four hundred square kilometers, seemed rather large given the size of the population. The sheer size of the steelworks and the presence of several other large factories made the distances between home and work enormous. Moreover, while the industrial area was growing to the north, the residential area was growing to the south, thereby enhancing the distances in the city. A system of public transportation struggled to cope.

The first tram line was put into operation in 1935 and had been the dominant form of public transit ever since. Like the steel plant, trams ran all night. It was striking just how much the tram defined the city, and not only because it accounted for 80 percent of passenger transport. The tram's wide and formidable tracks sharply divided all main thoroughfares, while the heavy cars rumbled loudly, giving Magnitogorsk streets the feeling of a train depot. All trams seemed to connect eventually with the steel plant or the two neighboring wire and cable factories. A ride from any of the principal residential districts to the city's three largest factories, a distance of between twelve and twenty kilometers, varied in time from forty-five minutes to more than an hour.

During commuting hours the red-and-white double streetcars, already loaded down with passengers well beyond capacity, could be seen approaching a stop where the throngs positioned themselves in anticipation of arrival. When the doors opened those getting off burst forth like water from a hydrant; those getting on jostled and clawed their way up the steps, pressed by others from behind, like trash in a compactor.

"From the theater to my home it's four tram stops; ten minutes," explained Viktor Shraiman, director of the Magnitogorsk puppet theater. "Every evening at the end of the working day I cover this distance, like an obstacle course, in forty minutes. . . . I do not now (nor will I ever) have an official automobile. The same goes for a personal one. Thus, I make it home like all Soviet people. Or almost all. By tram.

"When all is said and done, the hell with them—the ripped-off buttons. Stores are full of them (in contrast to laundry detergent and soap). . . . No, truthfully, the issue here is not torn-off buttons. Simply, when you fight for a spot on the doorway steps, pushing aside your fellow citizens, and then you get your nose stuck in someone's work clothes at belt level, you stop feeling like a human being. . . .

"And yet, this isn't the point. There are the lines to the cash registers in the shops, where out of six registers, two are open. Or our public cafeterias . . . where the cooks greet us in filthy smocks, where the trays are greasy, and where the silverware is dirty and wet. . . . And the boorishness! Tram operators, hospital admittance staff, salesclerks—young girls! What is going on with us? It is not right to build something new and to live in it like swine."

In addition to streetcars Magnitogorsk was served by a bus system, which until 1976 ran in the black. Then, owing to chronic personnel shortages, human ticket takers were replaced by self-operated *kassas*, into which a rider upon boarding was expected to deposit a coin and then tear off a ticket. To discourage cheating, controllers were supposed to make random spotchecks. The fine for riding without a ticket was three rubles. Magnitogorsk employed fourteen people to patrol dozens of bus and tram lines all day, every day, 365 days a year.

The average hourly citywide intake on buses had fallen by 1988 from nine rubles to between five and six (the cost, six kopecks, remained essentially the same, while the number of riders increased dramatically). Approximately one-third of all passengers were thought to ride without paying. The cumulative effect of these "rabbits," as they were called, was a shortfall of more than two million rubles a year. A ride on the tram cost even less—three kopecks—and a monthly pass good for unlimited riding could be bought for only two rubles. Nevertheless, the number of "rabbits" on trams was thought to exceed significantly that on buses.

In 1989, even during off-hours, trams and buses seemed to be as crammed as ever with people, most of whom were standing and almost all of whom were carrying bundles filled with the scant trophies of purchasing wars. Although planners had produced detailed charts depicting the distances traveled between work and home, no one had yet taken the trouble to draw a graph that portrayed the immense distances traversed as people combed the city in search of something to buy.

■   ■   ■

Even though most Magnitogorsk families interviewed in a newspaper poll said they felt two children were ideal, the city average was 1.5. (Almost no one expressed a desire to have more than two.) Thirty percent of all couples had one child, 51.5 percent had two, and 6.5 percent had three. Eighty-five percent of all preschool children went to day care. Indeed, in surveys of the factors inhibiting marriage or the bearing of children, housing, not day care, always came out on top.

"Housing is a big problem," acknowledged Mikhail Lysenko during an interview in 1987. "There just isn't enough. We're building, building all the time. By the year 2000 everyone ought to have an individual apartment—that's our goal." Vilii Bogun pointed out that during those years the city also needed to build another fourteen schools, thirty-two children's institutions, several medical clinics, libraries, movie houses, a theater, a bank, dozens of stores, and a few cafés, even as many existing projects had yet to be finished.

According to Bogun, of the city's nineteen microregions, only six were considered complete. The rest still awaited roads, sidewalks, stores, and other necessities. A fourth bridge to be built across the industrial lake to the south in order to shorten the commute to work for the already large and expanding population of the new microregions was at least a decade behind schedule. Furthermore, some uncomplicated construction, such as that of the standard-design covered market, took more than a decade to finish. Even such a high-priority job as the impressive party and government building, known locally as the Pentagon, sat on a piece of property whose roads were not finished. Such a track record did not bode well.

Bogun recalled that the 1957 housing program proclaimed an end to the housing shortage by 1970. After a decade of feverish construction, with the goal still far off, the target date was simply extended to 1980. Then, during the 1970s, the program was quietly dropped and remained unheard of until its recent revival. Alongside ambitious undertakings to reform the country's political and economic systems, long-standing social programs plod on much as before. If current population trends were taken into account, to supply every Magnitogorsk household with an individual apartment by the year 2000, Magnitostroi, the largest construction trust in the USSR, would have to build 2,070 apartments a year. It was actually building about 1,000. V. Anikushin, chief of the construction trust, told the newspaper that his organization could not build apartments any faster because of limitations in the "capacity" of the local cement panel factory.

Given the inherent limits to construction, attention tended to focus on allocation. All residents were required to submit their housing situation for approval to the police authorities, but complaints about the misallocation and misuse of housing were frequent. The agency charged with insuring compliance with the laws, the city's Bureau of Housing Exchanges, sanctioned up to fifty-seven hundred apartment exchanges a year. All work at the bureau was done by hand by a staff of three.

Housing scandals were regularly reported. For example, in the summer of 1987 the former chief of water purification was caught renting out space in the agency's office building for use as living quarters and pocketing the money. Similarly, an investigation prompted by a letter to the Central Committee of the Communist party ascertained that the chief of the medical department at the Magnitogorsk Works had assigned apartments to friends and relatives by falsifying documents.

Even though abuses in the city's housing registration system were regularly decried, as with other illicit behavior it was difficult to know how widespread such abuses were. A citywide occupancy reregistration was carried out between January and April 1989. Everyone who hoped to remain on official housing lists had to have his or her living situation verified. In addition, the first housing "census" since 1960 was taken along with the population census in January 1989. The results of these important operations had not yet been publicly announced. But however either survey turned out, the desperate housing shortage would not be alleviated by more accurate registration.

■   ■   ■

At the neighborhood women's clinic the long line to get an abortion was far shorter than the one next door for sausage, and much quieter. More than 80 percent of all women in the USSR will have undergone an abortion by the end of their childbearing years, usually two to four abortions each. *Perestroika* did not mean anything new in that regard.

In 1920 the Soviet Union became the first country to legalize abortion, but in 1936 legal abortions were proscribed. In 1956 came relegalization. By 1989, according to most estimates, the Soviet Union, with less than 6 percent of the world's population, accounted for perhaps as much as 20 percent of the world's yearly abortions. (Such estimates were difficult to make because perhaps 50 percent of abortions were performed outside state channels.) In the USSR for every live birth there were probably at least two abortions.

Even though the state provided abortions during the first trimester at no cost to "working" women (those who did not work outside the home paid a nominal fee), many women continued to pay anywhere from 50 to 100 rubles for anesthesia, cleanliness, confidentiality, more personal care, and everything else not available at state clinics during regular working hours. Perhaps the main reason for paying, however, was the desire to avoid the mandatory three-day hospital stay after a legal abortion.

The women at a state clinic one day in April 1989 were not very talkative. The atmosphere was unmistakably slaughterhouse. Pain, humiliation, and disgust emanated from the faces of those returning from the "conveyor." Counseling was unheard of. When asked why they did not seek a "private" abortion, those still waiting stared in contempt. "Money," someone finally snapped. "It's no better on the 'left,' " another disagreed. "I know. You just have to pay. It's the same butchers."

Some of the women were young; many were not. A sizable number wore wedding rings. Soviet sociologists estimated that from 25 to 75 percent of all couples did not regularly employ any form of contraception. A Soviet version of the pill was no longer produced (side effects were prominent), and imports were insubstantial. Soviet-manufactured intrauterine devices were extremely unpopular; infections were widely reported. Domestic-made diaphragms seemed to come in two sizes, at most, and, in any case accompanying jellies and foams were not always obtainable. "Galoshes," or condoms, were cheap but not always available; in any case, they were ludicrously thick, rarely lubricated, and thus despised by men. Abortion was the last option.

Everyone acknowledged the shortage of effective contraceptives. The cynical pointed out that those who might be expected to inform women about birth control options—namely, obstetric gynecologists—profited handsomely from private abortion practices. Even so, it was accidentally discovered that a supply of American condoms given to an educated Magnitogorsk woman in 1987 was unused two years later, despite every indication of sexual activity. The expiration date on the packages had long since passed.

■ ■ ■

"There's only one way to 'capture' goods, as we say," explained one seasoned shopper. "You have to know the stores, know when the shipments are coming in. You keep in touch with people in other neighborhoods; you get friends at the steel plant to make meat purchases. For some items there's no choice but to travel to Moscow. The best deal of all, of course, is to work in supply oneself."

"Shopping" is a misnomer for the acquisition of food, clothing, and other goods in Magnitogorsk; "scavenging" would be more accurate. Stores did not compete with each other. Prices for any item were identical everywhere. Discounts or markdowns were not permitted, even if goods were not selling, and there were no special or seasonal sales. Competitive brands did not exist: there were "children's" shoes, "women's" boots, "men's" coats—when available. Color and style varied, but rarely within a single year. Only the periodic appearance of Hungarian chickens, East German shampoo, or rare Finnish boots—goods known by the magical expression *importnoe*—offered a real choice to the Soviet consumer: the coveted opportunity to reject Soviet-made goods and still acquire something.

Without the option of buying elsewhere, consumers vented their frustrations on sales personnel. Letters denouncing employees in the trade network flowed endlessly to the Magnitogorsk newspaper, typically accusing sales help of rudeness, laziness, deception, and theft. Angry customers also took advantage of the "complaint and suggestion books" available in all stores. One "complaint book" I consulted in a large grocery store contained the following entries:

"I stood in line while the salesgirl fixed her hair."

"After waiting forever I had to endure the insults of the insolent staff when I asked why there was no more milk."

"There is never decent meat, and yet the salespeople are all overweight."

Violent shouting matches between frustrated customers and surly sales help were not uncommon. These deeply felt animosities were fed by scandals over corruption in trade, which broke out regularly. In the summer of 1988, for example, the newspaper reported that the chief of the entire provincial trade network, V. G. Sidoi, was under investigation. Both the police and the Procuracy were also implicated. "He who sits nearest the pot," remarked one Magnitogorsk wag as she and I sat down to a plate of boiled potatoes, "eats the most kasha."

Notwithstanding consumer demand, the state trade network in Magnitogorsk remained woefully underdeveloped. Although there were no separate shopping districts, many neighborhoods had few or no stores. The United States, with 85 percent of the population of the USSR, had three times as many people employed in retail trade as the USSR had in all kinds of trade. Inadequate numbers of sales personnel were only part of the problem. In Soviet terms retail trade was perhaps the least advantageous profession from the point of view of obtaining housing, yet trade employees were resented.

According to Vera Riadchikova, a department manager in a Magnitogorsk clothing store, "Lately it's become impossible to work. Utterly nerve-wracking. No goods, yet the [trade] plan looms. Prices are rising, and customers look at us. We have to hear complaints and foul language. Towels come in for sale at 6 rubles each. Before, they cost 2.20. We're blamed. . . .

"How long is this going to continue? There are no knitting needles. People say, 'You probably hid some under the counter.' But there aren't any, period. . . . But where is social justice if salespeople are not permitted to place priority orders on goods? . . . We who work at this store have no place to eat lunch. Nothing but investigatory commissions.

One after the other. What are they investigating? There are no goods. . . . [Yet] on TV all you hear is how splendidly trade employees live."

■   ■   ■

For every one hundred Magnitogorsk families, there were ninety-six radio receivers, ninety-nine television sets (most black-and-white), thirty-nine tape recorders, thirty-four photo cameras, ninety-two refrigerators, seventy washing machines, and five cars. The quality of these goods left much to be desired, but having them repaired often bordered on the impossible. Spare parts were commonly unavailable, sometimes even when a "premium" or bribe was offered. As a result, people rarely threw things away, hoping somehow to be able to reuse them. Many items acquired secondary purposes. Newspapers served as wrapping paper; old clothes became the basic material for new ones sewn by hand. Against this background the people of Magnitogorsk read reports of arms control agreements to reduce the number of intercontinental ballistic missiles.

Magnitogorsk banks, not to mention other businesses, operated without computers. Payrolls, inventories, and accounting procedures were done by hand. Almost all institutions, including the public library, were without photocopying machines. Cans were opened by repeated punctures in a circular direction with a knife. Indeed, basic household equipment was not taken for granted. Less than one-third of all families had telephones. Floor tiles and wallpaper encountered in Magnitogorsk kitchens were often obtained only after repeated foraging and installed by apartment dwellers themselves, unless they could find (and afford) a moonlighter. Cut glass, especially as a replacement for a broken window, was one of the most miraculous finds. Windshield wipers were removed by owners when leaving their cars; if stolen, the wipers were available only on the black market and thus were expensive to replace.

Even though 99 percent of apartments had indoor plumbing, Magnitogorsk residents had grown accustomed throughout the years to enduring a month or two without hot water every summer, when pipes were repaired and other maintenance work was performed. But interruptions in the supply of hot water had begun occurring year-round. Even cold water had become unavailable for stretches.

In an ordinary fifth-floor apartment in a five-story building in the center of town, hot water was consistently unavailable at least three times a week for a two-month period in the spring of 1989. Almost as frequently, all running water was shut off. Large buckets of water were kept in the kitchen and bathroom. Faucets were left in the open position. Whenever running water returned, there would be a rush to refill the buckets.

"They can't even manage to provide us with water! Tell me what here is *not* in short supply!" remarked a disgusted Evgenii Vernikov, managing editor of the city newspaper, while kneeling with a bucket over the tub, as the nightly news of much-ballyhooed political happenings emanated from the television in the living room–bedroom. "Smoke and dust," came the reply from Tamara Vernikova, a bookkeeper at the factory, who was busy in the kitchen concocting yet another minor miracle out of potatoes and a scrawny chicken.

■   ■   ■

As of 1989 life expectancy at birth in the Soviet Union, sixty-seven years, ranked thirty-second in the world (slightly above El Salvador and Tunisia). Infant mortality, 26 per 1,000—about equal to that of Barbados, worse than that of Mauritius, and twice as high as that of Cuba—ranked forty-ninth. Even though life expectancy and infant mortality figures for Magnitogorsk were not available, other eye-opening statistics from an investigation conducted by the Central Committee of the Komsomol were.

Every year the smokestacks of the Magnitogorsk Works emitted more than 870 million tons of atmospheric exhaust, or some 40,000 pounds per inhabitant. Only 50 percent of that total passed through cleansing devices, which removed just 33 percent of the dangerous gases. Moreover, at night pollution control devices at the factory were sometimes disengaged to circumvent their adverse effect on productivity. Fully 20 percent of the existing devices were out of service at any one time. In a three-week period in April 1988, for example, the few pollution control devices installed in the open-hearth shops were not functioning for one reason or another a total of 271 hours, or more than 50 percent of the time, according to data supplied by the steel plant.

Put another way, during the year each hectare of residential area in Magnitogorsk was covered by an average of 6.6 tons of airborne pollutants. (In the United States, the situation is considered serious if on one hectare of residential territory the amount of harmful substances that fall reaches 0.2 tons.) The incidence of harmful substances in the air (coke dust, phenol, sulphurous anhydride) significantly exceeded allowable scientific norms even thirty kilometers away. Soil samples taken from within twenty-four kilometers of the steel plant revealed zinc, copper, chrome, and especially lead concentrations five and ten times the "natural" rate. Extraordinary concentrations of these same metals were found in plants and vegetables grown outside the city limits. There was growing alarm at the possibility that even underground sources of water might be seriously contaminated.

The number of men retiring as invalids was increasing sharply. Upon retirement (at age sixty) the average Magnitogorsk male was said to live three more years. Thirty-four percent of the entire adult population (those aged fifteen or older) suffered from respiratory diseases. Almost 10 percent of all adults had a nervous condition. Rates for all manner of disease among adults in Magnitogorsk exceeded by more than 20 percent even the relatively high average for the largest one hundred industrial cities in the USSR. Of those diseases diagnosed, the vast majority were discovered in their later stages of development.

For Magnitogorsk children the rate for various diseases was 50 percent higher than that for the largest one hundred industrial cities in the country. Sixty-seven percent of all children age fourteen and younger suffered respiratory ailments. A majority of children suffered from bronchial infections. Bronchial asthma, pharyngitis, and ulcers among children were increasing at a phenomenal rate. Forty-one of every one hundred Magnitogorsk babies were born with pathologies. If parents of generally healthy babies bartering what they could for extra cans of condensed milk or some soap granules to wash a mountain of diapers could hardly be faulted for mocking the supposed promise of *perestroika,* what of the other less fortunate?

■   ■   ■

By the end of 1987 something did seem to be going right: visits to sobering-up stations had declined, according to Fedor Bulatov, chief of the militia, from more than thirty thousand a year to nineteen thousand. True, during 1987 almost thirty thousand people died nationwide from consumption of various alcohol substitutes ranging from cologne to antifreeze. And the drop in revenue from the sale of alcohol decimated the state budget. But meanwhile most people cheered that the presence of drunks on the street had been so effectively eliminated.

Then, beginning in 1988 the antialcohol campaign, just as it had finally started to reduce drunkenness, was reversed by Moscow. In the light of this development a public meeting to discuss the resurgence of alcoholism took place in Magnitogorsk on 13 April 1989. Anna Ianuz, the new chair of the sobriety society, delivered a report, her voice heavy with indignation.

Between 1984 and 1988, Ianuz reported, the sale of alcohol (vodka, beer, and cognac) in Magnitogorsk was reduced by a remarkable 50 percent. During the same period, she claimed, the sale of sugar—a chief ingredient in moonshine—rose only 2 to 3 percent (a figure consonant with population growth). Moreover, the number of individual gardens rose 30 percent, an increase that would raise the demand for sugar (to convert berries and fruits into preserves and jams). In other words, contrary to the estimates from the Ministry of Internal Affairs and the observations of almost all ordinary people, Ianuz asserted that there had been no growth in moonshine production. Even the initial surge in arrests for moonshining—a result, in Ianuz's opinion, of greater vigilance—was reversed, declining in the first months of 1989. And the number of "visits" to sobering-up stations had declined significantly, and crime was down.

Expressing great assurance that the campaign had been working, she admitted that not everyone was pleased. The antialcohol campaign begun in 1985 envisioned eventually cutting sales by 50 percent through yearly decreases of 10 percent, but in many places sales were reduced by 50 percent almost immediately, thereby causing huge queues and provoking widespread dissatisfaction. Ianuz went so far as to intimate that the unnecessarily steep cutback might have been calculated to discredit the campaign altogether.

Discontent did not arise over the unavailability of vodka. In Magnitogorsk about 30 percent of the population did not redeem its coupons for vodka; anyone who wanted extra coupons could easily obtain them. But even though the general availability of vodka was not an issue, *when* it was available and *how much* it cost were. Fedor Bulatov pointed out, for example, that vodka was freely sold—for twenty rubles a (one-liter) bottle, an eight-ruble premium—from gypsy cabs in the evenings after stores had closed. On top of this, beer sales were sharply reduced when the Magnitogorsk beer factory was closed owing to technical problems with the old equipment, and a decision was made not to retool it.

Against this background of allegedly overwhelming success yet mounting discontent, Anna Ianuz revealed that during the first quarter of 1989 sales of alcohol had by design been increased almost 20 percent. Moreover, plans for wine sales called for a 40 percent increase. All the hard-won gains were on the verge of being lost. Already in 1988 the effects of increased sales had been felt. Bulatov revealed that crime, which rose 26 percent in 1988 against 1987, after three months in 1989 had risen 46 percent. Beginning in 1988 and continuing into 1989 visits to sobering-up stations were up dramatically.

In the emotional discussion that ensued, much time was consumed discussing prevention of the sale of alcohol near schools and other institutions for children. Most speakers condemned this practice. No one pointed out that a prohibition on such sales would not have lessened the effects of alcohol abuse on children, who would still see the problem at home.

One speaker disclosed that the state construction firm, known to have many of the worst abusers, conducted a sociological study of approximately four hundred of its people. More than 20 percent openly admitted the existence of an alcohol-related "problem" in their families. Seventy-five percent supported either limitations on sales (60 percent) or a total ban (15 percent—virtually all women). The antialcohol constituency highlighted by these data, however, remained unorganized and thus had yet to act as an effective pressure group.

Someone proposed taxing cigarettes, which were not costly (about forty kopecks for common brands). Another suggested tying the sale of chocolate and coffee to vodka by making a single coupon redeemable for one or the other but not both—an idea that was greeted with scorn. No chocolate had been seen in city stores for more than a year. After an almost equally long absence from the shelves, coffee had only just reappeared—for twenty-five rubles a kilo, about three days' pay.

A number of speakers doubted the sincerity of the rationing system. At the end of every month in almost all retail outlets, they pointed out, vodka was freely sold in an effort to meet monthly plan targets. In various places, often directly from the back of trucks, vodka was freely sold throughout the month. One attending representative of the city authorities—Aleksandr Leislia, deputy director of the city soviet—was himself accused of carrying out such a duplicitous policy. Under attack, Leislia remarked that the first three years of the antialcohol campaign had adversely affected the state budget. Without increased sales of alcohol, revenues would not match expenditures. In order to pay workers' salaries, he flatly stated, the city needed to sell them alcohol.

There seemed no way out of the dilemma. The chair of the session, Ivan Galiguzov, professor of party history at the Mining Institute, closed the meeting by linking the elimination of alcoholism to the general cultural level, which, he emphasized, could be raised only through education. "It is our lack of culturedness," he shouted, pounding his fist on the table, showing the frustration that had characterized the public gathering where about half the fifty people in the hall had spoken, most with considerable emotion and a sense of urgency in their voices.

For four years the inhabitants of Magnitogorsk had been searching for *visible* signs of change, wanting so much to hope. There was, however, little cause for comfort, aside from the antialcohol measures, and even these were by no means universally popular. Then the very success of the campaign backfired by decimating the state budget. Once again, it seemed, *perestroika* notwithstanding, it was time to dig in for the long haul.

■   ■   ■

Owing to the peculiarities of its development, Magnitogorsk became two cities connected by three bridges that traversed the one-kilometer-wide artificial lake. Giving an indication of its geographical position in the Ural Mountains, a plaque on one of the bridges over the Ural River bore the words "Europe" and "Asia," with a slash in between. Of the city's 438,000 people, about 60,000 lived in the left-bank part (Asia), with the remaining 378,000 in the right-bank part (Europe). An overall limit on the size of the two-continent city was fixed at 500,000—a bureaucratic formality given the very slow rate of growth (mostly through in-migration). In any case, although the city was not growing much, the urgency for new construction was felt as never before.

As Vilii Bogun was fond of pointing out, all periods of Soviet architecture and urban development were on display in Magnitogorsk: the initial period of the 1930s; the "golden" period of the late 1940s and early 1950s; the period of the prefabricated five-story apartment buildings built under Khrushchev and after; and the contemporary period of twelve- to fourteen-story prefabricated apartment buildings.

In 1930 the Soviet government invited the internationally renowned German architect Ernst May to design several new cities, including Magnitogorsk. May had achieved wide acclaim for his highly successful workers' housing settlements in the city of Frankfurt and had been attracted by and enthusiastic about the possibilities of urban planning in the Soviet context. He proposed the then fashionable idea of a "linear city," a design based on the parallel development of residential and industrial zones separated by a greenbelt, which would permit the shortest possible distance between work and home while overcoming the detrimental health effects of industrial activity.

But on the ground May's planned linear design ran into unforeseen obstacles. The site of the steel plant, on the left bank of the Ural River adjacent to the iron-ore deposits, had long ago been settled. Moreover, a huge artificial lake created to supply the factory with water effectively wedged the plant between the hills and the lakeshore making the parallel development of "production" and "residential" zones impossible. The only space remaining for the city on the left bank of the Ural River was a small patch of land to the southeast of the factory. Although the hilly and difficult terrain of this land tract limited the size of the city that the site could accommodate, the original designs for the factory did not necessitate a large town. The projected size of the factory was soon increased, however. In addition, it was promptly discovered that all of the harmful smoke and fumes from the factory blew directly toward the area of the proposed city. The left bank seemed inhospitable to the idea of accommodating a city, linear or otherwise.

There was another option. The city could have been located on the other side of the industrial lake, to the west of the factory, on the right bank of the Ural River. This would have necessitated a two-kilometer bridge connecting the city with the factory and an effective mass transit system to move the workers to and from work. The level of transport technology at the time, however, was low, and the system would have been severely taxed to move so many people such a distance efficiently and reliably. In addition, building the bridge and the transport system would have been costly and extremely difficult, to say nothing of the problem of carrying out construction far away from the economic base provided by the factory.

After inconclusive debates, decisions, and counterdecisions, it was decided, despite the well-known problems, to build the new socialist city on the left bank, to the immediate southeast of the factory. But much valuable time had been lost. By the time the decision was taken, there were more than one hundred thousand people living in temporary installations on the factory site itself.

The critical advantage of the right-bank variant had been that the city would have been relatively well protected from the industrial zone. Building on the left bank, by contrast, meant that the city, literally right on top of the factory, would become drenched with soot, smoke, and chemicals. For this reason, despite the long and agonizing debate that had led to the decision to build on the left bank, and despite the work that had already been carried out, as early as 1933 the Soviet government reversed itself yet again and decided to build on the right bank after all. Although a few permanent apartment buildings and a school were built by early 1941, building on the right bank did not begin in earnest until after the war.

Of that left-bank city, May succeeded in designing and having built only one small settlement, the so-called first *kvartal,* or "superblock," of the socialist city, which was severely criticized for the boxlike appearance of the housing. Attacked venomously in the Soviet press, May soon left the USSR, a disappointed and bitter man. He would later write that he had been handicapped from the start by the unavailability of important construction materials, by the low technical and organizational level of the Soviet building industry, by a lack of finances, and by the notorious Soviet bureaucracy.

After May's departure, Soviet architects took over and built a second superblock of more outwardly impressive structures arranged perpendicularly to form inner courtyards. With the exception of the special settlement for foreigners later occupied by the local Soviet elite, these two superblocks were the only areas with permanent housing built in Magnitogorsk before the war. Well into the second decade of the city's existence no more than 15 percent of the population lived in permanent housing.

Alongside the socialist city, a different city arose. This was the temporary city, a city first of tents, then barracks, mud huts, and two-story carcass buildings. It was in such housing that the overwhelming majority of the population lived, with open sewage, without plumbing, and even without marking by which to distinguish one barrack from the next in the endless rows. Sections of the "temporary" city, wrapped around the factory like an outer layer of human insulation and in many cases built right on the factory grounds, remained in place through the 1970s. Parallel industrial and residential zones haphazardly took shape—only without the greenbelt.

World War II brought an influx not only of evacuated factories and equipment from Leningrad, Moscow, and the Ukraine but also of refugees and large numbers of deported Volga Germans. These people put an already strained housing situation under still more pressure. Tents were seen again, more barracks went up, and people crowded together more than ever. Because the evacuated factories were located near the steelworks, virtually all the newly arrived people were settled close by on the left bank. The bulk of the population continued to live in extremely close proximity to industry.

Although there had been no fighting near Magnitogorsk, the haphazard arrival and settlement of whole factories and large groups of people made it seem as if there had been. The reconstruction effort that followed the victory over the Germans proved to be enormous. Almost immediately work on the right-bank city resumed, and a new superblock, the third, was also built in the old socialist city. Although many of the original apartment buildings of the 1930s were large and rather nice, the housing built in the first decade after the war stood out.

The section of the city on the right bank built after the war was rightly known for its human streets and gracious, individualized buildings; its spacious apartments with high ceilings; and its well-planned layout, allowing for maximum sunlight, green space, and squares. Designed by Leningrad architects and made to resemble the architecture commonly found in that city, it would eventually offer a stark contrast to subsequent building in Magnitogorsk. But even after this relatively successful right-bank city was completed, the majority of people still lived in barracks. With the death of Stalin and the emergence of Khrushchev, a new housing policy was introduced.

Irina Rozhkova, who for more than twenty-five years, from 1954 to 1980, was the chief architect in Magnitogorsk, recalled that one year after Stalin's death a law was passed forbidding the design and construction of individualized apartment buildings in favor of prefabricated concrete buildings of a single design. The advantages were obvious: lower cost and a shorter construction period. As Rozhkova remarked, it was an urgent policy of "faster, faster, build housing faster, and move those people out of the barracks."

With barracks being torn down on the left bank, on the right bank whole new superblocks of prefabricated housing, called microregions, were springing up. More and more people were able to move out of barracks or mud huts and into apartments. Between 1956 and 1964 the city's permanent housing stock doubled. Older people recounted to me how the joy of acquiring their first real apartment brought tears to their eyes. The last inhabitants of barracks were finally able to move out at the beginning of the 1980s.

But the monotony of the new settlements, the lack of variation in either the shape or the color of buildings, as well as their flimsy construction and cramped interiors, combined to make them unpopular with the next generation. "You can't hide a bad building in the drawer like you can a bad decree," quipped one self-appointed architectural critic in a letter to the newspaper. While Stalin was still fondly remembered for the impressive and cavernous apartment buildings erected during the latter part of his rule, Khrushchev remained a subject of derision for the "boxes" built under him, colloquially known as *khru-*

shchoby—a pun on the word *trushchoby,* meaning "hovels." The even taller prefab buildings built under Brezhnev were perhaps even less popular than the five-story Khrushchev-era ones.

Meanwhile, at the very end of the 1950s the city center moved across the industrial lake to the right bank. The drama theater, other cultural institutions, and the political and administrative offices soon followed. The old park was abandoned and allowed to deteriorate, while the beloved sound movie house was converted into an ordinary workshop. Further construction on the left bank was expressly forbidden—in effect isolating the many tens of thousands of people still living there. Advertisements for housing exchanges, carried by hand or posted on a board outside the covered market, reflected the varying desirability of an apartment's location and its era of construction. Many came with the proviso "Left bank need not apply."

Through all the changes in city-planning style, one important practice remained constant, namely, the superblock. This building technique involves the arrangement of apartment buildings so that they face in on each other and form a large inner courtyard. Here, between the buildings and protected from harsh winds or street traffic, one finds schools, day-care centers, stores, and playgrounds composing (ideally) a semi-independent community. Each microregion, consisting of twenty thousand to thirty thousand people, is then connected by mass transit to all the others and to cultural institutions and public areas.

When the principle was carried out faithfully, the results were excellent. Particularly impressive were the neighborhoods, in which children were safe to play and to roam. Although some people clearly felt a lack of privacy with neighbors knowing one another and all generations mixing together, an authentic sense of community often developed. True, space inside the buildings remained at a premium, not everyone could obtain an apartment, and stores, roads, and other facilities were left unfinished. All the same, even if the execution had been seriously flawed, walking through the completed microregions and superblocks of both old and new Magnitogorsk imparted a clear feeling of the value of this building technique in the Soviet context. For the inhabitants of Magnitogorsk, the word *courtyard* (*dvor*) evoked comforting thoughts.

Not all the residential structures in the city were apartment buildings. A substantial part of the housing stock was made up of "individual constructions," which in essence were bungalows. At various times their construction had been officially encouraged as one way to combat the chronic housing shortage, despite the ideological awkwardness of individual home ownership.

Sometimes with gas and plumbing, although often without, these one-story self-built homes were spread out in a villagelike arrangement called a *posiolok*. Looking out over a landscape littered with small bungalows, cows, chickens, and agricultural plots, with the colossal structures of the steelworks in the background belching out clouds of smoke and tons of hot molten steel, one got a full picture of the telescoped history of this onetime peasant nation turned into a superpower.

In addition to the city's 8,963 "individual homes" (occupied by 10,800 households), a little more than ten thousand families owned cooperative apartments (the construction of which was financed by a sizable down payment). Together these two home-owning groups made up about 15 percent of the population. The remainder of the population lived in state-owned apartments for which they paid rent, calculated by the amount of space, with additional charges assessed for utilities. Families with two to three average-sized rooms usually paid the trifling sum of between twenty and thirty rubles a month—an obvious bargain.

By late 1987 the city was owed 150,000 rubles in back rent. Forty percent of the delinquents were classified as alcoholics and work-shy elements, 3 percent as pensioners, 13 percent as those who forgot to pay but would do so when reminded, and 10 percent as people away on vacation or business trips, those subject to delays in getting their wages, and the ill. The remaining 34 percent comprised individuals characterized as "malicious delinquents unwilling to pay." "When I feel like it, I'll pay," one obstinate tenant told a reporter conducting an investigation.

After three months, the city could appeal to the accounting department at the delinquent's place of employment to have arrears deducted from wages. But the paperwork involved was often overwhelming, and such people often changed jobs. Anyway, rent arrears paled in comparison with the cost to the state of the construction and maintenance of apartment buildings for which such a nominal rent was charged and from which eviction, even for wanton negligence, was well-nigh impossible—both among the most taken-for-granted benefits of Soviet life.

■   ■   ■

All agreed that few sights in Magnitogorsk were more pitiful than the rows upon rows of half-bare shelves in the shops. No less disquieting were the many store departments overflowing with supplies of goods whose use remained a mystery to all but the central planners. For the most part, however, store space was grossly underutilized, giving a distinct last-days-going-out-of-business impression.

Goods in demand were being sold as they were unpacked, without even making it onto the shelves. Many goods were being sold directly off delivery trucks, as surging crowds surrounded them. It was often the appearance of such a crowd that alerted inhabitants to a new arrival of goods, which were bought in bunches. For as long as anyone could remember, impulse buying had been the rule, although it seemed to have grown even more widespread after *perestroika* began.

One day in the spring of 1989 people began lining up at stores for matches and salt. They bought as much as they could carry, then went back for more. The commotion drew others. The crowds swelled. Rumors flew. Panic set in. Nikolai Gurzhii, the city official in charge of trade, drove around the entire city, from store to store, attempting to reassure people in queues that the city had plenty of salt and matches. "We went to as many places as we could," Gurzhii related in an interview. "We talked to people. The didn't believe us. We assured them: warehouses are well stocked. But they know there are no cleaning goods for sale, so they didn't believe our words about salt and matches."

Gurzhii knew he had to do more than speak personally to the people in queues. "We used the newspaper and radio to calm the panic," he explained. "This did the trick. The panic lasted only three days, thank God. It began on Thursday, peaked on Friday. By Sunday it was over. For now." He added that "it was mostly older people, not younger ones. Older people lived through the war and know that in bad times, salt and matches disappear."

Despite strenuous efforts to attribute the worsening hardships to the legacies of Brezhnev's stagnation and Stalin's terror, most people, even those who most favored reform, concluded that the culprit was really *perestroika*. Indeed, Soviet economists estimated that after four years of tinkering with the economy an unprecedented 240 of the 270 consumer goods manufactured in the USSR were "absent from the shelves" for extended periods of time during 1989. With such a dismal state of affairs who could blame people for their skepticism toward policies to set things right?

Yet although goods may have been unavailable through state stores, this did not mean that they were wholly absent from the country. Scarce goods could be purchased at the state-sponsored peasant markets—and other less official market channels—although not at state-subsidized prices. For example, when the minister of health announced the existence of acquired immune deficiency syndrome (AIDS) cases in the USSR, he indicated that the only effective defense was the condom. In the next few days, condoms literally disappeared from state shops. Soon, however, those same galoshes began to reappear—at the peasant markets, where they could be bought in unlimited quantities.

Few people believed that collective farmers had harvested condoms on their private plots. Instead, it was suggested that employees of pharmacies, in cooperation with "entrepreneurs" of the shadow economy, had acted decisively in anticipation of an impending rise in demand. Condoms at peasant markets sold for more than ten times the state price—an illegal practice referred to as "speculation," which aroused much public anger. Because severe shortages invariably brought "speculation," rationing was widely viewed as an equitable way to distribute the hardships and an important buffer against the full threat of scarcity glaring out from empty shelves.

In addition to the trade on gray and black markets, many hard-to-find items were "distributed" through enterprises and institutions, meaning that they were sold at low state prices to employees and staff during working hours. Such bonuses, called "special orders," ranged from meat and butter to perfume and men's suits. Although the content or availability of special orders could not always be predicted, whatever became available was more than could be obtained in the stores.

As a rule, the more powerful the organization, the greater the likelihood that it would be a regular site of distribution; the more powerful the individual, the more plentiful the allotment. Moreover, as goods became ever more scarce in state stores, officials with clout worked that much harder to ensure the goods' availability at organizations under their responsibility. Accordingly, with the effects of shortages unequally felt, the supply system had grateful, although discrete, supporters. As their supplies remained stable while those of the less fortunate without an enterprise supply pipeline underwent a marked decline, beneficiaries of "distribution" redoubled their backing for the status quo.

Among the populace, the practice of extending favors was not questioned, but the issue of who got them and why was a major bone of contention. Some "privileges," such as those of party officials (which were not even publicly acknowledged by the regime), were considered less than deserved, as were the benefits extended to "outstanding" workers. Unlike the privileges of functionaries, those of special workers were openly broadcast to serve as an incentive for others, but the possibilities for politically motivated manipulation of the bonus system cast a cloud over the awards of these workers.

One group whose privileges—such as they were—remained above question was the elderly. Each store in Magnitogorsk carried a sign indicating that "veterans of war and of labor" were to be served without waiting in lines. Although not every owner of a veteran ID card chose to take advantage of this privilege, those who did rarely met with objections from those whom they bypassed.

But like workers, not all older people who qualified for favors qualified equally. Magnitogorsk maintained a restricted-access store for a special group of "veterans": not only those who fought in the war but those designated "honored citizens" and those singled out by the state for service (so-called personal pensioners). "Our store serves a certain contingent of pensioners," explained T. D. Ilina, the deputy manager of the veteran shop where "absolutely everything the city ever sees can be bought: tea, sugar, medicines, and more. Are these privileges justified? I think they are."

"Consider personal pensioners," Ilina continued, referring to recipients of higher benefits. "Among them, and I know many personally, there are outstanding people, those who did a great deal for the good of others. More than us, the rank and file. For example, I. P. Logunov, a surgeon at the steel plant's hospital, performed an operation on me and also on my daughter. I'll be grateful to him my whole life. He's a personal pensioner not because of his position [*kreslo*] or connections [*blat*] but because he worked his whole life on behalf of us, the people of Magnitogorsk."

Not everyone agreed. T. I. Balandina, a senior staff person of the Magnitogorsk social welfare office, pointed out that "in death everyone is equal—but not for us. If a personal pensioner dies, we pay the family a sum amounting to two times the monthly pension. If a regular pensioner dies, we pay the family twenty rubles. And if a collective farmer dies, we don't pay a single kopeck. How can we accept this from the point of view of social justice?" A similar attitude on a related theme was evidenced by E. Repetko, who retired after working almost half a century. "Like many veterans of war and labor I feel sort of uncomfortable when I pick up stuff at the veteran store," he confided. "I try and push the cans of scarce goods way down into my bag before going out into the street."

But Repetko was an exception. As widespread and as deeply rooted as the feeling of social justice was, few individuals openly expressed guilt over any privileges they might have, however small, and most people, guilty or not, clung to what little advantages they had been able to secure.

■   ■   ■

In Magnitogorsk more than 90 percent of the economically viable population of *both* males and females worked full-time—a total of 240,000 people. Except for a tiny handful of people in cooperatives, everyone—teachers, doctors, steelworkers, bus drivers, journalists, salesclerks, artists, even soccer players—was an employee of the state. As state employees, people expected a wide range of social welfare benefits to flow merely from the fact of their employment.

N. F. Nasledov, an apprentice steel smelter, expressed concern about high prices, the lack of soap, and the quality of medical care. "In this shop colds are not rare," he stated. "I was sick and sent back to work four times, but it turned out that I had pneumonia. We have a special machine that makes diagnoses. Who needs this kind of diagnostic capability? Medical equipment is hopelessly old, and for treatment there are only pills.

"In the shop we have favorites—priority furnaces, or, as we call them, government furnaces. They always have the right of way, and the rest of us must wait while these designated leaders take charge. So much for social equality. There are the same 'lighthouses' [supposedly exemplary workers] we had in the stagnation years. . . . One's pay depends on results. Opportunities ought to be equal."

Like most Magnitogorsk workers, Nasledov assumed a kind of total relationship with his enterprise and in one breath linked his assumed entitlement to good health with his right to just working conditions. Women workers displayed similar attitudes, although many of their concerns were specific to their roles as housewives and mothers.

L. V. Kushnir, like hundreds of other women, operated a tram. "Work's gotten both easier and harder," she told a journalist asking in April 1989 if anything had changed in her life. "The trams are new and good. It's nice to operate them. But we don't only drive them; we have to clean them. And in all kinds of weather. Normally you clean them during work time, but now you don't get paid for it. And you clean by hand.

"We got a pay raise. What do you buy with it? We're women after all. We have to dress ourselves, and perfume—which was cleaned out from the stores—is a necessity. Even the expensive perfumes have disappeared. Before they blamed drunks, now who? It's hard to dress your children."

Because credit played virtually no role in the lives of Soviet citizens (for example, housing was mostly distributed rather than purchased with the aid of a bank), loss of employment did not threaten workers with loss of their principal possessions. In any event, layoffs were un-heard of. At any given time a small number of individuals were between jobs for a duration, on average, of less than twenty-five days. There was no "reserve army." Near-absolute job security was taken for granted. More than that, guaranteed employment was assumed to entail social guarantees founded on principles of social justice that were part of an unwritten social compact between regime and people.

■   ■   ■

For as long as anyone could remember, prices in state stores had been kept remarkably low: bread never cost much more than fifteen kopecks a loaf; milk, thirty to thirty-five kopecks a liter; a kilo of potatoes, thir-teen kopecks; a kilo of beef, two rubles. "For a long time and with great pride we have said that the low prices for basic necessities, urban transit, and rent have not changed," a Magnitogorsk reporter explained and then asked, "What's wrong with this? Is this not social justice?" Most people would have said yes.

But an official from the State Planning Commission quoted in the same article labored to point out the obvious: "Those prices include state subsidies. The more one obtains at state prices, the more one is subsidized. Those who do not have the opportunity to purchase state goods are in effect paying subsidies to those who do [have that oppor-tunity]." Because goods at state prices were often not sold in stores but were "distributed" through enterprises, institutions, and acquaintances, precisely those with the most connections ended up enjoying low state prices most often—hardly a just system.

At the same time, the official lamented, mere mention of possible price increases for state-sold goods provoked passionate anger among the populace. This was the catch-22 of regulated prices: a system per-ceived as providing for social justice in practice reinforced inequities; suggestions for freeing up prices, which in the long term could be more equitable, were viewed as betrayals of the commitment to social justice.

The planning official might have added that the majority of consum-ers paid a second time when, met by empty shelves in the shops, they were compelled to turn for produce to "peasant markets," where prices were more or less determined by supply and demand. At the markets, a kilo of potatoes cost three rubles, rather than the thirteen kopecks in state stores; a kilo of beef, seven to ten, rather than the state price of about two rubles (which might as well have been one kopeck given how rarely any was for sale there). Indeed, despite state-subsidized prices for food, a Soviet family spent a little less than 40 percent of its budget on food and beverages, slightly more than its counterpart in Ecuador (36 percent), slightly less than in Kenya (42.5 percent), and about equal to Thailand (40.9 percent).*

But only the few people with high salaries—the very people with greatest access to goods at state prices—could afford to shop regularly at peasant markets. Everyone else was condemned to hunt for staples at state stores, returning to them as often as it took, standing in line as long as it took. A Soviet citizen queued up for food and other products an average of two to three hours a day. Nevertheless, the knowledge that bread, milk, meat, and other staples were cheap brought a weary population some solace, reinforced by deep fears at the thought they could one day rise.

■   ■   ■

In Magnitogorsk basic education, considered a right, was provided free of charge; higher education, also free, afforded a chance to move up in society. One-third of the city's high school graduates attended higher education (roughly the same percentage as in the United States). The rest either entered the labor market straightaway or delayed their entry slightly by first obtaining vocational training. The ambitious could try to sign on for work in the most prestigious shops of the steel plant or other large enterprises, but the demand for these privileged spots was high, and access, even at the lowest level, was a long shot.

Although highly prized for providing social mobility, education rarely afforded geographical mobility. Fully four-fifths of the graduates of the Mining Institute moved on to an engineering or management position at the steel plant—in Magnitogorsk terms, viewed as a considerable achievement. Here they could expect to spend their entire lives. Meanwhile, most graduates of the Teachers College could anticipate spending at least their first three years after college working at a village school. For these people, getting back to Magnitogorsk was often a victory. A handful of Magnitogorsk youth were fortunate enough to gain

---

* Of the rest, 17 percent went to clothing and shoes, 10 percent to rent and utilities, 9.5 percent to various taxes and fees, and a little more than 10 percent to "savings."

acceptance to university in Sverdlovsk, the "capital" of the Urals, or even to Moscow University. Yet even this select group often found itself back in Magnitogorsk upon graduation, unable (in some cases unwilling) to secure the necessary official permission to remain in the larger city.

No Magnitogorsk resident could simply move to another city. The largest and most desirable cities, such as Moscow, were officially "closed." (Although exceptions were made for certain categories of individuals, only very few could pursue this option.) And even when a city was "open," without having some kind of housing there (meaning relatives), one was not legally allowed to obtain employment. Yet one obtained housing only as a result of inheriting from one's parents or after working many years at a single enterprise. "Housing," quipped one employee of the Magnitogorsk museum, in a paraphrase of Stalin, "decides everything."

To move to a city such as Cheliabinsk, the provincial capital, one *already* had to possess an apartment in Magnitogorsk for which someone who lived in Cheliabinsk was willing to swap. Of course, it took a decade and often far longer to get an apartment in Magnitogorsk. Moreover, although some advertisements by residents of Cheliabinsk looking to exchange their apartment for one in Magnitogorsk offered a one-bedroom-for-one-bedroom deal, others looked to trade up for more bedrooms. Why else move to a smaller city? One-bedroom apartments in the even larger Sverdlovsk could be had for nothing less than a three-bedroom place in Magnitogorsk—a prize few had and even fewer could afford to relinquish.

If there was a ticket out of Magnitogorsk other than signing up for work on one of the remote Siberian construction projects, it came through the Communist party apparatus or the steel plant's administration and usually only after slowly working one's way up over the years to the highest levels. Such people could be counted on two hands. And although party apparatchiks and economic administrators could usually get their children to schools in Sverdlovsk or Moscow, this was often merely a temporary escape. With rare exceptions, anyone born in Magnitogorsk could expect to be buried there. In the meantime, higher education brought its relative rewards.

■　　■　　■

During the summer of 1988, with the special party conference having just ended, V. Stepanov, a shop chief at the Magnitogorsk steel plant, reiterated some of the everyday concerns that had prompted the meeting of Communists and that continued to haunt the party and the country in the conference's inconclusive aftermath. "How much hope we placed on the opening of a milk plant. The newspaper wrote about it. And once again, either there's no heavy cream, or sour cream, or curds. What kind of meat do you get for your ration coupons? Fat and gristle. When meat is delivered [to stores], sales personnel leave the counter to 'sort it.' . . .

"I'm in Magnitka for the fourth decade," he continued. "Without question it's better than it was. But we travel to other metallurgical cities. Why is our supply situation worse [than theirs]?" Magnitogorsk's supply situation may have been worse than that of other towns located in richer agricultural regions, but what about in comparison with that of cities in "capitalist" countries? Stepanov did not suggest a comparison of his standard of living with that of steelworkers in Western Europe (although many others did), yet even in his formulation the standard of living theme came across as explosive.

Amid the potentially dangerous stirrings around the politically charged issue of living standards, A. Malov, an economist for Gosplan, wrote an article carried by the Magnitogorsk newspaper in which he tried to demonstrate that the living standards of the Soviet population had improved over time. As his basis for comparison Malov chose the recent Soviet past. Claiming that while prices for basic food, clothes, other necessities, public transportation, and rent had remained relatively stable, Malov asserted that the average nominal monthly wage had risen from 96.5 rubles in 1965 to more than 200 in 1987. The implication was that in the absence of inflation, purchasing power had increased dramatically.

Moreover, Malov argued, whereas in 1970 the average Soviet citizen consumed 47.5 kilos of meat per year, consumption had risen to 62.4 kilos in 1986. That people were better dressed than previously Malov felt was obvious just from observing them walking on the streets. And, he added, practically every family owned a refrigerator and television set; every third, a stereo; every fourth, an automobile. Material progress appeared undeniable.

Malov acknowledged, however, that with a monthly subsistence level of 80 rubles per person, 35 percent of the population lived on less than 100 rubles. But, he pointed out, one had to take into account housing: in the USSR "poor" families often had a better housing situation than did families whose income was significantly higher. And schools were free. Nevertheless, despite substantial progress made over the previous decades, apparently more than 33 percent of the population lived at or below the poverty level, leaving aside the question of how that level stood in relation to other countries.

Malov further revealed that another 31 percent of the population lived on 150 or more rubles a month. He chose not to differentiate this group, although it obviously included people whose income was as much as eight or ten times the cutoff. Nor did he mention that the remaining 34 percent must have been living on between 100 and 150 rubles a month. In any case, Malov demonstrated, even if he did not himself make the point, that 69 percent of the Soviet Union's population, almost two hundred million people, lived on less than 150 rubles a month. What did this mean?

At the official exchange rate set by the state, 150 rubles amounted to $225 —a paltry sum, to be sure, but one made irrelevant by the inconvertibility of the ruble. At the time of Malov's article, Soviet citizens who wished to exchange their rubles for dollars could do so only on the black market, where they were paying not 67 kopecks for $1 but up to 15 rubles. Thus, if they sought to assess the relative value of their earnings, 69 percent of the Soviet population could discover that they were living on less than $10 per month.

Underscoring the bitter truth of the black market, other Soviet economists publishing in the central press offered alternative ways to evaluate Soviet living standards. One shorthand method, readily comprehensible to the population, if deceptive, consisted of a simple calculation of how much time one had to work to be able to purchase a kilo of beef: in the United States, a little more than 40 minutes were necessary; in the Soviet Union, 120 minutes—and the number was rising rapidly. To drive home their point, these same Soviet economists questioned the notion that annual average meat consumption in the USSR was anywhere near sixty kilos per capita, suggesting that the method of determining what constituted "meat" was generously inclusive and that the state's statisticians failed to account adequately for spoilage.

Be that as it may, Malov's analysis did confirm, however obliquely, that a tiny minority of people enjoyed various degrees of luxury, a sizable mass lived in relative poverty, and the rest made up a broad "middle" group that was far closer to those in poverty than to those in luxury. The overwhelming majority of people were particularly vulnerable to inflation.

Malov also indicated, although without drawing out its true significance, that differentiation within the vast majority of the Soviet population was based not on income but on the possession of an individual apartment, an automobile, and, less significantly, a color television and that none of these measures of status could be bought freely, regardless of how high one's salary might have been.

Moreover, still finer distinctions in living standards were predicated on variable access to everything from yogurt to children's shoes. A family's fortunes could rise and decline without a change in income, as contacts in supply came and went or fell in and out of favor. Everyone acknowledged that continual networking and conniving for favors were tiring, but many people welcomed the smallest opportunity to soften the hardships inflicted by widespread shortages and feared the prospect of having what little they had taken away. Living standards might have been unsatisfactory, but at least people knew what to expect and how to cope.

■   ■   ■

Entrenched alcoholism, recurrent shortages of consumer goods, a severe housing crisis extending well into the future, a ubiquitous black market, a crumbling or nonexistent urban infrastructure, almost unfathomable pollution, and a health catastrophe impossible to exaggerate—such was the predicament of this once-showcased Soviet steeltown. Nothing more ambitious than trying to make it through the day was enough to grind down even the most spirited individuals. While all but a tiny minority of people were deeply touched by the hardships, the burden fell heaviest on retirees with small pensions, families with small children who required special foods and who outgrew clothes every year, and women.

A major by-product of such an existence was aggressive public and private behavior. Moreover, the warlike quality of daily life further fueled a deep resentment of the smallest of privileges thought to have been obtained unfairly or through deception. Yet at the same time almost everyone felt compelled to struggle for the slightest advantage, even if just temporary, and these petty and not so petty advantages could add up, providing, along with rationing and special orders, a much-appreciated cushion. And exhausting as it was, daily life took place in a familiar world with a sense of community, job security, access to health care and education, stable low prices, nominal transit and rent costs, and a future secured by retirement benefits. Although this system was far from being entirely free of negative aspects, its attractions should not be underestimated. A fragile sense of well-being amid difficult circumstances was further strengthened by the absence of homeless people or beggars on the streets.

Social tension in Magnitogorsk seemed perpetually near the boiling point, but along with frayed nerves the population displayed a resigned practicability in such actions as making rooms multipurpose and growing food for consumption or sale. It could not have been otherwise. Even black marketeering could be understood as a skillful response to challenging circumstances, as well as an indication that seemingly strict prohibitions could somehow be circumvented or ignored. Life was hard and tense but somehow manageable, and further sustenance was derived from the belief that however hard your lot, your children would live better by benefiting from your sacrifice.

To be sure, people in Magnitogorsk suspected they were not well off and wondered how their vaunted welfare net compared to West Germany's, but as long as they knew so little concretely about the outside world, their social compasses flickered only slightly when a handful of Western and Japanese radios began somehow to make their way into town. Similarly, restlessness on the part of a younger generation seemingly unappreciative of the supposed advantages of Soviet life, alarming as it was, could be dismissed as the eternal yearnings of youth rather than recognized as an ominous sign of an impending social revolt.

Yet precisely in the deepening alienation of youth some people began to recognize the existence of a profound moral degradation ultimately more serious than the inconvenience posed by life on the treadmill. And this debility extended beyond wayward youth to embrace all reaches of society. But these same people harbored a deep-seated fear of change, a word in the Soviet vocabulary synonymous with upheaval. Much of this reflexive resistance to things new stemmed from legitimate self-interest. Workers, to take one example, wanted a better life, but not at the expense of job security or as a result of working harder. There were also strong vested interests against change. Many officials insulated from consumer hardships lived relatively well. And even if there had been a social consensus on the *need* for change, the questions remained: What *kind* of change was necessary? And how and by whom would it be brought about?

In the face of this bizarre amalgam of contentment and desperation, resentment and shameless conniving, conservatism and moral disgust, the central leadership launched in stages the most far-reaching package of reforms seen in the country since the failed effort of the 1860s, a failure that helped pave the way for the revolutions of 1905 and 1917. Magnitogorsk inhabitants, at the end of their ropes but clinging to their precarious way of life, needed substantial prodding before they were ready to consider seriously the necessity of reform.

It did not help matters that previous Soviet reforms, announced many times before, never seemed to amount to much and more often than not were quietly dropped. Then when *perestroika* seemed to bring at first only greater material hardships, enthusiasm dimmed even further. No better metaphor for the paradoxes brought to the fore by the current reform efforts could be cited than the admission at a public meeting in Magnitogorsk that the government, after having waged a deeply unpopular antialcohol campaign for three years, had to turn around and sell workers more alcohol in order to pay them their wages. Even plans born of the best intentions seemed incapable of altering structures.

Indeed, as we have seen, the reform process, of which antialcoholism was merely the opening gambit, was hindered not simply by popular conservatism or entrenched interests but by structural impediments. Political pluralism proved to be incompatible with the rule of the Communist party, and the centrally controlled economy, the source of the party's patronage and thus its power, revealed itself to be incapable of the kind of dynamism the reformers originally envisioned. Yet the badly battered and tarnished system lived on, propped up not simply by indecision at the top but also by the social structure and even the way of life.

One source of the prevailing system's ability to endure was Stalinism's creation of its own social base, at the top of which stood the *nomenklatura*, the priority recipients of the advantages society had to bestow (a topic explored further in the afterword). Another was ordinary people's ability to find a tolerable niche in which to conduct their lives. Not without justification, the inhabitants of Magnitogorsk suspected they had much more to lose than to gain from change.

But the common people's adherence to the prevailing system was limited by the numerous indignities they had to endure, material *and* spiritual. Under the added weight of having to make speeches they knew to be full of lies, or read reports they knew to be false, people began to wonder if life could continue much longer in this state. What was more, within the womb of the basic social structure inherited from the 1930s a new class of urban professionals had taken shape that was more interested in technical proficiency than in Communist party dogma. It comes as no surprise, therefore, that the one aspect of the reforms that did take hold was ideological: namely, *glasnost*.

In Magnitogorsk the newspaper expertly conducted the campaign to expose the fatal flaws of the existing system but did not offer any suggestions about how to put the pieces back together again, other than to pursue the truth and to support Mikhail Gorbachev, whatever he might be up to. But if it was unrealistic to expect tangible and quick material improvements as a result of *perestroika,* no one in the top leadership said so. On the contrary, in trumpeting its new program, the leadership raised expectations of improvements in people's lives that it could not fulfill and thereby squandered a measure of the trust that had been gained by *glasnost*. Nonetheless, journalists did not give up.

"Why do I work for the newspaper? What keeps me here for the twelfth year?" wrote Tatiana Leus, the paper's ace social reporter, in a moment of unsolicited self-justification. "The chance to change something in our lives. To change things for the better. Do I believe this? I believe. Despite the difficulties, I believe." There could be no doubt that she did. "Who is not concerned about social issues?" Leus continued. "This is our most vital thing. People judge the quality of Soviet power by how the mass transit is operating, what's on the shelf, whether the free medical care can prevent their illnesses. They verify the soundness of the advantages of our system, about which they hear from birth." They did, indeed, and that was the problem: the newspaper was full, but the shelves were empty.

Emboldened by the newspaper's example, many people became outspoken, exercising the freedom to voice their frustration and disgust. "People have stopped being afraid; everyone can say anything that's on his mind," explained A. F. Kusakin, a worker who was secretary of his shop's party committee, during a discussion published in the summer of 1988. "Yeah, we have plenty of talk," agreed I. A. Bodakov, a worker and party member in Kusakin's shop, with more than just a touch of irony. A colleague of Bodakov quickly added, "But where is *perestroika?*"

Materially, in fact, what change there had been occurred mostly in the direction of chaos and breakdown, thereby fostering a sense of impending collapse and further reinforcing the innate conservatism of the population. Then when leading economists began to assert in 1989 that fundamental improvement in living standards might be as many as twenty years away, people were stunned. "If the authorities admitted to twenty," one Magnitogorsk teacher shrieked, moved to tears while looking at her two teenage daughters, "that meant they were secretly contemplating forty." To be on the treadmill oneself was one thing; to conclude, as many people did as a result of *glasnost,* that despite all the sacrifices, one's children (and even grandchildren) could expect nothing better was another matter.

To combat the widespread sense of hopelessness, Leus counseled persistence. "Keep hitting at the same place," she advised, in reference to the city's monumental problems, "until the matter is resolved." But it was hard to find many others who shared her enduring optimism; one was more likely to encounter bitter pessimism, made more concrete by the incessant revelations of corruption, incompetence, and disaster, from train crashes to airplane hijackings, industrial explosions, AIDS contamination, bloody ethnic strife, and radioactive fallout.

Against this gloomy national canvas, comments from desperate Magnitogorsk families in search of ever-scarcer goods, workers sick of ever-deteriorating working conditions, and officials exhausted from the unfamiliar pressures in their publicly challenged positions fed on each other. By 1989 many people from all walks of life formerly caught up in the excitement of *glasnost* were claiming that they had stopped reading each new revelation and sensation. "What's the use?" they asked, in the same breath inquiring if I had seen an article in the newspaper or a copy of the latest issue of one of the leading national monthlies.

Aleksei Tiuplin, one of the younger reporters at the city newspaper, remarked, "I wonder what you see here," his voice heavy with frustration. "We're used to this life. We breathe this air. We can somehow take it. I haven't seen the West, so I withhold judgment about that question. But here I can assure you, nothing fundamental has changed. Nothing you can see, touch. Perhaps in people's consciousness, a little. We are locked in one place. We constantly try to change within this enclosed space. Seventy years. We get no results.

"We all know that we must break through structures. We sit around, speak these truths out loud, breathe a bit easier, soothe our souls, and then go out again. Nothing results. This pattern repeats itself endlessly. This is our life. It is not necessary to dig 'deeper,' to dig down to the roots. All our problems and their causes are visible on the surface. Just look at the idiocy! Idiocy begets further idiocy."

"I disagree," a colleague of Tiuplin interrupted. "Our American friend is right. The problems are deeper. They lie, as you yourself said only a moment ago, in the roots of the system. But this whole circus of Gorbachev was worth it if only because the people have discovered that you can't simply solve every problem in a short period of time. Some problems you can't solve at all, no matter how much time you have.

"I'll tell you something else. There's been a pattern to the catalogue of enemies. In 1985–86, it was the drunkards and lazy workers. Then in 1987–88, it was Stalin and the conservatives. In 1989, it's the financial people and, lately, the journalists. Who'll be the next enemy? I'll give you a hint: they have horns." It must be said, however, that even though some people could be overheard referring to the newspaper as the "synagogue" and many Jews had taken to "sleeping on their suitcases" as they waited anxiously for the routine bureaucratic processing to emigrate, this prediction of overt, aggressive anti-Semitism had yet to be borne out. The next enemy looked to be despair.

Cynicism was never stronger, paradoxically because of the newspaper's unwavering commitment to openness in the service of reform. Yet in the end, there were those, perhaps a majority, who still clung to an inner hope founded on a deep reservoir of patriotism. Nadezhda, a young woman who helped maintain the city archives and whose name meant "hope," lived with just such resigned tenacity.

After having been graduated from the local Teachers College, Nadezhda taught English for three years in a nearby village school. "I loved the early classes," she recalled. "The children's faces, their brilliant eyes, their genuine interest. If you are able to communicate with them, you can see them learn and grow. This is happiness.

"Out in the village a single woman has a tough time. And there was absolutely no one with whom I could practice my English. I got tired. I just couldn't do it anymore. Through a friend I got a job back in the city, at the archives. My son and I live with my mother in the two-room apartment where I grew up. I have no husband. I make a little more than 130 rubles a month. Mama, a widow, gets a tiny pension. Each year my son needs a new winter coat, and I sew one for him myself.

"These last two years of intensive reading have really opened my eyes. I suppose I kind of knew a lot of this before, but somehow I didn't put it together. I remember those arguments we used to have back in 1987. I was very offended by much of what you told me. A lot of water has been drained from the swamp since then. That's for sure. It's all true, but you see, it's our country. Leaving is no help. We must stay and repair our own house."

Despite the deep disillusionment that four years of failed reforms had brought, the leadership's decision in early 1989 to hold multicandidate elections to seats in a new state structure, the Congress of People's Deputies, brought a flicker of hope to the hearts of a weary populace convinced of the impossibility of anything coming out of the process but still waiting and praying desperately for signs of a way out of the increasingly grave domestic crisis.

CHAPTER FIVE

Socialism Is Dead!
Long Live Socialism!
Regeneration through Elections?

Few people in Magnitogorsk ever expected to see such a variety of signs posted everywhere in the city, but there they were. "Vote for Petrov!" "Vote for Andreeva!" "Riabkov is your man!" "Only Romanov knows what a deputy ought to be!" An election campaign with different choices? More than one candidate running?

There had *never* been a competitive election for public office in Magnitogorsk in the sixty years of its existence. Of course, there had been innumberable "elections" before, but they were not political contests so much as orchestrated affirmations of legitimacy lubricated by the lavish provisioning of normally scarce food and drink.

As for the filling of offices, previously candidates in "elections" to the city soviet and the *oblast* soviet in Cheliabinsk, where there had always been exactly as many people running as there were positions, had come preselected by the city party committee. And with the party running city affairs, none of those "elected" to the three district soviets in Magnitogorsk were expected to do anything. As for the "elections" to the Supreme Soviet in Moscow, the reigning director of the steel plant simply added the title to his many others.

This time the food was still there, as was the drink (although it was nonalcoholic); but politics was added in the form of multicandidate elections to the proposed Congress of People's Deputies, a kind of parallel state body that would be empowered to transform the existing state administration. At stake was nothing less than the nature of the Soviet political system.

Notwithstanding the torrent of reform legislation in the three decades following Stalin's death, by the time Gorbachev became general secretary local soviets, in whose name power was seized in 1917, remained without effective authority. On paper soviets had far-reaching rights and responsibilities; in practice they were reduced to supplicants. A similar impotence characterized the top organ of state power, the Supreme Soviet, which was eclipsed by the Politburo.

Paradoxically, in a country renowned for its all-encompassing state, strictly speaking there were no functioning formal state structures. The state had been swallowed up by the party, which enlisted the economic ministries to govern. The proposed task was to decouple the state and party and create a free-standing state administration whose control might become the object of competing political forces. These state reforms would start from the top (with the Supreme Soviet, which was to become something of a real parliamentary body), but they were designed in such a way as to involve and reinvigorate the populace—hence, the competitive elections, which were viewed as the key to everything.

The proposed overhaul of the state machinery was seen as complementary to the ongoing but sluggish party reform, one of whose chief intentions was to remove the party from day-to-day administration (as well as from "meddling" in the economy) and allow it to tend to what were called "political and ideological" matters. In Magnitogorsk party functionaries, unchallenged by an organized opposition, interpreted the call for a renewed commitment to politics as a direct invitation to get involved in the elections, even as their involvement in economic matters and day-to-day administration did not lessen. Reform of the state structure, itself an implicit recognition of the failure of party reform, was caught in the same matrix, although the process threatened momentarily to burst the boundaries of Communist party domination of the city.

■　　■　　■

In early January 1989 the Magnitogorsk newspaper explained the new rules for the elections to the congress. Candidates would be permitted ten deputized surrogates (*doverennoe litso*), agitation would be "wide open," and those elected would serve a five-year term. No one was obligated to vote, the head of a household was prohibited from voting for other members of the family, and private voting booths were mandatory.

Nominations could be made by "working collectives," public organizations, or neighborhood meetings of at least five hundred people. After the deadline for nominations, a meeting of "electors" was to take place to compose the final list of candidates. At the electors meeting an equal number of representatives for each nominee, regardless of the size of the nominating "collective," would be guaranteed. Sufficient space was to be reserved for journalists, and overall participation was to be determined by the number of seats in the auditorium. A strict pass system was to be enforced to insure the integrity of the process.

From the newspaper account there appeared to be no limits on the power of the electors, except that there had to be more "final" candidates than positions being contested. Nor was it clear who these electors would be. The paper reported that no less than half the electors would have to be from "neutral organizations"—that is, from groups not on record as supporting any of the candidates. Precisely how such people would be chosen remained a mystery.

That same day, 5 January, the newspaper reported that the nomination by the steel plant party committee of factory director Ivan Romazan had been seconded by the *oblast* party committee. Romazan would be a candidate "from the party"—that is, his candidacy would be voted on by the party's Central Committee, not the public at large. One-third of the 2,250 seats in the proposed congress were reserved for nominees from so-called social organizations ranging from the party and the Central Executive Committee of Trade Unions to the Academy of Sciences and the unions for writers, filmmakers, and journalists. From Magnitogorsk, along with Romazans's nomination through the party, Valerii Kucher's name was put forward by the journalists union. Neither candidate would come before the Magnitogorsk electorate for a vote, but both eventually recognized their need to win the electorate's approval.

Another one-third of the seats were apportioned to population centers, or "districts," based on size. Magnitogorsk received one such seat. Beginning in the second week of January, it was reported that the Teachers College had nominated its rector, Valentin Romanov; city hospital no. 1 put forward its director, Anfisa Andreeva; the wire factory in conjunction with the cement, repair, and glass factories, the Lenin district branch of internal affairs, and the rail yard nominated the worker-hero Iurii Petrov; the Mining Institute recommended the candidacy of Aleksandr Arzamastsev, chair of the philosophy department.

Finally, one-third of the seats were apportioned by so-called national-territorial districts in an effort to insure proportionate representation by nationality. Magnitogorsk was placed into a national-territorial district made up of the Cheliabinsk and Kurgansk *oblasts*, which were dominated by ethnic Russians. Although it was by no means certain that a Magnitogorsk candidate would be able to compete for a seat covering a huge territory that included the provincial capital of Cheliabinsk, the Magnitogorsk newspaper reported that the Mining Institute had nominated Vitalii Riabkov.

Thus, under the new system, Magnitogorsk, which normally had one representative in the Supreme Soviet, could have as many as four in the congress: Romazan and Kucher from "social organizations," one from the city district, and Riabkov from the overlapping national-territorial district (see table 1). The spirited campaign for this bewildering lineup of seats had begun.

■   ■   ■

The period from mid-January to mid-February was one of intense political activity that included meetings with constituents, leafleting, speechmaking, and public debate. The newspaper was extremely active, carrying "spotlights" on each of the candidates, including some newly nominated.

Aleksandr Perminov was described as a work-brigade leader in coke and chemical assembly, fifty-two years old, and a party member. He had worked abroad, first in Iran between 1970 and 1973 on the construction of a steel plant and then in Nigeria in 1984. As for his "platform," Perminov responded tersely: "Housing, transit, food, and, of course, ecology."

N. V. Kuznetsov, a forty-four-year-old brigadier, was nominated by the local construction company Magnitostroi. When asked about his program, Kuznetsov, who was born in a nearby village where he completed seven years of elementary schooling, offered none. "If candidates are really concerned about the interests of their electorate," he told the newspaper, "then their programs cannot be different from one another."

One could see the care with which the newspaper, easily the most powerful force for influencing the minds of the voters, sought to remain

Table 1. *Candidates in the Magnitogorsk Elections*

Social Organizations		City Districts	Overlapping "National" Districts
Central Committee slate	*Union of Journalists slate*	*Territorial district no. 339 (Magnitogorsk city)*	*National-territorial district no. 32 (Cheliabinsk and Kurgansk oblasts)*
Ivan Romazan, director of the steel plant	Valerii Kucher, editor of the *Magnitogorsk Worker*	Anfisa Andreeva, director of city hospital no. 1	*Round 1*
		Iurii Petrov, worker at the wire factory	Vitalii Riabkov, director of the Mining Institute
(1 of 100 for 100 slots)	(1 of 15 for 10 slots)	Valentin Romanov, director of the Teachers College	Igor Velichko, director of a military factory in the city of Miass
		[Aleksandr Arzamastsev, chair of philosophy, Mining Institute (eliminated along with 4 others at the electors meeting)]	*Round 2*
			Vitalii Riabkov
			Baronenko, school principal from Kopeisk
			Vasilev, locomotive driver from Kurgma

objective as it presented the candidates. Each candidate received the same opportunities to reach the voters through interviews published on successive days; each was asked mostly get-acquainted questions and allowed to review the results prior to publication. Upon seeing the transcript of her interview, Andreeva strongly objected to its publication and demanded that she be allowed to draw up her own material. Although deeply indignant, the newspaper nevertheless complied, publishing her material exactly as received, with a note to that effect.

■   ■   ■

In February the newspaper reported that an attempt in the city's right-bank district to hold a nominating meeting fell considerably short of the five-hundred-person minimum. Similarly, an attempt by Counter Movement to call a neighborhood meeting to register the nomination of their leader, Timofeev, could produce no more than eighty people.

Meanwhile, the inhabitants of the Lenin district, after trying for two days and assembling no more than two hundred people, unexpectedly brought together almost one thousand. No doubt holding the meeting at the Mining Institute contributed to the large turnout. Nominations were made, and the votes of 933 people were recorded, with the following results: Arzamastsev, 203; Petrov, 641; Andreeva, 89; Khokhlov (identified only as a driver), 0. In other words, the one neighborhood meeting that achieved the five-hundred-person minimum voted on three candidates already nominated by working collectives, endorsing one of them.

The newspaper reported that the Lenin district meeting also "unanimously" supported the candidacy of the institute's rector for the national-territorial slot. It seemed scarcely coincidental that Riabkov's colleague from the institute, the far more radical Arzamastsev, failed to win nomination even to a seat different from the one Riabkov sought on their mutual home turf.

In these events I could not help but recognize the handiwork of the adroit Lenin district party committee. Later when I suggested this to various party officials, they smiled knowingly. "Just an example of exceptional activeness," one party insider from a different Magnitogorsk district averred, using one of Gorbachev's main rallying cries in the push for party reform.

■   ■   ■

The city soviet in Magnitogorsk does not exercise fiscal control over the business conducted within its jurisdiction. Almost all local enterprises in Magnitogorsk are subordinated directly to a Moscow ministry, meaning that the allocation of their profits, including that portion that is turned over to the Magnitogorsk city soviet, is determined by Moscow.

All Soviet towns are company towns in that they owe their continued existence (and often their origin) to the presence of factories. But in comparison to most other industrial cities in the Soviet Union, Magnitogorsk is fortunate in at least one respect. In other cities with several medium- and large-sized enterprises of varying profiles, as many as a dozen ministries may be exercising autocratic powers over "their chunk" of the town, with no coordination. By contrast, because of the profile of its industry, Magnitogorsk has to contend chiefly with one ministry: ferrous metallurgy.

To a ministry, enterprises in a given locality are suppliers of components to other plants in the national network, rather than suppliers of finished output to local markets. To the Magnitogorsk soviet, the Ministry of Ferrous Metallurgy is a rich but miserly uncle. Of the 1 billion rubles profit generated by the Magnitogorsk Works in 1989, 6 percent—60 million rubles—were returned for use by the city soviet.

The Magnitogorsk city soviet, like most local soviets, derives its revenues primarily from the turnover tax. The rest of the budget is composed of transfers from the budgets of the *oblast*, republican, or the all-union (Supreme) soviet. Moreover, these higher bodies control not only the size but the specific composition of a local soviet's staff. Paperwork flows in torrents down the pyramid.

Technically responsible for the construction and maintenance of health care facilities, schools, and communal services, the Magnitogorsk city soviet is compelled to rely on the steel plant and other large enterprises to attend to the urban infrastructure. For example, a bridge under construction across the Ural River connecting the city's two halves is part of the budget for the construction of the steel plant's new converter shop. The same is true of the "city" hotel being built. It is the factory, not the city, that owns and operates the urban tram and bus systems.

Industrial budgets have historically carried niggardly sums for what are called "social needs." And even these small sums are invariably reduced, if not eliminated, as the industrial budget runs over. The new Magnitogorsk bridge, like the new hotel, was alternately included and scratched from the steel plant's construction budget for more than twenty years before work finally began in 1989.

Moreover, financial reforms in industry have brought even more problems for the city soviet. Previously the steel plant turned over more than 10 percent of the new apartments it built to the city soviet. With the proposed transition to full profit and loss management, the factory will no longer do so. At the same time, the city soviet remains without the means to construct its own apartments for the teachers, doctors, artists, and others on its growing housing list.

The election campaign for a national congress designed to alter state structures aimed first at the top, but in Magnitogorsk both the electorate and the authorities also had their eyes on the bottom. The slogan "All power to the soviets" was endorsed by every candidate.

■   ■   ■

Ivan Romazan was born in Magnitogorsk in 1933, four years after the arrival of the first settlers. He was graduated from the Mining Institute and in 1954 became an apprentice foreman at the Magnitogorsk Works. Some thirty years later, in 1985, he became its director. In 1986 Romazan was made a candidate member of the Central Committee; in 1989, a full member. For all of Cheliabinsk province, Romazan was the only person aside from the first secretary of the *obkom* who was a full member of the Central Committee.

By virtue of his membership on the Central Committee, Romazan had greater authority on paper than did the first secretary of the Magnitogorsk *gorkom*, Lev Stobbe. But Romazan's considerable power derived more from his control over vast resources, human and material. His standing in the committee reflected the weight of the Magnitogorsk Works in the country's economy and gave him leverage to fight for the plant's position within the centralized economic system against the competing claims of thousands of other enterprises.

Even before Romazan became a member of the Central Committee, he was not merely the boss in Magnitogorsk; he did not need to answer to the *obkom*. The steel plant was subordinated not to the provincial authorities but directly to the all-union Ministry of Ferrous Metallurgy.

While his candidacy on the party slate was under consideration, Romazan said little publicly. Some quotations appeared in the steel plant newspaper, such as when Romazan asserted that "for Magnitogorsk's inhabitants, the reconstruction of the steel plant is the conversion into reality of the principles of *perestroika*." In these scattered and tiny hints of his views, Romazan rebuffed calls to reduce production, arguing that Magnitogorsk metal could be used to trade for such dire necessities as foreign hospital equipment. He urged that the factory be valued as a resource when it was freed a bit from the ministry's tight control. Moreover, he insisted that he would not follow his predecessors, all of whom had eventually been promoted to Moscow; just as he was born in Magnitogorsk, so he intended to be buried there.

▪ ▪ ▪

In early February the newspaper announced that the election commission had verified compliance with the rules in the nominations of eight candidates for the city district slot. The electors meeting was set for 13 February. According to the newspaper, representatives would be invited from the eighty-three working collectives that declared their support for one of the candidates (another three hundred remained "neutral"). Exactly who would select them and what the selection criteria would be remained unexplained. Moreover, although it was mentioned that representatives of the party, city soviet, and the press would also be invited, the newspaper did not disclose by whom or how many. "Everything depends on Magnitogorsk inhabitants themselves," declared Aleksandr Kostin, head of the Magnitogorsk election commission, "on their activeness or, on the other hand, on their passivity." On the contrary, it seemed that only a small and not well-identified group was invited.

Dissatisfaction with the organization of the electors meeting began to be aired. Readers wrote to the newspaper asking why the city soviet hall, with a capacity of 630, and not the circus, which could hold 2,000, had been chosen. They also wanted to know why there were no plans to transmit the proceedings outside over loudspeakers. Kostin, asked by the newspaper to reply, answered that the circus did not permit proper security, and that the large and secure hall at the Ordzhonikidze palace of culture owned by the steel plant was too expensive to rent. He indicated further that the city soviet hall, the site of the recent thirty-third city party conference, was perfectly suited to the occasion, although he gave no reasons. As for broadcasting the proceedings, Kostin answered that placing loudspeakers outside the soviet building would constitute too big a disturbance of the neighbors. That noisy outdoor events were frequently held on the large square adjacent to the city soviet building had apparently slipped his mind.

▪ ▪ ▪

It was announced on 3 February that the election commission in charge of national-territorial district no. 32 of the Russian republic had met in Cheliabinsk to consider nominations. Several nominees report-edly withdrew, including Boris Yeltsin (the rules stipulated that a can-didate could run only in one district, and Yeltsin chose national-terri-torial district no. 1—Moscow). Others were found not to have been nominated according to the rules and thus were disqualified. That left only two: Igor Velichko, the fifty-five-year-old director of a "closed" factory in the city of Miass and a candidate member of the Central Com-mittee, and Vitalii Riabkov.

Information on the national-territorial campaign published in the Magnitogorsk newspaper was not as plentiful as that for the city district. An interview with Velichko that appeared on 1 March gave his program as "ecology, food, national cultures, religions, power to the soviets, chil-dren, health," and so on. It was the only piece of news about him; he made no appearance in Magnitogorsk, apparently conceding the city to Riabkov in order to contest the smaller towns, villages, and, of course, the big prize: the one-million-plus city of Cheliabinsk.

■　　■　　■

On 13 February the electors meeting for the Magnitogorsk territorial district took place. Five days later a long and detailed report by Aleksei Tiuplin appeared in the newspaper. Describing the setting and proce-dures with care, Tiuplin noted that the conference hall contained exactly 501 electors. "The severe pass system," he wrote, "did not let in a single extraneous person."

Eight candidates had been officially registered. Each was allowed five minutes to be introduced by a supporter, another ten minutes to present a program, and as many as fifteen minutes to answer questions. Those desiring to speak during the discussion period were given five minutes (three for a point of information). Every hour and a half or two hours there was a break. The order of candidates was alphabetical, first up being Dr. Anfisa Andreeva.

According to Tiuplin, Andreeva presented a six-point program: for the soviets, full power through territorial self-financing; for enterprises, radical reconstruction; for Magnitka, clean air and contemporary tech-nology; for mothers and children, priority attention; for youth, new schools, sporting facilities, and a youth center; for veterans, concern and charity. Andreeva was asked her opinion of the proposal to build a nuclear reactor in the province. "Any nuclear technology is danger-ous for people's health; therefore I'm opposed," she answered. What about medical cooperatives? "I have had to answer this question many times. I'm against them," she explained, because "they are costly, draw away staff from state hospitals, and do not carry any guarantee of service." There were many other questions: about ecology, about her age.

Aleksandr Arzamastsev spoke next, stressing the necessity of reforming the political structure of the country in order to reform the economy and living standards. "Last year I spent ten days in Finland," he said. "For these ten days I was ashamed for the USSR. . . . I understood that I could no longer stand in the wings. I resolved to do everything that came within my powers at the first opportunity. Such an opportunity is now before me." He was challenged from the floor: "You got your degree during the stagnation [Brezhnev] period and now your views have suddenly turned around—just because of one trip to Finland—or were there other, more serious reasons?" Arzamastsev asserted that his current views were a logical development of his past ideas. As for Finland, "let's say it sort of had the effect of 'pulling the trigger.' "

Iurii Isaev, in Tiuplin's rendering, did not seem to have much of a program. He did, however, question the nominating process, which he charged in some cases had been influenced by pressure from above. "This is office [*kabinetnaia*] democracy," he griped.

Iurii Petrov singled out three problems: housing, concern for women, and the powerlessness of soviets. When asked whether it was possible with a one-party system to arrive at authentic democracy, Petrov answered that "the people have power [*vlast' narodnaia*], so I think we'll get there." He was also asked what he did for women compelled to work the night shift at his factory, given that he was a member of the All-Union Trade Union Council. He said he got them extra pay. Someone asked critically if the city needed a pleader (*khodok*) or a politician. Others wondered if a worker was up to the job.

N. V. Kuznetsov was introduced by his supporter, with emphasis, as "nonparty." According to Tiuplin, this did not seem to have the intended effect on the audience. An attentive reader could not fail to note that with this aside, Tiuplin had managed to convey the important message that the hall was dominated by party members—something that should have been stated directly. A. F. Perminov spoke next, mentioning housing, transport, and food supplies without, evidently, making much of an impression (at least on Tiuplin). Two candidates had yet to speak.

"Well known in the city, Valentin Fedorovich Romanov was greeted with applause," Tiuplin wrote, adding that Romanov spoke with emotion about his program: the necessity of restoring a just approach to Magnitka, given its role in the past and its contribution to the motherland; the solution of ecological problems; faster construction of housing; medicine; food supplies; the social defense of youth's rights; and other social problems. Someone challenged Romanov, comparing him to Arzamastsev, but unfavorably. "Arzamastsev got lucky: he was in Finland. But Valentin Fedorovich, your academic career was also made during the stagnation period." Romanov answered dubiously that because he had worked on "foreign issues," he was "not affected" by the stagnation.

The last candidate to speak, A. A. Serebriakov, addressed what he considered "the issues of the concerns of construction workers," as well as the state budget and the ecological situation. "How do you feel about the multiparty system?" he was asked. "I do not intend to destroy our party," he replied.

Of the eight candidates, it was clear from Tiuplin's report that four—Andreeva, Arzamastsev, Petrov, and Romanov—were in the running. And yet, "there was no debate as such, neither during the nominating process nor at the electors meeting," Tiuplin wrote. "The candidates' programs (and this is obvious) differ from each other only in details; in principle, they are the same. . . . More than that, the problems touched on by the candidates are familiar to all Magnitogorsk inhabitants. So the question seems justified: why precisely were these candidates and not any others nominated?" He provided no answer and thereby aroused suspicions.

In any case, he continued, "if you take the big picture, the programs of only two candidates—Romanov and Arzamastsev—stood on their own. There are even principled differences between their positions." Therefore, Tiuplin implied, one would have expected a useful discussion to have taken place. "But the party secretary of the Mining Institute motioned to proceed directly to voting without discussion. This was a violation of election law," yet "no one from the election commission 'batted an eyelash.'" Two hundred thirty-nine voted for the proposal to dispense with discussion; 186 against.

At this point, according to Tiuplin, a district procurator, P. P. Gess, stood up and read article 38 from the election law: everyone has the right to participate in discussion. "Here is one of the paradoxes of the times: not every dictate is harmful," Tiuplin remarked, noting that a discussion was announced following a break. "Democracy was saved. Everyone wanted to take part in the discussion, especially those who had voted to preclude it.

"The battle was joined primarily around three candidates: Romanov, Andreeva, and Arzamastsev," wrote Tiuplin. "The other nominees did not seem to have any support." Tiuplin suggested that the individuals selected to represent the nominating work collectives on behalf of the other five candidates were chosen without regard for their oratory or political skills.

For a long time those in the hall argued about the process of the vote. They finally settled on two rounds: first, to choose three of eight; second, to choose two from these three. Despite the insistence of several people on the need for one round with a final result of three or four candidates, the first-round vote went forward. Romanov polled 441 votes; Andreeva, 379; Petrov, 283. (Arzamastsev came in fourth, although his total went unreported.)

The second round was interrupted by district party secretary Savitskii, who wondered, "Does this make sense? All three candidates received the votes of more than 50 percent of those present. All made it." The voting went forward anyway: Romanov, 435; Andreeva, 332. Petrov was eliminated.

Voices were immediately raised to protest that the Supreme Soviet, the highest organ of state, ought to have a representative of the workers, meaning Petrov. Yet, as Tiuplin pointed out, "the supporters of the other three worker candidates did not seem to think so." They evidently did not vote for Petrov during the second round after their candidates had been eliminated.

According to article 37 of the election law, a decision was considered binding if a majority of those present at the meeting voted for it, but the exclusion of the only worker candidate who, after all, had passed the first round with a majority of those in attendance prompted the election commission to reconsider. The meeting was adjourned uneasily, and the next day the newspaper carried a notice that as a result of the violation of election procedures, the electors meeting would be repeated 22 February.

At the second electors meeting attendance mysteriously dropped to 444 people. It was decided to have a single vote: whoever got a simple majority would be included in the ballot to be presented to the public. The paper reported the tally as follows: Romanov, 363; Petrov, 285;

Andreeva, 250. The vote counts of those who received less than 223, the total needed to advance, were not made public.

■   ■   ■

By the time I arrived in Magnitogorsk in mid-March 1989 (I had been in Moscow since mid-January), the election campaign was in full swing. Absolutely everyone was talking about it, especially how unusual it all was, and virtually everyone was taking the elections seriously. Many people had not yet made up their minds. There was no mistaking the impressively high level of politicization and the intense newfound passion for politics.

A few days before I arrived Andreeva had scheduled an open meeting in the city's main cultural center for 5:30 P.M. to drum up support. Outside there was a kind of counterdemonstration. According to the newspaper, as people arrived they were greeted by a vehicle equipped with loudspeakers and stationed near the entrance. Those coming to hear Andreeva were besieged. "In Magnitogorsk more than half the inhabitants are workers! Put one of your own in the government! Vote for Petrov!" "Vote for Andreeva and you'll get the same mess in the country that we've got in city hospital no. 1."

Andreeva met with hostility inside the hall, too. "What can you personally recommend, right now, this minute?" someone shouted at her. "In city hospital no. 1 there is no order at all. How do you propose to manage matters at the state level?" Andreeva maintained her composure. "I consider the question a provocation. The hospital is forty years old. Yes, problems have accumulated. But to say that all is in a horrible state is to insult the entire collective of the hospital." Maybe so, but insults seemed one of the chief modes of dialogue in the campaign.

When questioned about her attitude toward the idea of a multiparty system, Andreeva remarked that "there should be some kind of factionalism created within the party . . . and if yet another party appears, it should have the right to exist." Neither Petrov nor Romanov would go so far.

■   ■   ■

An article in the steel plant's newspaper, *Magnitogorsk Metal,* charged that buses owned by the wire factory had delivered supporters of Petrov to the nomination meeting of the city's Lenin district. (It was also asserted that the party committee of that district, led by Anatolii Makeev, mobilized its forces to pack the auditorium with supporters of Riabkov.) Sergei Shchetnikov, party secretary at the wire factory and an organizer of the Petrov campaign, denied busing in supporters but admitted that the campaign was pursuing what many viewed as an excessively aggressive strategy.

"People fault us for employing such tactics as dropping leaflets from an airplane or using the services of an orchestra," Shchetnikov conceded late one night on an empty Magnitogorsk street corner, as we were waiting for the tram after an evening at the wire factory's discussion club. "But this is politics; these are what elections are all about. Should we not try to get our man elected?" There seemed to be no limit to what the twelve-thousand-worker wire factory, living for decades in the enormous shadow of the steel plant, would do to have its presence acknowledged.

■   ■   ■

Before his defeat at the electors meeting, Aleksandr Arzamastsev summarized for a Magnitogorsk reporter what he called the two prevailing views on what a deputy should be: "a large-scale facilitator [*tolkach*] who can get in the door of the big-time offices and wrest concessions out of those at the top versus a political actor who can see ahead; can understand people, economics, the political situation of the country; and can fight for countrywide solutions." With Arzamastsev out of the running, this analysis was appropriated by Valentin Romanov.

Romanov had had the reputation during the Brezhnev period of a relatively progressive figure, a popular teacher who did his best for students. With the advent of the Gorbachev period, Romanov had enjoyed an upsurge in popularity. But listening to him speak during a chat in his office after I had given a lecture at the Teachers College, I had a hard time reconciling the man in front of me with the image.

Romanov assembled various officials of the Teachers College in his office. In response to one of my questions, Iurii Polev, chair of the party history department and deputy rector, argued forcefully that "Magnitogorsk was not a clear example of socialism but rather of the retreat from socialism, the retreat from Leninist principles." Romanov strongly disagreed with his subordinate, insisting that Magnitogorsk was "the clearest possible example of socialism, of its weaknesses and strengths. Socialism was especially good during wartime situations." Polev became silent. The conversation turned to the contemporary situation.

"We have complete ideological confusion," Romanov bellowed. "Too much social nihilism has led to increases in crime. All we hear is negative, negative, negative. No one can recall the positive sides of our history, of which there were many. We are in danger of losing an entire generation by our misguided attempts to uproot everything at once. They are learning all the wrong things.

"We are on the brink of social chaos. How much do strikes cost us? Billions of rubles, not to mention the ruin of our industry. How realistic is a multiparty system under socialism? Have people who advocate such a thing really thought through what they are proposing?

"We go overboard in our criticisms of centralism. Democratic centralism in our country was wrongly applied. There are different ways to achieve centralism. Japan, for example, represents an intelligent application of centralism, which does not mean complete monopolization but coordination. It is dangerous to advocate total democracy. This will lead us to chaos. Sure we need democracy, but there is no democracy without discipline."

■   ■   ■

On the evening of 21 March 1989 Cheliabinsk television broadcast what it called a "dialogue with voters" in district 339. In the studio the three candidates—Romanov, Andreeva, and Petrov—were asked to respond to questions from callers and from the moderator. Questions ranged from how to make the new Supreme Soviet "real" and how to eliminate the state budget deficit to the possibility of a multiparty system and convergence between the USSR and the United States.

Petrov adopted a mildly populist position and questioned the bureaucrats and directors who wielded unlimited power, a stance reminiscent of the campaign of Boris Yeltsin, the successful Moscow "populist." But when queried about Yeltsin, Petrov retreated, responding cautiously that "we have very little information about all our leaders." He came out against the multiparty system, as did his two opponents (a reversal for Andreeva), but he offered no arguments.

Romanov, the college rector, spoke about the need to address the problems of youth. He warned about the dire consequences of neglecting the education and upbringing of today's generation, a generation confused and demoralized by the "excesses" of present-day reporting (rather than, presumably, the "excesses" of the Stalinist era being reported). Although visibly nervous on camera, Romanov spoke at length and displayed a capacity for logical reasoning, in striking contrast to Petrov.

Andreeva's strategy was more elaborate. With a calm, yet passionate, voice, she spoke about the importance of attending to issues of social welfare and put forth proposals about what could be done. Of the three candidates, she was the only one to discuss the problems of women. Then she attacked Petrov's campaign tactics.

Andreeva claimed that Petrov's backing by the wire factory, an institution considerably better off than the hospital, made for gross inequality in the resources the candidates could muster. She also lashed out at what she called the "pressure tactics" of Petrov's "forces." Citing derogatory posters holding her responsible for the sorry state of the city hospital, harassment on the phone by unidentified callers, and naked abuse in the wire factory newspaper, Andreeva called Petrov's campaign an example of "terrorism."

The affable Petrov appeared shaken by the accusations, none of which he denied. In response to a question about a van equipped with a loudspeaker that not only traveled around the city piling abuse on Andreeva but did so in front of a building where Andreeva was about to give a campaign speech, Petrov said it was "just agitation." Andreeva had clearly thrown Petrov on the defensive for his campaign tactics, but she did so at the cost of appearing aggressive herself. In the end, her allusion to the Petrov slogan—"If you want the whole city to resemble the hospital, vote for Andreeva"—remained the most memorable moment of the program. Much of the audience had experienced the atrocious hospital firsthand.

■   ■   ■

Little news of the "campaign" for the seats from the party ever materialized until the announcement in mid-March that Romazan, along with the other ninety-nine candidates vying for the one hundred slots allotted to the party, was elected to the congress.

Meanwhile, the campaign for the fifteen seats allotted to members of the journalists union took Magnitogorsk editor Valerii Kucher in mid-March to Kiev for a meeting of the Ukrainian, Belorussian, and Moldavian branches. Kucher's nomination was supported by all eleven branches of the journalists union in Cheliabinsk province. The union received ninety-six nominees, fifteen of whom were "registered" and included on the ballot by the presidium for their ten allotted slots. The elections were set for 21 March.

Born in Kiev on 8 July 1941, Kucher's first job was as a reporter for the Magnitogorsk steel plant's newspaper. Later he worked as the Magnitogorsk correspondent for the Cheliabinsk newspaper, before leaving for party work. Soon he returned to journalism, becoming editor of the main Magnitogorsk daily in June 1983.

In Kiev Kucher sounded the same themes he had in Magnitogorsk. "The paradox [of journalism today] consists in the fact that a huge mass of people support the paper, but it is evaluated by only a few," he was quoted as saying. "And this evaluation at times does not coincide with the feelings of the urban inhabitants." He insisted on the need for a law guaranteeing everyone the right to information.

Kucher also touched on what he would refer to in conversations with me as Moscow's "colonial policy" in the Urals. "Magnitogorsk is a classic example of the harmful policy of extremely centralized administration. A city with so many huge profitable enterprises ought to solve its local problems independently from the center. We are capable." Of all the candidates in the various different races, only Kucher pressed this issue.

"Magnitogorsk patriotism has begun to change," Kucher confided during our many discussions. "Previously, whatever the center demanded, we gave. We were proud we could do so much for the country. Now we still want to do our part, but we expect to be treated fairly in return." These comments were echoed by Tatiana Leus, one of Kucher's ten designated surrogates, who often spoke more bluntly, arguing, for instance, that the "city is in a sorrowful state. . . . We need to fix it, to end the frightful dependence of the city on the Magnitogorsk Works. No one will disagree that the country, just like fifty years ago, needs metal. But not at any price." On 22 March the paper carried the news that Kucher had been elected, joining Romazan.

■   ■   ■

In the 23 March issue, the newspaper published the responses of all three candidates in the city race to four questions:

How do you propose to solve the state budget deficit?

What is your opinion of Boris Yeltsin?

If a voter approached you with a request for help in obtaining medicine for a sick child, what would you do?

You have just learned that plans for the long-awaited construction of a hospital in Magnitogorsk are canceled; what would you do?

To the first question all the candidates recommended eliminating planned gigantic industrial projects, decreasing the size of the apparat, and demilitarizing the economy. But there were differences of emphasis: Andreeva stressed the benefits to accrue from a reorganization of the economy; Petrov called for turning over unprofitable enterprises to worker cooperatives; Romanov advocated compelling work-shy elements and other parasitic types to work.

As for the second question, all three were cautious, avoiding excessive praise of Yeltsin and expressing no criticism. Similarly, little real disagreement emerged in the answers to the fourth question, as each candidate suggested involving public opinion and insuring that the status of a deputy was sufficiently high to be able to challenge ministries.

In answer to the third question Andreeva vowed she would do everything within her powers, as she has always done in the past. Romanov stated that a deputy should not be a "procurer" of medicines or anything else but rather should look at the larger causes and address them. Petrov proposed importing more medicine at the expense of all other items being purchased for foreign currency.

That same day the newspaper published the results of a "poll" taken from a random sample of two hundred people. The responses to the question, Whom are you going to vote for? were as follows:

Romanov	27.8%
Petrov	18.0
Andreeva	15.5
Undecided	18.0
Cross out all three	around 4.0
Will not vote; no one is worthy	14.0
Will not vote, indifferent	around 3.0

A second question—Are you satisfied with the campaign?—elicited a majority of negative responses. The newspaper divided people who claimed to be dissatisfied into three groups: those who distrusted the organizers ("There is no full democracy; this is just a show [*igra*] put on by the apparat"); those who remarked on the country's lack of experience with democracy ("We know all the secret details of Bush and Nixon, but not of our own candidates"); and those who indicted themselves ("We're used to a signal from above; we're not ready"). Some people were nostalgic for the old elections. "Previously," one voter told the newspaper's pollster, "we went to vote as to a holiday, with the whole family. And there was beer."

In conclusion, the newspaper emphasized that "a virtual majority of those surveyed answered questions gladly. And their answers, we daresay, were honest." Change was on everyone's mind. To one voter's comment that "we're waiting for changes," the newspaper suggested as an alternative, "We're taking part in changes."

·   ·   ·

With two days left before the vote, Iurii Petrov scheduled a meeting with the electorate in the Old Magnitka settlement (*posiolok*). There are a number of such rural-looking neighborhoods in Magnitogorsk, particularly toward the outer city limits, where one can see cows, chickens, and flourishing, if small, agricultural plots. But Old Magnitka is different.

Founded in 1743 as a Cossack outpost, Old Magnitka was the site of the region's first church (submerged in 1930 when the plain was flooded after construction of a dam). It was also the site of the original cemetery, long since torn down.* In 1962 a decree was issued forbidding further construction of cottages in the settlement, with the hope that it would slowly wither away. It has not, although now it is surrounded by forlorn blocks of colorless high-rise apartment buildings.

Petrov's meeting, held in a rundown sports and cultural facility, was attended by fewer than two dozen people. Aside from four teenagers in the back who, after making noise, soon left out of boredom, those in the audience were elderly. They pelted him with questions about a road that was promised but never built, a wall that was going to be replastered, more frequent bread deliveries to the one store in the entire settlement. People had desperation in their voices; some were moved to tears. Petrov showed extraordinary patience and empathy. "That was rough," Petrov exhaled in the car, as we hurried down the bumpy dirt path out of the settlement on our way to his next scheduled campaign appearance at the Mining Institute. We were already late because Petrov had insisted on staying until everyone who wanted to speak had been heard.

"This is the most neglected part of the city. The people have lived here for decades without anything being done," he remarked. "They had nothing but complaints and demands [*odny pretenzy*]. I can't blame them. How often do they get the attention of someone in authority? It shows the bankruptcy of our local soviets. Did you notice that none of these people could even name a single one of their deputies to the district soviet? It's a shame, really."

---

* Recently the old cemetery grounds were earmarked for new housing construction. During the groundwork scattered collections of bones were uncovered. Prompted by irate local activists from the construction trust, the newspaper published a scathing article on the scandal. City architects apologized and promised to restore the cemetery.

Petrov admitted that he was not a political figure of "state proportions" and that he had a lot to learn. He expressed his willingness
to learn, his openness to new ideas and solutions, and his commitment to carry out his social duty should the people place their trust
in him. Claiming he felt very much like the underdog, he regretted
the confrontation with Andreeva on television and his failure to respond adequately. "Sometimes," he said, "I don't always find the right
words rolling off my tongue, like Anfisa [Andreeva] seems to all the
time."

We finally reached the beginning of the paved road. "I've now spoken
in every settlement in the city," he sighed. "I tell you, it was a real learning experience. I had no idea about many of the things people have in
their hearts. When I first started this campaign, I thought I knew our
city. Now I know better."

●　　■　　■

Instructions for the 26 March vote were given in the newspaper: each
voter was to receive two ballots, one for the territorial district, one for
the national-territorial district. There were three names on the first ballot, two on the second. The voter was advised to cross out the names of
those candidates *not* wanted, leaving the desired candidate's name alone.
This system meant that each candidate would receive votes both for (untouched) and against (crossed out). A ballot with more than one candidate untouched or with everyone crossed out was to be considered
invalid. Write-in candidates were not permitted. And a candidate could
not win the election unless he or she received at least 50 percent of the
votes cast.

On 25 March, the day before election day, a demonstration of sorts
organized by Counter Movement took place in front of the music
school. Including undercover and uniformed police, about two hundred people, most of whom were men middle-aged and older, milled
around on this crisp, chilly Saturday afternoon. Speakers represent-
ing all the candidates were invited by the organizers, but only ones for
Riabkov and Andreeva (who were running in different races)
showed.

Makeev, the first secretary of one of the city's three district party committees, remarked on the comprehensiveness of his man Riabkov's campaign: visits to more than two thousand voting places in two provinces.
Authoritative and clear, Makeev elicited neither approval nor condemnation.

Next up was a woman who mentioned her name only to have it drowned out by the sustained groans that had greeted the first words out of her mouth: she represented Andreeva. Her attempt to explain that the sorry state of the hospital was not Andreeva's fault, but rather ought to be laid at the door of stingy bureaucrats, met with derision. Whistles and shouts of "We don't need a woman on top" forced her from the stage.

People were agitated. "Who's to blame? They are," one pensioner from the crowd shouted, pointing to the huge office building down the road. "They build party cathedrals. How much money did they sink into that Pentagon of theirs? You can't even count the number of offices they have there. We could have built three children's hospitals with the money."

"The Magnitogorsk Works is a trampoline," another elderly man howled. "Every boss comes along and tells us how much he cares about the city; then he springs, whoosh, into a ministerial chair in Moscow. We never hear from him again, except to learn that he advanced himself further by writing a dissertation on the smoke here."

Organizers from Counter Movement circulated, gathering signatures on a petition that they intended to present to Gorbachev, calling for more attention to ecology. Meanwhile, Valerii Timofeev, one of the leaders of Counter Movement, climbed onto the platform. Pacing, his hands wrapped tightly around the large microphone, Timofeev, a short man with a long, stringy beard, worked the crowd with melodramatic gestures and "shocking" revelations. He droned on for more than one hour. It was difficult to discern his message, but after a while his rantings, intended to stir up an angry mood, had the effect of dissipating the crowd's energy, and people began leaving.

■   ■   ■

News of the outcome in the Magnitogorsk territorial district election was finally reported the morning of 28 March, three days after the polls closed (the results for the national-territorial race were delayed several more days):

	FOR	(%)	AGAINST	(%)
Andreeva	36,473	(15.9)	181,893	(79.0)
Petrov	79,888	(34.7)	138,478	(60.2)
Romanov	97,114	(42.2)	121,252	(52.7)

No one having received a majority of the votes cast, the election rules stipulated that the two top vote-getters, Petrov and Romanov, face a runoff.

Of the city's 297,466 eligible voters, 230,250 (77.4 percent) went to the polls. (Nationally the figure was 89.8 percent.) In Magnitogorsk almost twelve thousand ballots (5 percent) were pronounced invalid, although it was not reported how many had been invalidated for mistakenly leaving more than one candidate's name and how many for having purposefully crossed out all three.

A reporter chose one of the city's voting places, located in school no. 18, to conduct an informal "exit poll." "I don't believe in the democratic nature of these elections," stated S. K. Butorin, an employee of a technical assistance center. "These are just preliminary attempts, yet all the same they are a step forward. I detected certain defects during the agitation. There were 'directive' phone calls from the *raikom,* but I voted for Romanov—an informed [*soznatelnyi*] selection." Others were quoted as having cast their ballots for Andreeva or Petrov. Some complained about the organization of the elections.

"I, for example, did not receive my voting notification in the mail," Zoia Turbanchininova, a retired worker from the steel plant with many prestigious labor awards, pointed out. "Meanwhile, in our stairwell one family that moved away five years ago received their voting notices. I ran into my young neighbor Oksana Torfimova, who was in a panic, not knowing where to vote. In our stairwell there are many like her."

The same reporter traveled to another polling place at school no. 56, where members of the younger generation were queried. "I didn't vote for any of them; I didn't think anyone was worthy," declared S. Iashchenko, a student at the Mining Institute. "Why? First, all three were promoted during the stagnation period; second, their programs were virtually identical and vague; third, the campaign did not inspire trust." By contrast, for E. Novoselova, also a student at the Mining Institute, the vote involved an important choice. "Romanov is the only one who can change anything," she insisted. "He was nominated by youth. He's believed because he's known. He is a man of action. He will defend us and raise the cultural level in Magnitka."

The newspaper coverage concluded with assurances that the process had been overseen closely and that all ballots had been counted as cast. There were, however, a number of mishaps. For example, appearing at his designated polling place, Aleksandr Kostin, the chair of the electoral commission, discovered that his name was not on the list (he was allowed to vote anyway). "A second round," as it was called, was set for 9 April, twelve days away.

■   ■   ■

One Magnitogorsk taxi driver whose services proved indispensable to me on many occasions was anything but shy about voicing his opinions on current events during the election campaign. "This whole country, it's one big concentration camp," he liked to remark, speaking in a colorful vernacular. "We want to feel free, even if we're not rich. Open the borders. Get rid of these stupid restrictions. So many bosses and rules.

"We told ourselves the whole time we're the best. Now look. It turns out we're in the same company with poor slobs of the Third World. We said we're for peace. And then Afghanistan. What 'international duty'? Why did our boys have to die there? How the hell did we get involved?

"Elections you say? I crossed out some names because I knew them well. I crossed out the rest because I didn't know them. We learn about our leaders only after they're dead. When Gorbachev dies, it's going to be interesting. He's trying to turn the whole machine around. But he needs helpers. Gorbachev has no helpers. Others resist. The apparat— now that's something original. Does any other country have something like that? We'll never put things right until we get rid of the one-party system.

"Why did it turn out so badly? They didn't think it through to the end, I guess. They started something, and then, well . . . The people themselves are good. They help each other, lend a hand, look out for others. I'm optimistic. It can't possibly get any worse, can it?" The deep disgust and the wholesale condemnation of the powers-that-be were the same as in 1987, but in 1989 the indictment was more focused. Such were the fruits of *glasnost* and the election campaign.

■   ■   ■

On 31 March the results for the "other" contest in Magnitogorsk, national-territorial district no. 32, were given as follows:

	FOR	(%)	AGAINST	(%)
Riabkov	1,134,404	(40.3)	1,547,158	(54.9)
Velichko	1,322,259	(46.9)	1,359,303	(48.2)

Neither won a majority of the 2,817,537 votes cast (85.9 percent of those eligible), meaning that no one was elected. But, because there were only two candidates (and not three), an entirely new nomination process would have to be held before a second election could take place.

■   ■   ■

Aleksandr Arzamastsev apologized for having had to cancel our interview the first time with the words, "I was summoned to Cheliabinsk by the *obkom*." "Why didn't I just tell them I was busy?" he repeated slowly and with a smile, evidently savoring a thought he chose not to share. "You must know that as a member of the party, I am obliged to report whenever they call me, regardless of the amount of advance warning."

Arzamastsev described himself as a "full-scale democract" in both the political and social senses, emphasizing equally "the need to safeguard the opinions of the minority and the need for those in the workplace to have a say in the management of their work." He was asked to explain his defeat at the Magnitogorsk electors meeting.

"Two hundred seven voted for me; some 300 were against," he replied. "It was the conservative party stratum. I am too bold for them, too unexpected. They don't want any fundamental changes, changes in structures. I speak out at every party meeting for pluralism and radical change. These are the first open discussions we have had here in many, many years. The ice has been broken. People have been awoken out of their slumber. The process cannot be stopped. Pluralism is the future. I feel a silent majority on my side during every argument."

Arzamastsev reached for a book called *Barracks Socialism,* a scathing analysis of Chinese Communism he had written that was published in 1974. "Our attitude toward China at the time permitted publication. But as anyone could see, I was speaking not just about China but about our country, too." He claimed that the book demonstrated his long commitment to fundamental change of the Soviet system, not to mention his courage and cleverness for being able to publish an (indirect) indictment of the USSR while Brezhnev was in power.

Born in 1931, Arzamastsev went to work in one of the Magnitogorsk rolling mills at age seventeen. From there he was selected to study at Moscow University, where he obtained the candidate degree (one up from a bachelor's) in 1965 and was assigned to the philosophy department of the Magnitogorsk Mining Institute. He has taught there for more than twenty-five years.

Arzamastsev lectured about power. "All forms of it," he explained. "There are seventeen or so of them: autocracy, aristocracy, bureaucracy, gerontocracy, theocracy, militarocracy, plutocracy, democracy, and so on. But when you analyze each one, you see that there are basically only two forms: democracy and autocracy, with all others being different manifestations of the latter. I need hardly add that it's obvious which form we have.

"Our history is not separable from world history. We must know and properly evaluate world experience, and our own. Right now we need an NEP [New Economic Policy]: the motor for economic development provided by property combined with political pluralism. The biggest task before us today is to destatize our economy, our society, our life.

"Our path is difficult. The social and class structure has changed since the nineteenth century. We must think this through. We need a new Marx, a new *Kapital*." (In the meantime, he expressed gratitude for a Russian-language edition of Trotsky's biography of Stalin, which I presented to him and which, of course, he had never before seen.)

"The key issue for the upcoming Congress of People's Deputies," he continued, "will be political power: on the one hand, how to limit and redefine the role of the party, and, on the other, who can be active and how can people participate in decisionmaking.

"We need to observe our own constitution: all power to the soviets. If the soviets right now do not have power, who does, on what basis, and how did they get it? These are the questions the congress ought to resolve. I am an optimist. Life itself will compel the changes. The party could very well become nothing more than a discussion club."

■   ■   ■

On the eve of the runoff in the contest for the city electoral district, the newspaper published interviews with Romanov and Petrov, as well as Andreeva, even though she was no longer on the ballot. This was a calculated gesture of conciliation on the newspaper's part; not merely the adversity inherent in a competitive election but the fact that someone *had* to lose took much getting used to by both the candidates and the electorate. Andreeva rose to the occasion. "I don't consider it a defeat," she stated. "We directed public attention to the problems of health care. Isn't this the most important thing?" She vowed to continue her work, attending to the matters of city hospital no. 1.

Petrov spent most of the interview carping about the hostility his campaign had met with. When several of his representatives went to

Vladimir Kichenko, the trade union organizer for the construction company, to set up a campaign appearance, they were allegedly told by Kichenko that "I myself am for Romanov, and it is useless for the others to agitate here." In conclusion Petrov claimed Kichenko said that "the right-bank district party committee had given the order to agitate only for Romanov." According to Petrov, this tactic of being refused access to working collectives by their bosses was encountered repeatedly.

Defending once again his use of airplanes and leaflets, Petrov also sought to clarify his relationship with the higher authorities. He maintained that contrary to the rumors, assistance from the city party committee did not account for the active nature of his campaign. He then brought up a matter from the past, unprompted by the interviewer but evidently in response to certain conversations around town: "Five years ago I was summoned by the city committee for an important matter. They suggested that I get up in front of the workers and call for the work norms to be raised. I refused. Our norms are already among the highest in this branch of industry. Hearing this, they were amazed in the city committee."

Romanov, asked about the slogan advanced by his competitor, "For a workers' Magnitka, a workers' deputy," offered blunt remarks. "This is the slogan of bureaucrats and party functionaries calculated for simpletons, to put it mildly," he charged. "Not long ago certain powerful leaders hiding behind the name of the workers committed illegal acts." Romanov had smeared Petrov's campaign managers indirectly but unmistakably with Stalinism.

Like Andreeva, Romanov asserted that because he and his team were not released from their regular jobs during the campaign, they could not devote much time and energy to it. This comment was clearly directed at Petrov's campaign. "I resisted the temptation of bringing in an army of students," Romanov added. "Our campaign expenses were minimal, just for 'pencils and paper.' In general I don't think superfluous pomp in agitation yields much of an effect. This is a lesson for the future." In conclusion Romanov appealed to youth, noting their many problems and specific needs, which he vowed to help solve.

■   ■   ■

Judging by the conversations with voters as election day neared, Romanov's campaign was winning. On 11 April his victory was announced:

	FOR	(%)	AGAINST	(%)
Petrov	86,267	(40.8)	123,400	(58.3)
Romanov	119,644	(56.6)	90,003	(42.5)

As expected, participation for this round declined slightly, but it remained at an impressively high 71.4 percent.

The day after reporting Romanov's victory, the newspaper continued to carry TASS dispatches on the "complex situation in Tblisi," where a few days earlier the army had been used to break up an unsanctioned ongoing demonstration. Everything was unclear, except that there were casualties, among them women and children. On the same page Aleksandr Leisla, deputy chairman of the Magnitogorsk city soviet, responded affirmatively to questions about the need to ration soap and detergent.

■   ■   ■

With Romanov having joined Romazan and Kucher as Magnitogorsk delegates to the Congress, Vitalii Riabkov announced on 14 April his intention to run in the upcoming second round of the national-territorial district. Having spent weeks crisscrossing two provinces and holding more than one hundred meetings with voters, he "refused to give up." Riabkov offered a reporter from the newspaper impressions from his campaign travels.

"What I saw was very sad, especially in the villages of Kurgansk *oblast*," stated Riabkov, who was raised in Magnitogorsk. "To live in a village is to be without the most elementary comforts. The same can be said about small towns, which are half-built, forgotten worker settlements attached to factories. I was also struck by the ordeal of women's work. Women are used for the hardest of jobs." Magnitogorsk readers were not used to being told they had it much better than those elsewhere. This not only shook up many people; it reinforced the supposition that the country's crisis was deeper than they had previously thought.

As for the pending election, Riabkov offered little by way of a program. Instead, he mused that he did "not expect an easy time of it. Last time I had one opponent. Now there are already twenty-four. In any case, this does not change the situation. A battle is a battle. Easy ones don't exist." But Riabkov omitted mentioning that his main rival, Velichko, had declined to reenter the race.

Little was heard of the campaign or of the all-important electors meeting in Cheliabinsk. A samizdat account of the repeat electors meeting for the national-territorial district prepared by M. Kriukov, chief of the Cheliabinsk Civil Construction Agency, gave an embellished but nevertheless essentially accurate appraisal of Riabkov's cakewalk. The author was a supporter of Arzamastsev, who had sought to get on the ballot in the national-territorial district after having failed to do so in the Magnitogorsk city district.

"On the day of the electors meeting three organizations actively supported Arzamastsev, passing out flyers and copies of his article for the Mining Institute newspaper, 'Political Pluralism.' You should know that the censor expunged a paragraph in which Aleksandr Mikhailovich compared the constitution of the USSR with that of fascist Germany.

"Pavlenko, deputy electoral commissioner, opened the electors meeting at 10:00 A.M. Campaign managers were given five minutes to introduce their candidates, who then spoke for seven minutes and answered questions for five minutes. This procedure took five hours.

"A proposal to include all twenty-four nominees on the final ballot to go to the public and adjourn the meeting was defeated. Yet those present also voted to eliminate the discussion of programs, a clear violation of the election laws. In any case, even when this was overturned, many candidates, such as Riabkov, made no mention of a program. He chose instead to discuss his erudition.

"Twenty-one people were put on the list for consideration by the meeting (three voluntarily withdrew). You could vote for as many of them as you liked. At 7:30 P.M. they finished tabulating the results. Only Riabkov's name appeared on more than 50 percent of the 570 ballots.

"The chair of the meeting unexpectedly handed over the microphone to Riabkov for a final word and then closed the meeting. Riabkov, instead of insisting on the need for a multicandidate ballot, gratefully accepted the electors meeting recommendation of only his candidacy. Someone shouted, 'How can that be, only one?' The presidium left the hall, promising to return. People threatened to begin a hunger strike. 'They deceived us, like sheep.'

"Pavlenko returned to the hall twenty-five minutes later, requesting ten more minutes. He returned again and agreed to continue the meeting if a quorum was still present. The count revealed some 440 people; the meeting reconvened.

"Pavlenko proposed including three candidates for the final ballot. Someone from the hall shouted, 'Why not five? Let's take a vote.' 'You entrusted us with the task of running the meeting,' Pavlenko responded. 'Don't disturb us. We suggest three. Let's vote.' Four hundred voted in favor of having three candidates; 45 voted against.

"The presidium proposed Baronenko, a school principal from Kopeisk, and Vasilev, a locomotive driver from Kurgma. 'Who is for Baronenko? Two hundred thirty.' To shouts of 'Let us speak!' from the hall, Pavlenko shouted back, 'Don't disturb us from conducting the meeting.' 'For Vasilev? Two hundred seventy-one.' In conclusion, Pavlenko remarked, 'No one tricked you. You yourselves voted only for Riabkov, and then you began to make noises. It's necessary to know the electoral laws.' Everyone left more or less satisfied.

"And so 440 people decided for 4 million who is worthy and who is not of inclusion on the ballot. Who sent these 'representatives'? How were they selected, at least the ones from Magnitogorsk? But trying to find out from the authorities who was sent, by whom, and in the end who actually went proved impossible." Three candidates having been approved, the election was set for 14 May.

On 6 May the Magnitogorsk newspaper published a short statement by a representative of Vasilev and one by Baronenko himself, the only material on Riabkov's opponents that appeared in Magnitogorsk. The other candidates apparently conceded the city to the native Riabkov.

■   ■   ■

Cheliabinsk province forms part of one of the major industrial heartlands of the USSR. Factories in the province produce thirty million tons of steel annually, not to mention 70 percent of the country's pipes and 50 percent of its tractors. It is the most militarized region in the country, with more than five hundred major factories devoted to defense. Put another way, Cheliabinsk province produces nearly 4 billion rubles' worth of profit annually, one of the highest values by a single province in the Russian republic. Only a tiny percentage of that output consists of consumer goods, however. Moreover, Magnitogorsk is only the tenth leading producer of consumer goods in consumer-poor Cheliabinsk province.

For three days in January 1989 a conference convened "on the condition of the environment and the safeguarding and improvement of the health of Magnitogorsk citizens." Local leaders and scientists from the Magnitogorsk Mining Institute were joined by representatives of the Ministry of Ferrous Metallurgy and the Central Committee of the Komsomol, which organized the gathering. Judging by the newspaper account, published in February, participants tried to outdo each other in presenting the shocking facts about the ecological catastrophe. The forum also offered a rare opportunity for Magnitogorsk to confront its boss, the Ministry of Ferrous Metallurgy.

At the meeting Mayor Mikhail Lysenko took on a deputy minister in attendance. "We're building again like we did in the 1930s: the factory, the factory, the factory—without attention to social needs," he argued. "Mill 2000 will cost 10 billion rubles [a sum almost triple the original estimate for all reconstruction work], yet only 80 million have been allocated for social needs. Who needs a cold-rolled steel mill and a BOF converter with starving steel workers?

"The director of the steel plant says that the ministry siphons off all the money. And what does that mean for us!? We lose years dragging from office to office! It is impossible for us to work this way any longer! This is a criminal disgrace!

"The city's water situation has become catastrophic. . . . And these two huge industrial objects under construction will also need water in the future. On Saturdays and Sundays we turn off the water in twenty to thirty superblocks. There is no water in the city! Can it be that no one in the ministry understands this! We demand: reduce by 10 percent state orders for the Magnitogorsk Works, and we'll exchange our metal for meat, sausage, and candy."

As a result of this long-dreamed-of and dramatic showdown with the ministry on Magnitogorsk territory, Lysenko got a commitment of two million rubles to expand the city's water-pumping facilities. As for the steel plant, the ministry promised to allow it to keep all the profits from its above-plan production, but the plan targets were not reduced.

For Lysenko the confrontation was the culmination of several years of ostentatious shoe-pounding and yet another confirmation of his guiding maxim that he who makes the most noise wrings the greatest "concessions" out of Uncle. But for other inhabitants of Magnitogorsk the spectacle offered little consolation. "The ministry still takes out everything that can be carried, leaving behind only the poisons," a lecturer from the Magnitogorsk museum remarked later. "And these poisonous emissions are mutilating not just the present generation but future ones."

■   ■   ■

On 17 May the outcome of the second national-territorial balloting, with 71.2 percent of the eligible populace taking part, was announced:

	FOR	(%)	AGAINST	(%)
Baronenko	589,070	(25.6)	1,672,051	(72.5)
Vasilev	652,006	(28.3)	1,609,115	(69.8)
Riabkov	955,582	(41.5)	1,305,539	(56.6)

Again none of the three had garnered the requisite 50 percent! Vasilev and Riabkov faced a runoff, the third election for this one seat. It was scheduled for 21 May—only one week after the last one and just four days before the opening of the congress in Moscow.

■　　■　　■

In early May Valerii Kucher, dictaphone in hand, rode the ten kilometers from the offices of the *Magnitogorsk Worker* to the factory administration building. He had an appointment for an interview with Ivan Romazan. The two most powerful men in Magnitogorsk had both become "people's deputies" to the new congress, although neither had been elected by the people. But whereas it was obvious from reading the newspaper what Kucher's views were, Romazan's were a complete mystery.

> *Kucher:* ... I will say it plainly. From the first days of fulfilling my new duties I sensed not only the vital interest of the majority but at the same time a certain gentle doubt of the mandate bestowed to deputies by social organizations. ... Sometimes people have said, "So you are a people's deputy but the people did not vote for you." It is possible that for you this is unpleasant to hear, but the majority of questions the newspaper has received were occasioned by the fact of your election from the party. . . .

> *Romazan:* The new system of elections . . . was discussed, and the basic mass of our population agreed with it. I'd like to point out that . . . elections from social organizations were conducted in our country for the first time. In the new system there are great pluses and, no doubt, certain shortcomings. I think that the system will doubtless be perfected. . . . But I want to underline the genuine democratism in which the elections took place.
>
> The nomination process by the Communist party had in principle a mass character. . . . It would be unjust to consider me or another candidate from the party self-appointed. For example, I was nominated by the collective of the steel complex. With this I am saying nothing new. History formed in such a way that Magnitogorsk grew on the basis of the complex. . . . Traditionally it has happened that the leader of the Magnitogorsk Works has represented

the interests of Magnitogorsk inhabitants before the highest organs of Soviet power.

I consider it a normal phenomenon when the leader of such a huge enterprise is located in the center itself. . . . I should say that in order to represent the interests of all strata of the population of our city and to be able, I'll be candid, to fight for these positions in the highest organs of state administration, it is necessary to have a person who, if you like, has the authority [*polnomochie*] to step up to any level of the highest leadership of our country, whether that be the chair of Gosplan, the Council of Ministers, or the minister of finance. Real access to such places is possible only for a person possessing real authority.

This is all the more important now, when the tasks before the director of the steel complex are wider than they were ten, fifteen, twenty years ago. Today the main issues are not only the increase of the production of metal, raising its quality, but above all social tasks: food, the construction of housing, ecological problems. . . . We came of age, were taught and worked without hearing that it was dusty and smoky. We literally did not notice any of this, considering it a normal phenomenon. Of course, this is not so. Today we understand this. . . .

Kucher: I detect a certain contradiction in your answer. The works and its leaders have always had tremendous power and for the most part determined the fate of the city. . . . Is it justified once again to put the question in such a way that all responsibility will belong to the works alone? We are convinced that life in our city is complicated and not simple. . . . You must agree that from Moscow, from the offices of ferrous metallurgy, not everything is visible, even to leaders who are concerned with the life of our city.

Does it not seem to you the time has come for the steel works to relinquish its absolute power and share power with the local soviet? The chairman of the city soviet, M. M. Lysenko, has always journeyed to Moscow to beg for money for life necessities for the city, and he continues to travel, lately even more often than before. . . . The ministry has real power; it has money, resources, and so on; while the city soviet has nothing but a slogan about the need to transfer power to it. How can we make it so that the ministry decides how to develop the city not through its director but through the organs of Soviet power? Doesn't it seem paradoxical to you that the city can get something new only as part of the construction of some industrial objective? . . .

Romazan: The question you raise is complex and distinctive. It is necessary to do everything for the needs of the people. This is the main thing in the stages of *perestroika*. Those individuals who today promise that tomorrow things will be better, that people will awake and manna will drop from heaven—such individuals are misleading the people. . . . Only on the basis of high labor productivity will we be able to attain those material advantages, which can then be divided in society. Now we're dividing what we don't have. . . .

And how to divide political power [*vlast*]? I don't need such power. I don't have such power. But there is disciplined responsibility. You must do that work for which you are paid. . . . Every week you must look back and ask yourself what you did for people and what kind of legacy you're leaving. For me this is a question of honor: in what shape will I turn over the steel complex to the next leader? . . .

Kucher: Ivan Kharitonovich, the people of Magnitogorsk view you at times as a representative of the Ministry of Ferrous Metallurgy, as a man who executes the policies of that body, and not always as a citizen of this city. . . . During my meetings with the electorate people asked me, "Why are meat and other products sold at the steel complex? What about us doctors and teachers who don't have such options?"

Romazan: The director of the steel complex ought to be thought of as a man of the ministry. This is correct. I am not offended by this remark. But in my heart I sometimes am disturbed when people try to . . . see me as the slave of the ministry. . . . I think that previous leaders of the complex carried out the work that the party and government put before them. . . . What happened during the so-called stagnation period, when more was wrung out of Magnitka than should have been, is not the fault solely of the former leaders of the factory. I will work, just like my predecessors, as much as my energy allows. But now is a different time. There are different priorities in economics and politics. . . . The directorship of the factory and the inhabitants of the city make up one whole. . . .

Kucher: Understand me, I don't want to catch you on the possible imprecision of your answers . . . but you just said that your predecessors unwaveringly followed the directives of the party and the government and that you yourself intend to show the same steadfastness in following this rule within the new directions. . . . Are you sure that the present policy of the ministry in relation to the steel complex is a people's policy [*narodnaia*]? . . .

Romazan: It is impossible to live without faith. There must be faith. And discipline. No state, whether socialist or capitalist, can live and develop itself if there is no internal discipline. . . . In my opinion everything depends on discipline. Not only has discipline not been raised to the requisite level, but it has fallen. This is connected with a leveling tendency [in wages]. . . . There exists a lack of responsibility in the fulfillment of one's duties and in pay. As a result, people think that they should be paid simply for showing up. . . .

Kucher: People often ask what we deputies personally expect from the congress. . . . What do you think?

Romazan: The congress will be organizational. . . . But, no doubt, things will be called by their names, and the people will be told what we actually have, what we have achieved thus far in industry and agriculture, and how to apply concretely our current resources to get the maximum effect at the present stage. It is necessary to avoid general phrases. . . . It is possible and necessary to speak about what happened seventy years ago. But at this congress it is time to evaluate what we are doing right now; how we are concluding the economic year, with a plus or a minus; and what must be done to fix matters. . . .

Kucher: . . . What qualities do you think a leader must have?

Romazan: Unquestionably, a leader must have the trust of the people. If a director does not have the people's trust, the people sooner or later will remove him from his post. . . . Second, a leader must have the proper qualifications. Also a leader should be modest personally. . . .

I became a full member of the Central Committee only recently. The rules are as follows: a candidate member has the right to speak but not to vote. . . . But I'll tell you honestly: I'm little known in the Central Committee. I attend the plenary meetings. This means, as a rule, a one-day trip to Moscow. . . . I am not torn away from production very often. . . .

Kucher: Ivan Kharitonovich! At the congress the interests of different strata of the population will be represented. It is not excluded that within the congress initiative groups could form. . . .

Romazan: My position is as follows: I am not a partisan of groups, groupings, or associations that try to influence critical state matters, the political system of the country, using personal emotions. I do not want multipartyness. The party of Communists ought to be the party of Communists. It should be a party of like-minded thinkers and not a group of people who today are for socialism and tomorrow monarchism. . . .

Kucher: What can unite us if behind me is the word and behind you are money, technology, and metal?

Romazan: I am pleased that in our city a collective of deputies has formed. We have the same task: to do everything in order that life in Magnitogorsk makes people happy. We can do a lot in this direction, and the people will support us. . . .

Seeing the interview, many readers marveled at how Kucher had pulled yet another rabbit out of the hat, extending the frontiers of *glasnost* in Magnitogorsk to a new and decisive dimension: the utter subordination of the city to the steel plant. But as for the thoughts and thought processes of Magnitogorsk's "big boss," laid bare for the first time, people were appalled by his primitiveness of mind and alarmed by the import of his remarks.

When a transcript of the interview was shown to the deputy editors of the newspaper, all were sure Romazan would refuse to allow its publication. According to Kucher, Romazan gave his okay willingly and even suggested that they meet more often to discuss the city's problems.

.   ▪   ▪

As expected, on 21 May Riabkov trounced Vasilev, becoming the fourth Magnitogorsk deputy. In addition to vying for a seat in the new Congress of People's Deputies, Riabkov had been a delegate to the previous summer's special Nineteenth Party Conference in Moscow. Furthermore, he had suggested himself (unsuccessfully) as a candidate for the position of first secretary at the thirty-third congress of the Magnitogorsk city party committee in November.

"I am a person without ambition," Riabkov had told the newspaper in January 1989, when, in his words, he gave his "assent" to run for the congress. After more than five months and three separate elections, he had emerged victorious, clearly a rising political figure to be reckoned with.

▪   ▪   ▪

Back in late March the election results for the rest of Cheliabinsk province were announced. Running in the Troitsky electoral district, N. D. Shverev, first secretary of the *oblast* party committee, received 37,129 votes for and 153,284 against. Both of his opponents more than doubled Shverev's total, advancing without him to a runoff election. Inconclusive as the results were generally, there was no mistaking this one: the top man in the provincial party organization had been sent packing, a scenario repeated throughout the country.

Elena Karelina asked *raikom* secretary Anatolii Makeev in mid-May to explain the poor showing of various party leaders during the elections. "There are a number of reasons," Makeev answered, seemingly nonplussed. "Too little movement in the economy. The shelves are not filling up. The incident with Yeltsin at the March plenum [of the Central Committee] did not raise the authority of the party.*

"Lately, top party leaders have unfortunately indicated that good decisions are being issued from the top but are badly implemented below. This assignment of responsibility, to put it mildly, is untrue. [And] our forebears lived differently and gave cause to doubt their modesty.

"I know many party workers who were crossed out, and I'm sure that people did not cross them out personally, but their positions. I think

* The Central Committee launched an investigation of Boris Yeltsin for his obvious flouting of party discipline in several freewheeling speeches questioning the leadership's ability and willingness to carry out real reforms. After a public uproar, the investigation was quickly dropped, but not before Yeltsin's growing popularity had received yet another unintended boost.

nothing horrible has taken place. It's necessary to draw lessons, roll up one's sleeves, and go to the people." This was one view inside the local apparat; there were others.

"We elected philosophers," remarked Nikolai Gurzhii in disgust. "Romanov, Riabkov, they can deliver speeches, but what have they ever done? They are not people who have been solving problems day and night for years on end. Mikhail Lysenko does more for Magnitka than anyone else, yet he has no chance now of being elected.

"These are illusions. The public voted for professors, hoping against hope that 'bright' people could figure things out. All blame is laid on the reigning apparat: we do nothing; we live well. The open recommendation of the party has become a candidate's death sentence.

"The 'informals' are a bunch of noisemakers. They do nothing but talk, yet you read about them all the time in the newspaper. Journalists never come to talk to me. I know what is going on in the city, what the problems are, what is being done about them, who is at fault. What the journalists write is taken as absolute truth. They should not be as gods."

Gurzhii's comments were those of an embattled apparatchik, angry with the feeling of being hung out to dry. Makeev shared Gurzhii's sense of having been betrayed by the center, but in contrast Makeev hustled to make the best of the new situation. Of all the members of the Magnitogorsk apparat, none maintained a higher profile during the election campaign than Makeev, even when that meant having to answer embarrassing questions.

Whereas Gurzhii's closest associate (Lysenko) chose not to risk running in the face of a likely humiliating defeat, Makeev's confederate (Riabkov) became a candidate and won. And Gurzhii's bitter remarks notwithstanding, a viable candidate from high up in the party was dearly valued by some far-seeing individuals in the apparat.

•   ■   ■

When the Congress of People's Deputies opened on 25 May, there were high expectations. On the first day, before discussion, Mikhail Gorbachev was elected president (chairman) of the congress, in a defeat for the nascent "opposition" led by Andrei Sakharov, who had not opposed Gorbachev's candidacy but who had demanded discussion *first*. But the discussion came soon enough, as the congress, billed as a means to get the stalled reform process moving again, turned into an extended talkathon.

One after the other delegates rose to reveal a mind-boggling state of disarray in every region of the country. A handful of speakers made shockingly frank remarks about the misrule of the Communist party and the "secret empire" of the KGB. Amid the sensational revelations and the flow of cathartic talk there were many calls for unity and a closing of the ranks. But with the entire two-week congress broadcast live on television and virtually the whole nation watching, the "liberals," although a minority unable to prevail in matters put to a vote, stole the show. Two weeks of the congress, coming on the heels of four years of *glasnost,* were enough to erase the effects of decades of state propaganda. If in a food queue in 1987 I heard all manner of frank complaints about the horrors of the Soviet system, in a similar line in 1989 I heard ordinary citizens asserting that nothing would ever improve until the country abandoned the one-party system.

None of the Magnitogorsk delegates spoke. Although Kucher and Romanov were signed up on the list, their turns never came. Romazan typically adopted a low profile, while Riabkov spent most of his time trying to get into the new 542-member Supreme Soviet, a quasi parliament, which was "elected" by and from the congress (he failed). Of the four, only Kucher felt intrigued enough to attend one of the open meetings of the (misnamed) Moscow Group (which later became the Interregional Group and then Democratic Russia), but he chose not to join forces with the liberals.

Before the congress the existence of political differences among the Magnitogorsk delegates went unnoticed. Not long into the session Kucher and Romanov clashed in private discussions so fiercely—over political differences!—that they were no longer on speaking terms. This previously unthinkable development inside the Magnitogorsk delegation, which mirrored the split in the national party between conservatives and centrist-liberals, went unmentioned in the detailed Magnitogorsk press coverage of the congress provided by Kucher. It would most likely remain muted until top-level Communists overcame their aversion to the appearance of disunity and allowed institutionalization of such a division at the top.

■   ■   ■

In Magnitogorsk 85 percent of more than four hundred households surveyed by the newspaper claimed to be dissatisfied with their material position. In another local poll also conducted in 1989, 80 percent of the sample expressed dissatisfaction with their housing. And yet hundreds of conversations during the election campaign demonstrated time and again that official corruption rather than living standards was by far the most explosive political issue.

Surprisingly, none of the candidates attempted to make serious political capital out of the deep popular disgust at apparat privileges (aside from one brief moment with Petrov on television). Nor did any of them seek to affix blame for the miserable living conditions. Instead the candidates competed with each other to show how seriously they were committed to giving the proper attention to the admittedly long-neglected social sphere. Most striking of all, despite the multiplicity of candidates there was essentially only one political program. Each candidate strove to represent *the* general interest, *the* common good, rather than the competing interests of certain groups. Even the possible conflict between the interests of Moscow and those of Magnitogorsk was downplayed in the campaigns of everyone but Kucher. And all seemed to take for granted that the general future direction of the country had already been pointed out: change led by the party.

Once Arzamastsev was screened out by the electors meeting, the elections in Magnitogorsk were conducted over who best would implement the reform program of the Communist party. But the election campaign had the unintended consequence of making that program appear less and less sustainable. The Soviet political system itself was the overriding campaign issue, and it was losing. "Socialism is dead," quipped one middle-level manager in the midst of the Magnitogorsk election campaign. "Long live socialism!"

The campaign in Magnitogorsk had been extraordinarily lively, and, not surprisingly, the local party machine had played an extremely active role. Petrov was backed by the wire factory, which fell within the Lenin district. Even though the district party committee devoted itself to Riabkov, the wire factory had both the size and the clout of a district party committee. Andreeva had the support of the party committee in the Ordzhonikidze district, where the hospital was located, although the committee's efforts on her behalf appeared less than vigorous. Romanov was backed by the right-bank party committee, which had jurisdiction over the Teachers College.

One has to wonder how it came about that precisely these candidates and not others were nominated. All working collectives had the right of nomination, yet far from seeing a proliferation of candidates there were only eight (before the electors meeting reduced the field to three). Of the eight, the candidates whose nominations were publicly announced earliest were the three who eventually were put on the ballot.

Conveniently, each of the three candidates was from a different district of the city; and one was a woman and another a worker. It was also helpful that the two most powerful political figures in the city, Romazan and Kucher, were "taken care of" by having been nominated through social organizations. Interestingly, at the summer 1988 plenum of the city party committee, held just prior to the Moscow special party conference, three and only three people were promoted from candidate to full membership on the city party committee: Anfisa Andreeva, Iurii Petrov, and Valentin Romanov. Coincidence? Possibly; more likely, these three party members were being singled out for a greater future role.

To become convinced that the apparat at the very least closely oversaw the nomination process it is necessary only to recall that "working collectives" are headed by party and trade union officials. Yet the suggestion of the apparat's strong involvement in the elections by no means implies an absence of conflict. In fact, the elections brought into the open the otherwise invisible tensions within the apparat, especially the competition among the lower level district committees as district secretaries sought to make names (and careers) for themselves and their allies. By fielding strong candidates in two races, the Lenin *raikom* was able to achieve a high profile. Similar ambitions by the wire factory party organization were less successful.

Although the city apparat clearly sought a low profile, there were moments when its heavy involvement behind the scenes came to the fore, such as when Arzamastsev was defeated at the electors meeting. And in the end Romanov's main sponsorship came not from the right-bank *raikom* but from the *gorkom*, as some political insiders acknowledged.

"What I can't figure out," remarked Evgenii Vernikov during our regular late night discussions in his apartment, "is what the apparat needs Romanov for." But in the course of the election it became clear that of the three candidates, Romanov's views were the most orthodox *and* the most stable. If Andreeva suggested at times that she was not opposed to a multiparty system and Petrov's evident pliability left that issue up in the air despite his pronouncements of the moment, there was no mistaking Romanov's uncompromising stance on the need for one-party rule.

Even without *gorkom* backing, Romanov would likely have won the election, given the high "negatives" of both Andreeva (a woman running a dilapidated hospital) and Petrov (a worker aristocrat in a town with a working-class electorate)—once these two were his only opponents. It is, of course, mere speculation whether the city committee set up Romanov to win. What is clear is that Romanov would not even have become a sanctioned candidate without the apparat's approval.

Ultimately, however, the dominant new political figure on the Magnitogorsk scene was clearly Vitalii Riabkov. Whereas Kucher could be classified as slightly left of center, Romanov and Romazan as right of center, and Arzamastsev as on the left (i.e., liberal), Riabkov was pure opportunism. Highly educated, articulate, and miraculously perceived to be untainted by close connection to power, Riabkov mastered the vocabulary of *perestroika* and the skills of public politics.

Precisely the "guilt by association" suffered by the old political leadership cleared the way for the eager Riabkov to rise on the wings of the equally ambitious Lenin district committee. If first secretary Lev Stobbe was acknowledged to be an "economic apparatchik" incapable of mastering the new politics, he was in any case stained by his deep involvement with the existing "system." City soviet chairman Mikhail Lysenko, although a self-styled and outspoken "man of the people," was nevertheless also seen as "marked."

And yet inside the apparat Romanov and Riabkov's victories were— with notable exceptions—viewed as victories, given the long odds for party candidates. Indeed, whereas the *obkom* suffered a serious blow when first secretary Shverev ran and lost, the apparat in Magnitogorsk did not suffer a ringing public defeat; better sensing the mood of the population, it chose not to run directly, but through a surrogate. Following the clear vote of no confidence against him, Shverev immediately fell under intense pressure from Moscow to resign his position (which he eventually did). But in Magnitogorsk, despite the antiparty tenor of the election, the local ruling clique was not damaged.

Nevertheless, the elections can be seen only as a temporary victory for the Magnitogorsk apparat. There will certainly be more multiple-candidate, secret-ballot elections, including those for the city soviet, with an electorate likely to reject anyone who smacks of being the apparat's candidate. In the choose-your-sobriquet atmosphere, rumblings could even be heard about the necessity of a Nuremberg trial for the party. Ultimately, the only unambiguous results of the elections, which were carried out against the astonishing deepening of *glasnost,* were to discredit the prevailing Soviet system of one-party rule and magnify the general disgust with all political authority.

Moreover, after the elections there was talk of removing the filter of

the electors meeting, meaning that the next time a figure such as Arzamastsev could well be able to put up a good fight for (nominal) local
power. Certainly his antiparty views had wide support, if only because
a vote for them offered a way to strike back at the formerly unassailable
bureaucrats. Of course, what Arzamastsev would do with the city soviet
should he vie for it and succeed was unclear; nor would his election have
been easy. Any change of the guard would more likely have brought
Riabkov into local office.

While the apparat struggled to remain in step with the rapidly moving times and the balance of power in the middle and upper layers of
the apparat was being reshuffled, resentment of Moscow and especially
of Gorbachev increased dramatically. Local party functionaries were
ever more wary of Moscow and ever less willing to push for reform,
although careful to protect themselves by keeping up appearances. True,
they had been compelled to seek out and promote local officials who
could speak the new language of reform while protecting the interests
of the entire apparat, and they were not entirely happy with who
emerged. But the alternative—the rise of an antiparty figure who might
set about trying to overturn everything—chastened them.

As for reform of the state administration, the original motive for the
election campaign, Magnitogorsk showed that however genuine the desire to distance the state system significantly from the party, such a sep-
aration meant little at the local level in the absence of a well-organized
opposition group able to offer the Communist party a strong challenge
for power. Indeed, with elections to city offices pending, Communist
functionaries in Magnitogorsk who previously ruled as if local soviets
did not exist began eyeing them aggressively even as the "parallel" party
administration backed by its command over enormous resources was
not being dismantled.

If the continued dominance of party machines constituted one obstacle to transferring "all power" to the soviets, the centrally controlled
economy constituted another. Making the soviets responsible for day-
to-day administration would amount to very little given the concentration of money and other resources in the industrial enterprises and the
tight central control over those enterprises exercised by the Moscow
ministries.

At long last severe central control was subjected to sharp public rebuke in the provinces, taking the form of an attack against Moscow's
"colonialism." Yet although the pressure for "decentralization" was
building in Magnitogorsk, local officials had as yet no legal basis for

such a move. And the views of the steel plant's director, Ivan Romazan, who although locally born and raised embraced the designation as the ministry's man in Magnitogorsk, seemed to preclude unsanctioned local action to force the center's hand. Until large-scale reform of economic administration was introduced by Moscow, the strenuous efforts of those in Magnitogorsk could lead to no more than periodic concessions from the ministry.

Moreover, wresting greater autonomy from the center would do little to effect the balance of power within Magnitogorsk. The preposterous imbalance in the relations between the steel plant and the city soviet would persist. There seemed no reason to assume that enterprises like the Magnitogorsk Works, really a miniministry unto itself, would be any more "people oriented" than the Moscow ministry had been. Not until some effective form of "municipalization" occurred would the city soviet be in a position to take advantage of any loosening in the ministry's grip—should that come to pass.

Decentralization might in theory have offered the possibility that localities could attend to their own needs, but in Magnitogorsk the ministry's authoritarian role could simply have fallen to the steel plant. More than that, a shift in the relations of power *within* any given region, however welcome, was not a cure-all; the Soviet leadership itself admitted that only a new economic system based on markets, competition, and private enterprise could begin to solve the country's problems.

As for the status of the Communist party, it was hard to know how long a rationale would persist for Kucher's middle position between Romanov's staunch advocacy of one-party rule and Arzamastsev's call for the dissolution of the Communist party and the advent of "political pluralism." In the meantime, it seemed likely that decentralization and municipalization would join ecology, health care, living standards, and social justice as volatile issues in the contentious battles over political office that in the new era of competitive elections would no doubt preoccupy Magnitogorsk.

CHAPTER SIX

A Stalin Mausoleum

The Past in the Present

It was, as the Russians say, no accident that in the historical novel *Children of the Arbat* (written in 1967, published in late 1987), one of the first literary works to come out of the drawer and see the light of day under *glasnost,* Anatolii Rybakov chose to sketch a portrait of the 1930s by contrasting developments in Moscow with those of a far-off five-year-plan construction site. Nor was it by chance that Rybakov modeled his fictional Stalin-era steel plant on Magnitogorsk.

Set in the period between September 1933 and December 1934, when the Leningrad party boss Sergei Kirov was assassinated under mysterious circumstances that point to Stalin's involvement, the novel revolves around the life of a young man, Sasha Pankratov, and his peers. Residents of the same apartment building in an exclusive central district of Moscow on a street called "the Arbat," the children come of age in the heady era of socialist construction, just before the onset of the great terror.

In a foreshadowing of the ominous Kirov murder, Sasha, an exemplary young man dedicated wholeheartedly to the country's grand crusade, falls under a cloud. Sasha's arrest and exile on concocted charges raise profound moral dilemmas for his companions, who are already preoccupied with the trials of growing up, falling in love, experiencing sex, going to school, and having anxiety about careers and the future. They know that Sasha is innocent, yet out of a sense of self-preservation and well-being, with one notable exception, they do not come to his aid.

Meanwhile, Mark Riazanov, Sasha's uncle, who is the director of the country's largest and best-known construction site, periodically visits Moscow on business, where he meets with various top leaders, including Stalin. Riazanov spends most of his time and energy battling not only the primitive conditions that threaten the success of the industrial venture, for which he knows he will answer with his life, but also the entangling web of political intrigue that complicates his every move.

Children of the Arbat, a richly evocative, multilayered, yet highly readable work, was a smashing success in Magnitogorsk. Despite the small number of copies that had been allocated for the city, it seemed that everyone had read it. For some, revelations about certain episodes in the history of Magnitogorsk came as an unwelcome shock. But for others the novel made concrete Gorbachev's calls for new historical inquiry and conferred the highest authority on the need to reexamine Magnitogorsk's past.

The definitive work on the history of Magnitogorsk, *The Flagman of the Fatherland's Industry: The History of the Magnitogorsk Metallurgical Complex,* co-authored by Ivan Galiguzov, professor and chairman of the department of the history of the party at the Magnitogorsk Mining Institute, and Mikhail Churilin, a journalist, appeared in 1978. The book's publication was timed to coincide with the city's fiftieth anniversary celebration for the following year. Yet the book is a history not of the city but of the factory. As such, it belongs to a genre of historical writing that defines Soviet reality by the construction and operation of heavy industrial plants.

In the book Magnitogorsk's history unfolds through a series of canonical affirmations: it was all Lenin's idea; everything that happened was begun on the initiative of the party; simple people, inspired by the party's summons, spared nothing in the struggle to do the impossible, which they did, in the process becoming heroes and inspiring others. Under the party's leadership no mistakes were possible, but enemies, including foreigners ostensibly there to help, worked to sabotage the proletariat's miracle. Fortunately, notwithstanding some serious incidents, overall success could not be denied; of course, certain negative phenomena associated with the cult of personality impaired the epic victory, but they did not fundamentally damage it.

To these tenets are added local details: the names of the youth who came from across the Soviet Union in the early 1930s to build a new world and become new people; the world record number of mixes performed by particular cement-pouring brigades in one shift, in freezing temperatures, without warm clothes, adequate food, and rest; the drama of the first hunk of metal to emerge from the new blast furnace, completed at breakneck speed against all odds.

The battle to shift to wartime production, a drama like the construction of the 1930s, occupies the center of the book. Galiguzov and Churilin become lyrical when describing the monumental victory over the barbarian fascist invaders, achieved at almost unimaginable cost. This moment, the greatest in the nation's history, would not have been possible, the authors suggest, without the steel plant, built together by the party and the Soviet people, who are united in their triumph.

For the postwar period, we are treated to a narrative of the continuation of labor enthusiasm, charted by a recitation of each production milestone (one hundred million tons, two hundred million, and so on). Biographies of worker-heroes, their achievements and their honors, often accompanied by photographs revealing a sport coat covered with medals, make up large sections of the chapters throughout the book.

Galiguzov and Churilin faithfully follow a formula so rigid that in the end, it seems they are left with little more than filling in the names of local heroes and saboteurs. As their history approaches the present, each new plan target assigned to the steel plant is fulfilled and overfilled; more and more worker-heroes, far-seeing leaders, and chests overladen with medals are depicted. Such a history foresees no possibilities for change other than ever-higher aggregates of production.

Historical works such as the one by Galiguzov and Churilin served as a tomb, encasing the past and closing off historical inquiry. But the narrative in the *The Flagman of the Fatherland's Industry* could not be dismissed as blatant falsehood. It formed part of the shared mythology that until recently pressed itself upon the consciousness of all but a handful of Magnitogorsk residents. More than that, it served as one of the principal sources of legitimacy for the unelected Soviet regime. To open up the past would mean calling into question fundamental beliefs and existing relations of power.

■　　■　　■

At sixty years of age, Magnitogorsk, which dated itself from 1929, was younger than Ivan Kokovikhim, one of the people who helped found it. Born in 1906 in the town of Viatka (now Kirov), the son of a baker, Kokovikhim came to Magnitogorsk in October 1929 and by the time I met him had lived there for fifty-eight years. When he arrived at the construction site he saw absolutely nothing except a few large white tents at the base of the hills where he would first live, enduring the severe winter cold. Soon he moved to a barracks: "Four walls made out of plywood and a big room with lots of cots. It wasn't much, but we were so pleased that we weren't in a tent anymore!"

Kokovikhim began as a construction worker, later becoming a foreman. He attended courses and in 1935 was graduated from the industrial trade school. He helped build many of the buildings still standing in Magnitogorsk, including the school in which his children were educated. He knew the specifications of the factory by heart. His parting words to me encapsulated his worldview: "We were victorious."

For people like Kokovikhim, the original settlers who built the factory and the city with their bare hands at incomprehensible sacrifice, history was a matter of heroism and victory, no more, no less. The October Revolution and Soviet power were the steel plant itself. The revolution and heavy industry were merged, the war cementing them forever. Such was their oral history, a tradition vigorously promoted by publications, lectures, awards, and holiday commemorations. For all their one-sidedness, the stories of these "veterans" were accorded tremendous respect by people of all generations and political viewpoints.

There was, of course, a different oral history, a history kept back by fear (until recently). For the most part this tradition survived around the kitchen table or in the privacy of individual minds, such as that of Nina Kondratkovskaia. Born in a village in the Ukraine in 1913, the daughter of gentry, Kondratkovskaia made her way to Magnitogorsk in 1934 and has been living there ever since. Known fondly as "Baba Nina," for almost thirty years she has directed a literary association in Magnitogorsk, providing a group of young writers who had gathered around her with guidance and official sanction. In 1987 I attended meetings of the Magnitogorsk literary association and subsequently met with Baba Nina in her apartment. Although not above nostalgia, she demonstrated an excellent memory, a lively mind, and a love for conversation.

"In the 1930s," she explained, "there were ten local members of the Writer's Union; today there are two (both are older than sixty). Back then the elite was cultured, and people strove with all their hearts to emulate them. Our leaders lent material and moral support to the de-

velopment of high culture. The theater was an absolutely sacred place."
She was the single most important living source in the city for all kinds
of information on life in the 1930s, ranging from the songs that were
sung in the barracks to the terror. Above all, she was courageous and
forthright in expressing what she knew—to a small, dedicated circle.

When asked if she would ever write about that period, she shot back,
"It is complicated, so complicated." Despite her sadness about the
events of those years, her words expressed a frequently encountered ambivalence. "Now all we hear is 'crimes, crimes,'" she continued, "but
this is also one-sided. What was Stalin's position? What were his
choices? I am not at all in agreement with those who justify his actions
completely, but we must consider the international context and the atmosphere in our country. Back then, we didn't know from which direction war would come, from the east or from the west, but we knew it
was coming. The country needed metal. We had to build. And yet there
were so many injustices."

■ ■ ■

Such was the state of self-understanding in Magnitogorsk as the city
entered the Gorbachev era: a formulaic, written fairy tale reinforced by
a corresponding oral tradition, on the one hand, and, on the other, elements of an unofficial oral history, spoken in private, based on the memories of a diminishing group of aging individuals with varying critical
faculties and degrees of civic courage. But two factors complicated the
picture and in their own way challenged the fantastic official story: the
survival of large numbers of peasant exiles deported to Magnitogorsk in
the 1930s and the return after 1956 of some of those who were arrested
and disappeared during the great terror of the late 1930s.

At the beginning of the 1930s about forty thousand peasants accused
of being "kulaks" had their property confiscated and were "sentenced"
to permanent exile with forced labor in remote regions; these peasants
were transported to Magnitogorsk in boxcars. It was one of the many
paradoxes of the Stalin era that Magnitogorsk, the most widely heralded
site of the new world under construction, could also be a place of exile
and thus in part an island of the Gulag archipelago.

During the first winter, when they were living in tents, as many as 10
percent of the exiled peasants died. During a time when hardship was
the rule for virtually everyone, they suffered additional deprivations of
food and warm clothing. Under police surveillance, they were confined

to an area on the outskirts of town known as the "special labor settlement." They performed much of the most difficult manual labor.

In 1936 the peasant exiles, who constituted about one-fifth of the local population, had their "citizenship" ceremoniously restored under the Stalin constitution of that year. They no longer lived or worked under armed guard, but few were granted internal passports, which after 1932 were required for travel within the country. So they stayed. Today, the odds of meeting either the children of dekulakized peasants or even the dekulakized themselves are still high. I met quite a number, including some who were enjoying professional careers. Although at one time the stigma placed upon them was strongly felt, they were gradually assimilated into Magnitogorsk life.

They or their parents had taken part in the "great socialist construction," they had helped build the blast furnaces and rolling mills of Magnitogorsk, and later they had worked in them. Many fought in the war. They pulled their weight, made their contributions, earned awards for heroism. Many long ago moved out of the barracks of the special labor settlement and into the city proper. The rest moved en masse from barracks into apartment buildings in the late 1960s and early 1970s. They were among the last to leave the barracks.

In conversation they often questioned the methods and execution of the dekulakization policy, pointing out, for example, that many exiled peasants had by no means been rich and that the process had been brutal. Some even went so far as to question the policy as such, but no one questioned the policy of forced industrialization, let alone the legitimacy of Soviet power. If they blamed anyone for their fate, it was "local blockhead leaders," who had not understood Soviet policy and had carried it out stupidly. Sometimes resentment could still be detected, but for the most part the deeply felt bitterness of the 1930s had subsided. The dekulakized had made their peace with Soviet power. Nevertheless, they stood as living testimony to the "errors" and "injustices" of Stalin's reign, even if as late as 1987, *glasnost* notwithstanding, their story remained to be publicly told.

The terror of 1937–38 hit Magnitogorsk like a cyclone: midnight arrests, torture, hysterical informing, venomous secret and public denunciations, suicides, disappearances without trace, executions. Such things occurred both before and especially after 1937–38, but that the terror in those two years decimated the regime's own elite distinguished the episode in the popular imagination.

Virtually no one in a position of responsibility escaped arrest, although some were later released. Most of the city's leading cultural figures disappeared. Every top-level party figure or factory executive who had ever worked in the city, with one exception, was shot, if he or she had not already committed suicide. The police themselves, those who zealously carried out the terror, were eventually arrested and shot. Few, if anyone, understood what was going on. The episode remains largely mysterious to this day.

Under Khrushchev millions of people were released from camps. The group of people who returned to Magnitogorsk after surviving long terms in the camps was small but important, as most of them had been prominent citizens and soon became so again. The best-known returnee was Boris Ruchov. A published poet and a popular figure in the city, Ruchov was arrested and vanished without trace in 1937. He was not heard from for twenty years. Some of that time he spent in the camps of the infamous Kolyma in the extreme northeast of the Soviet Union. In 1956, after the Twentieth Party Congress, he was "rehabilitated" and permitted to return to his hometown. Resuming his activities as a poet, Ruchov published several collections of his works, many devoted to the heroic days of the 1930s. After his death, his apartment became a museum dedicated to his life and work.

Not only did such former *zeks* (camp prisoners) as Ruchov return to active lives in the city; many actually discussed their camp experiences, especially during the Khrushchev years. After Khrushchev's fall and Brezhnev's consolidation of power, however, the camps once again became a matter best handled by silence. As more and more of the returnees passed away, their impact lessened. Very few were still alive in 1989.

During a guided tour of the Ruchov museum in 1987, Ruchov's repression, as it was called, was not concealed, although the young guide, Lidia Lapteva, did hesitate and ask my chaperone if it was appropriate to discuss. In any case, on the wall hung a poem Ruchov had written down on a scrap of paper while in the camps, one of the ways he had kept himself alive, according to the guide. Among the visitors to the museum were groups of schoolchildren.

Although the Ruchov museum was impressive, in itself it was an infinitesimally small reminder of the colossal repressions that had occurred; nor did it give any indication of their magnitude. And Ruchov was an exception: he *survived* and returned, enjoying a new life. There was no memorial for the multitudes who died in the camps. As for Ruchov himself, according to Nina Kondratkovskaia, "after he returned from the camps he completely justified Stalin. 'What were Stalin's options?' Ruchov used to say. 'We needed the gold of the north, but who would go there voluntarily? Someone had to be sent for it. Stalin did what he had to do.' "

.   ■   .

In the Soviet Union ideas have played a fundamental role—not only particular ideas as such but the very fact that one had to have ideas, that all political policies and programs had to be explained in terms of Marxism-Leninism. Even when violating Marxism-Leninism, a Soviet politician had to explain why the violation was needed and argue that, in essence, the violation was not fundamental. The debate in the press and on television over Soviet history—centered on the era of the 1920s or the so-called NEP and its contrast with the subsequent rule of Stalin—far from being an academic exercise, involved a search for alternatives within the framework of the Leninist revolution relevant to the present-day battles for economic and political reform. De-Stalinization involved much more than rewriting history textbooks.

To defend the status quo—the centralized planned economy, for example, or, more selfishly, the elaborate system of privileges—"conservatives" had to defend the Stalinist legacy wholesale, given the interconnectedness of the system's mutually reinforcing constituent parts. Conversely, those attempting to introduce reforms had to challenge the Stalinist past. Reformers had to show that the Stalinist legacy was not a given, not the result of some sort of natural law of socialism, that it came into being, had a history, and therefore could be undone. Reform politicians had a stake in controlling the inquiries into and revelations about the Stalinist past, for there was always a danger that the revelations could reach back further than Stalin to the roots of the socialist system. No matter how dogmatic and uninspiring the content of official history has been, history remained an effective political tool, although an explosive one.

To delegitimize existing political institutions in order to clear the way for new ones, the reformers posited an alternative model of socialism, a path of development that, although not taken, nevertheless could and should have been taken, as Lenin supposedly advised. First, however, reformers had to undermine the lingering popularity of Stalin and the epoch he represented. In their campaign for de-Stalinization, the reformers tried to perform an exorcism of the Stalin demon and a purification of the Leninist revolution.

In Magnitogorsk public opinion polls on the Stalin question were not conducted. But the appearance in 1987 of the much-discussed film by Tengiz Abuladze, *Repentance,* offered a unique if limited substitute. A deeply allegorical portrayal of Stalinism, the film revolves around the deeds of a local dictator, Varlam, and the conflict after his death of whether to confront or to hide his actions, a struggle encapsulated by the trial of a woman who has repeatedly exhumed Varlam's body as a statement of her refusal to let his crimes be buried.

Powerful scenes recall episodes in the terror of the late 1930s, such as long lines of women begging officials in vain for information about arrested husbands or the rounding up of an entire village as enemies of the people. Employing overt Christian symbolism, the film takes a strong moral stance against those responsible for the crimes of the Stalin era and their attempts to ignore or whitewash their past behavior.

In Magnitogorsk a significant segment of the audience was clearly unable to understand the highly allegorical portrayal of Soviet history. There was a great deal of puzzled chatter, such as, "Huh? What? What is going on? Do you understand what is happening? What is this?" To the extent that the film was understood—as an attack on Stalin—it was not popular. Some people walked out of the movie house well before the film had ended. Indeed, in less than a month after the film opened in Magnitogorsk, the number of daily showings was reduced by half. Through the middle of 1987, de-Stalinization in Magnitogorsk was slow in taking hold.

■   ■   ■

Not long after Abuladze's film began playing in Magnitogorsk, Rybakov's novel was serialized and produced a ground swell of historical inquisitiveness in the city. This revival of historical memory at first had little to do with the Stalin question, basing itself instead on a kind of antiquarianism.

Much of historic Magnitogorsk, a city of barracks, tents, and mud huts, simply disappeared over the years. Many fine old structures did survive, but they had been neglected. The city tourist bureau led the way in retrieving old street names and forgotten historical sites, from dilapidated buildings such as the original sound cinema, which had become an industrial workshop, to the city's first park, whose once vibrant attractions were rusted and overgrown with weeds.

After decades of wanton neglect there was talk of restoring historic structures. Plans were also afoot to reconstruct one of the 1930s barracks as a museum. (City financial experts remained skeptical.) In the meantime, there was much to be done just to take an accounting. Moreover, with the newspaper's assistance the newly activist tourist bureau rekindled an interest among the broader population through a project to reprint old clippings. Readers were astonished to read verbatim sixty-year-old articles about problems with the supply of soap or discussions of the amount of butter that could be obtained for one's monthly ration coupons.

Thus, as the old historical orthodoxy was being battered from the top, a broad-based historical curiosity was spreading, inducing a search for material. In conjunction with preparations for Magnitogorsk's six-tieth anniversary celebration scheduled for June 1989, a group of people decided to take another look at some films made a while back using historical footage. But at a screening of the films—*Blast Furnace Men, Build Magnitostroi,* and *The Steel Heart of the Country*—almost everyone felt ashamed by what he or she saw. The naive glorification of production, the fawning portrayal of a group of "prominent" workers, the simplistic notions of progress—Magnitogorsk life was reduced to quantities of metal smelted ahead of production deadlines through a series of heroic acts.

One way out of such a bind was to create new material, and some would-be historians discovered forgotten individuals. In the process, they followed the time-honored practice of consecrating a hero by means of a museum. Although the content might have changed, the form and goals remained essentially the same.

Liudmila Volnistova (1912–42) came to Magnitogorsk in 1931, a nineteen-year-old enthusiast. At first she worked on the construction of the central energy station, whose early completion was thought crucial to the further progress of the steel plant's construction. She was provided the opportunity in the mid-1930s to study at the Moscow Energy Institute, returning to Magnitogorsk upon completion, in 1938, a certified engineer. When the war came Liudmila went to the front, eventually ending up with a group of partisans in the occupied Ukraine. In December 1942 Liudmila, whose underground nom de guerre was Natasha, was captured near Gomilev. She was presumed shot by the Gestapo. A museum dedicated to Liudmila's memory was opened on 3 October 1988, the seventy-sixth anniversary of her birth, at a Magnitogorsk school by a teacher, Liudmila Abdullina, who had spent many years assembling materials entirely on her own initiative.

For the museum Abdullina put together a selection of the ores of

Magnetic Mountain and some of the belongings of original settlers: a pair of homemade bast sandals, a samovar, a phonograph, some brushes, an iron—artifacts that seemed reminiscent less of the 1930s than of the seventeenth century. Also on display were several dozen rusting cans, made from Magnitogorsk metal and donated by the steel plant, whose labels revealed food products no one in Magnitogorsk had ever seen. They were a big hit. A few photographs, letters by and to Liudmila, and the testimony of those who knew her formed the centerpiece of the exhibit.

Abdullina searched throughout the USSR for people who worked with Liudmila on the Magnitogorsk energy station in the 1930s. "In the process, I discovered other people who are worthy of such an exhibit," she said. "Museums are an important part of the educational experience. We can use them to teach children history, to cultivate an interest in the past, in the lives of individuals who gave of themselves and whose sacrifices and labor can inspire us today."

■   ■   ■

A massive nationwide frontal assault on Stalin was launched during the preparations for the special Nineteenth Party Conference called for July 1988 in Moscow. In a preconference interview with the newspaper, Vitalii Riabkov, a Magnitogorsk delegate, hit upon one of the main themes eventually sounded at the gathering: "I consider a regime in which a person is punished not even for his political views but for his scientific convictions to be the most reactionary regime. This is darkness; it is frightening."

A year earlier Riabkov had treated my attempts to document the Stalinist past of Magnitogorsk as defamatory and unwelcome. Now he led the way. "As a child of the Stalin times," he was quoted as saying, "I consider myself deeply deceived. We lived life among the people who built socialism, and Stalin and his deeds were hidden from us by an impenetrable dark curtain." In such language was individual responsibility deflected and a sweeping explanation for present ills asserted.

That same summer the city newspaper took up the de-Stalinization drive and organized a public discussion on Stalinism and its victims. A huge crowd attended, and more than fifty years of silence were shattered in an emotional outpouring that lasted well into the night. By August a local committee on the victims of Stalinism had been founded "to make public the names of rehabilitated people and when possible to tell the stories of them on the pages of the newspaper." Given space at the offices of the newspaper, the committee announced a weekly reception to which former victims, their relatives, and friends began to come. A savings account was opened for donations to a memorial "to the victims of the Stalinist repressions."

The Stalin theme began to dominate the pages of the newspaper. Viktor Shraiman, relieved that Brezhnevism was over, wrote that he remained far from euphoric about *perestroika* because he thought it would take several generations "to conquer the slave within us, to root out Stalinist thinking from our souls and minds. . . . Stalin will be in our memories a long time! In truth, 'the dead have seized hold of the living.' Thirty-five years he has not been with us, but the system lives on." Shraiman's was a common, but by no means universal, view.

"How much abuse is possible!" another letter writer complained. "Stalin was bad; Brezhnev was awful. Yet we lived until 1985, and we were happy. We had everything: condensed milk, cream, powdered milk, various candies, ice cream, oranges, tangerines, all sorts of sausages. And no one goaded us into cooperatives. We were led by party people of the 1930s. They were utterly dedicated to the party." Exposing precisely this way of thinking was the goal of the campaign, but could the newspaper be sure this was the only message getting through? "Can it be," asked A. Smirnov, a "veteran" of war and labor, "that someone still doesn't see that in speaking ill of Stalin, Khrushchev, and Brezhnev, we do not compromise them (they couldn't care less!); we compromise the entire history of the Soviet state and of the party?" Smirnov's question went unanswered.

Most people who wrote letters had suffered or members of their families had been arrested; these letter writers seemed less concerned about the political implications of the campaign than about the chance to come forward and have their stories heard. For example, A. Chechulina's husband was arrested, and then she was arrested while pregnant. Their child was born in a labor camp and died there of starvation. "I was so afraid of everything," she wrote, "that for a long time I concealed who my husband was. Only now—thanks to our government—have I been given the chance to look people in the eye." An editor's comment was appended, assuring readers that "these are her words."

But as important as finally being heard was for former victims, much more was at stake. "For decades," wrote a woman whose brother and father were both arrested and exiled, "people have been exhausted by the thirst for the truth. Truth is essential, like air, no matter how bitter. In setting straight our past we will be able to build our future without mistakes and crimes. . . . The denunciators and provocateurs are still alive, having destroyed many innocent people. . . . Here are the real 'enemies of the people.' " Such sentiments were echoed by others. "I agree with those who say that it is necessary to name the guilty for the repressions in our city," wrote I. Drapeko. "There are people who call themselves veterans, who take advantage of various privileges. They do not deserve them."

Not all communications on the Stalin theme, either for or against, were vindictive. A letter to the Magnitogorsk city newspaper from Zina Cherkasova was full of grief yet without accusation. She sought comfort in public recognition for those who suffered rather than vengeance for those who profited.

"In 1932 my father, an unassuming middle peasant, was excluded from the collective farm," she wrote. "We were kicked out of our house (true, by that time, my two older brothers and sister had their own families). Father without our family was exiled for five years, first to Cheliabinsk for the construction of the tractor plant and then to Tavda in the [neighboring] Sverdlovsk region, where he worked as a hauler at the logging plant. Our family was permitted to join him there.

"[At Tavda] living conditions were horrible: five or six families in a room, without any sort of dividers; famine claimed the lives of many of the prisoners. In July 1933, from strenuous work and hunger, father died. In August 1933 my mother and I, together with two of my brothers, went to Magnitka where my older brother Dmitrii lived. He was a worker at the ore agglomeration plant on the mine. In March 1934 Dmitrii died on the job as a result of an industrial accident. He was thirty-two years old.

"Dmitrii was buried in the original cemetery of what had been the Old Magnitka settlement. On that spot today stand high-rise apartment buildings. My younger brother, Anatolii, after completing the workers technical school in 1934, worked as an electric welder in the blast furnace shop. In 1937, unexpectedly and without the slightest reason, he was arrested. Twenty years old.

"Mama was devastated with grief. When she finally got hold of herself, she went to the gates of the prison, where there gathered an enormous crowd of people, mothers burdened with grief, fathers, wives desperately hoping to find out something, anything about their loved ones. No one ever said a word to them, but they stood and they stood, hours, days, months.

"Only much later, after 1956, did mama learn that Dmitrii had been sentenced 27 October 1937 to ten years without the right of correspondence, that as a result of an investigation nineteen years later his criminality had been removed, and that he had died 25 December 1946 of pneumonia. On the letter, in the space for place of death, there was a blank.

"Nor did the Patriotic War fail to touch our family. Three brothers of mine were drafted into the army. Two were at the front—one of whom, Peter, a lieutenant, disappeared without a trace near Rzhev in November 1942. He was thirty years old. The other returned from the front an invalid in 1943. My third brother, owing to medical reasons (he had a heart condition), was mobilized in June 1941 into the labor army. In 1945 at the age of thirty-one he died while still in the labor army in the rear.

"Such were the costs, the loss of sons that mama had to endure. All of this occurred in my lifetime. To this day I am unable to remember my cherished parents and brothers without tears. The idea of creating a memorial in honor of all those who suffered unjustly as a result of the Stalinist repressions I enthusiastically support. I'm ready to lend my hand in its creation. I also consider it necessary to establish a memorial for those who did not return from the war. These and the others—by name."

For Zina the past was more than just the record of an evil leader's crimes compiled for opportunistic condemnation in the political machinations of the present or a long-awaited chance to turn the tables and denounce collaborators. Even as it demonstrated the shuddering depth of the tyrant's impact, Zina Cherkasova's family history, a merciless succession of calamities deeply felt and somehow endured, extended beyond an indictment of Stalin's tyranny. Notwithstanding the magnitude of tragedy, the Cherkasov family's experience was not exceptional, even if Zina's narrative of it was.

■   ■   ■

The day celebrated in the Soviet Union as the end of World War II, 9 May, offered an impressive spectacle in Magnitogorsk. Half the city could be seen visiting the cemetery, laying wreaths, saying prayers, and remembering dear ones who died in the fight against the German invaders; the other half, people said, paid its respects during the days before the calendar commemoration of the country's estimated twenty million war dead.

On Victory Day in 1989 people rose early. A narrow artery leading to the distant cemetery was overflowing with family and kin, many on foot, most carrying flowers. At gravesides tears were neither spared nor concealed. Spasms of grief punctuated the cold morning air. It was a rare family without someone to call on this memorial day.

Speeches were made by various city and party officials. Familiar slogans—"No One's Forgotten; Nothing's Forgotten"—could be seen on banners and signs. But on this day, there was no abyss between rulers and ruled, no rancor. No one contested the point when one official making a speech singled out the party's role in guiding the country to victory.

"Today is a sacred day," Evgenii Vernikov whispered, as we surveyed the mix of grandmothers covered in shawls, grammar school students proudly attired in dresses and jackets, steelworkers decked out in their "Sunday best," and KGB officers in their soft blue dress uniforms with gold trim and immaculate white gloves.

Veterans of the war were accorded pride of place. This day, as every day, medals adorned their suits. Although each year fewer and fewer veterans of the Great Patriotic War remained to be honored, their ranks had lately been swelled by their grandsons, veterans of another war, Afghanistan. For most of the decade-long war there, people in Magnitogorsk did not really hear much. And what they heard never suggested that a real war was going on. But sons returned, some in coffins, others in wheelchairs.

Afghans, as these soldiers were called, took a prominent place in the procession, marching in camouflage fatigues. To see them, their walk, their manner, was to recognize unmistakably that they were a special breed. At first, when the war went unacknowledged, the graves of soldiers killed in Afghanistan could not mention where or how they died. Now officials have promised that gravestones would be changed, the indignity remedied. But the hurt lingered.

Veterans of the Afghanistan war were supposed to be served in stores without waiting in queues. Sometimes, however, they were ridiculed. "No way," shouted one shopper, shoving a veteran of Afghanistan aside, according to a report in the newspaper. "Look at this trooper, still wet under the nose and moving forward in line like a veteran."

The men confided that they could not become acclimated to being home. "The bizarrely calm, inanely quiet streets, the absence of engagement, the pretense and pomposity—it all seems incomprehensible, senseless," one said, as the others nodded in vigorous agreement. They stuck together. Many sought involvement in social causes.

At the tomb of the unknown soldier on Victory Day, one Afghan made a short speech, far sharper than those of the other speakers, be it apparatchik or veteran. The war there was condemned in no uncertain terms; responsibility for the folly was assigned without equivocation to the government. Fallen comrades were recalled by name. That participants from World War II were known as veterans while their countrymen who fought in Afghanistan were called Afghans underscored the contrast in the men, their experiences, and the way they and their efforts were perceived. This was Victory Day, but in Afghanistan there was no victory.

■   ■   ■

No more than a handful of professional historians in Magnitogorsk have studied the city's history. The author of the greatest number of works on Magnitogorsk, the original settler Valentin Serzhantov, resided in seclusion in Cheliabinsk. He was said to have been among those who signed denunciations of Boris Ruchov. Like Serzhantov, most other Magnitogorsk historians obtained their degrees under Stalin; all published the bulk of their work under Brezhnev. Acutely aware of the political constraints and resulting low prestige attached to Magnitogorsk history, almost no one chose to follow in their footsteps.

Given the sorry state of the professional historical guild in Magnitogorsk and the political role that revelations about the past played in the battles for reform, it came as no surprise that the revival of historical memory in the city was led by journalists. Journalistic treatments of Magnitogorsk history took the form of attempts to fill "blank spots," what George Orwell called "memory holes," in the city's past. One of the most dramatic blank spots involved the death of a former local party boss, Beso Lominadze.

In August 1933 Lominadze, once the first secretary of the Communist party of Soviet Georgia and a high official in the Communist International, was demoted to first secretary of the Magnitogorsk city party committee. On 18 January 1935, seventeen months after arriving in Magnitogorsk and just six weeks after the Kirov assassination, Lominadze shot himself. He died the next day. Most of his associates were removed, and a number of those removed were arrested. Denounced as a traitor, Lominadze was soon expunged from the history books.

Under Brezhnev, Lominadze became a person again. A short biographical sketch appeared in 1974 in the *Great Soviet Encyclopedia,* and five years later favorable recollections of him were published in the Magnitogorsk newspaper. Nevertheless, neither the encyclopedia article nor the crafted reminiscences of "the dedicated and faithful party man" said anything about the circumstances of his death. In the absence of reliable information, various rumors continued to make the rounds.

Purporting once and for all to unlock the mysteries of the man and his fate, Elena Karelina wrote several long articles based on the testimony of Lominadze's surviving son, Sergei, who lives in Moscow and who claimed that, although there was indeed a suicide attempt, Lominadze's death was a murder. Sergei narrated: "I was eight years old at the time, and I remember that day very well.

"Even now I can see the white, chalklike face of the driver in the doorway, when he brought my father. When they led him into the house he was fully conscious. He even joked, 'What a woman's shot!'

"Just before that there was a holiday atmosphere. A bright light, the glitter of goblets on the table, Chinese billiards, my father's friends, my smiling mother. At home there were always lots of people, drawn to my father, a highly original mind, a very lively person. Then suddenly there was a knock at the door. The bright light was extinguished; the voices subsided. All that could be heard was mother shouting, 'But he's alive?! Alive?!'

"My father was not carried but led, held up under the arms, and placed on the couch. I overheard that he was wounded and pictured to myself a wound, blood, but when they removed his shirt, it turned out to be a little red speck under his left nipple.

" 'And why is he here?' asked my father, pointing to me. 'Let him go to sleep.'

"What happened was something that occurs once in a hundred years. The human heart contracts (systole) and expands (diastole). At the moment of the shot, his heart contracted, and the bullet went right through.

"All night there was contact with Moscow. On the direct line Ordzhonikidze was called. He categorically forbade that anyone be allowed to come near my father. He promised to send expert doctors by morning. But in the early hours the chief of the NKVD, Iagoda, intervened in the conversation and began to insist on an operation. Mother assured that my father felt fine. Iagoda contended that he was losing blood. 'But it's not blood,' argued my mother. 'I gave him some Georgian red wine on the road. It's wine.' But what needed to be done was clearer to Iagoda in Moscow. The operation was being conducted not by doctors but by the NKVD.

"In the morning my father, on his own legs, entered the operating room. After receiving anesthesia he never awoke.

"Many years later, a doctor present at the 'operation' met my mother in the camps and told her that my father was administered a large dose of anesthesia. My mother died convinced that father was put under.

"And another meeting. It was in 1951, in a camp outside Igarka; I had already finished serving my sentence but didn't know where to go, having neither money nor a trade nor an apartment, and I was employed as a senior detail clerk at a camp station. Once a little man with feverish eyelids sat next to me at lunch and inquired, Wasn't I the son of the Lominadze who had been first secretary in Magnitogorsk? I nodded; the man looked me over thoroughly and quickly departed. Through friends I ascertained who he was. 'Gruzdev,' they had told me.

"After father's death mother often repeated this name. And I remember well those red, sore eyes. Gruzdev was the chief of the city NKVD, and I saw him in our house that night.

"We rebuke writers for overly intricate plots, but life concocts such plots as we can't dream. And I often reflect on that; indeed, camp life is larded with such 'chance happenings.' But, probably, things are not merely chance. Life simply reminds us over and over that everyone in the world is connected, that everyone is responsible for his or her own actions, and that nothing secret does not in the end become clear.

"The last days father was often home. This was unusual: father home during the day. In his nightshirt. As my mother told me, he had written a letter to Stalin and was awaiting an answer. He sat at the radio when they were transmitting the report of the Kirov murder case. My father knew him well. They had worked together in what was a very difficult time for our country—Kirov in Astrakhan and father in the Baku underground. Later I was able to read the account of the [Kirov murder] trial and learned that there were accusations against my father.

"Soon they summoned him to Cheliabinsk. My mother told me that the first secretary of the *obkom*, Ryndyn, had telephoned. Ryndyn usually treated father with great piety. But this time he spoke very rudely, literally shouted at him. Father understood everything and was shaken." Here the testimony, a mishmash of innuendo and hearsay, abruptly ended; no commentary was provided. But by publishing Sergei's problematic recollections and leaving them unchallenged, Karelina lent them authority.

Sergei strongly suggested but never directly stated that Lominadze was murdered. The only evidence for murder he offered was the secondhand testimony in the camps of a doctor. Moreover, the doctor told Sergei's mother, in Sergei's account, not that Beso had been murdered but that "they gave father a large dose of anesthesia." It was not re-marked whether such a dosage as Lominadze reportedly received was abnormal, only that it was large. That Lominadze could walk of his own accord into the operating room did not of course mean that he did not need an operation. That Gruzdev, the local NKVD chief and thus also a member of the city's ruling circle, had been in Lominadze's house that evening was to be expected. Nor is there anything so remarkable about the fact that Iagoda, head of state security, was fully informed of what happened. It is never easy to accept the suicide of someone close to oneself. In this case, there was the added complication that the whole family suffered at the hands of Stalin's regime.

Lominadze's wife, Nina Aleksandrovna Lominadze, née Kuvakina, was arrested in 1938. After serving her first sentence in the camps, she was given a new one. Sixteen years elapsed before she and her son were to meet again. Lominadze's older brother was shot as an English spy. Sergei's aunt on his mother's side, a singer at the Bol'shoi Theater who had taken in the parentless young boy, was herself "taken in." Sergei, too, was arrested "for counterrevolutionary terror and for trying to worm himself into the ranks of diplomats and in such a manner accom-plish demolition activity," just prior to his seventeenth birthday, appar-ently in 1944, one day after he had submitted an application for admis-sion into the newly opened department of international relations at Moscow University. He was released from the camps after Stalin's death. Could such a person be faulted for wanting to believe that Stalin, who murdered thousands of innocent and capable men and women, was also responsible for his father's death?

Karelina divulged that Lominadze shot himself "returning from Verkhne-Ural'sk," a small town about fifty kilometers north of Magni-togorsk, and not on the way to Cheliabinsk, as oral accounts claimed. But she did not discuss the summons to Cheliabinsk or the subsequent events up to the return trip from Verkhne-Ural'sk. This was important because the implication of Lominadze's having shot himself on the way to Cheliabinsk was that arrest awaited him there.

Karelina treated the issue of Lominadze's putative impending arrest only obliquely by reporting a meeting between Anastas Mikoian, an old friend of Beso Lominadze's, and Sergei Lominadze that took place after Sergei had been released from the camps. "It was good that Beso shot himself," Mikoian reportedly told Sergei. "Otherwise they would have tortured him." Yet contrary to Sergei's testimony, the implication here was that Mikoian—one of the highest ranking officials under Stalin and after—did not know that Lominadze had been murdered. Of course, Mikoian's ignorance did not in itself disprove the assertion that it might have been murder. And in any case, Mikoian might have known and simply not said anything. Or it might not have been murder at all. In the end, Karelina's attempt to set the record straight put forward less hard information and a less convincing scenario than did those given in memoirs of then highly placed foreigners. Furthermore, her desire to "rehabilitate" Lominadze's reputation resulted in an inaccurate portrait of the man and the meaning of his fate.

Lominadze, Karelina wrote, "belonged to that narrowest party stratum of the revolutionary intelligentsia that created the authority of the party in the eyes of the people. This party stratum of the intelligentsia, especially the Georgian, very much disliked the cobbler family's offspring, Koba Dzhugashvili." But as much as they might have disdained and ridiculed that uneducated commoner, better known as Joseph Stalin, old party loyalists like Lominadze were no match for him. More than that, their own actions in going along with Stalin and his policies contributed to their downfall. Beso Lominadze and others could not be seen as unfortunate victims. As even Sergei Lominadze admitted, "My father was a member of the Central Committee, which means that he, too, bears responsibility for everything that . . . took place."

■   ■   ■

Victory Day came on the heels of another state holiday, May Day. In 1989 no portraits of current Politburo members hung on the facade of the Mining Institute, as had been the case in 1987. In the crowd there were no portraits of anyone other than Lenin, and even those were few. Slogans spanned past and present, from "We Are for an Open Democratic Society" to "Thanks to the Party for a Happy Childhood."

A few banners for the first time crossed the line of acceptability, including two on ecology: "Hiroshima, Jewish Holocaust, Magnitocaust" and "Convert the Housing Settlement Adjacent to the Wire Factory to a Residence for the Ministry of Ferrous Metallurgy." These were anticipated by the authorities, who took no action.

The party, KGB, municipal, and managerial elite arrived together, laid flowers at the foot of Lenin's statue, and then assumed the place of

honor on the reviewing stand in front of Lenin. To each side were plat-
forms for the lower level functionaries, honored senior citizens and veterans, journalists, and one foreign guest (myself).

Floats accompanied the marchers, who were organized by city district; within each district, by enterprise; and within each enterprise, by
shop, as had been the case since the first local May Day parade in 1930.
Each district delegation was headed by its party secretary, who after
leading his forces past the reviewing stand walked over and climbed on.
Strict hierarchy was observed in the columns: after the first district secretary came the second, then the third; these were followed by delegations headed by the winner of "socialist competition" at the biggest district enterprise, the victor at the next largest, and so on.

It was difficult to judge precisely when May Day celebrations in Magnitogorsk began to lose touch with their original inspirations as International Workers' Day. In any case, in 1989 the parade lasted less than
two hours, by far the shortest ever. People on the reviewing stand commented on the thinness of the crowd. A young KGB officer adjacent to
the raised platform, standing at attention in dress uniform, recognized
me and, perhaps overcome with boredom, struck up an innocuous conversation while keeping his head facing straight ahead. Of all the groups
marching by, the only audible "hurrah" came from the visiting Polish
construction workers, who proudly displayed wide red and white banners with the word *Polska*.

Stobbe, first secretary of the city party committee, delivered a speech
composed of wooden phrases that, with the exception of half a dozen
words, could have been (and probably was) read ten or fifteen years
previously. It struck people not simply as old, stale, and uninspiring but,
above all, as false. The crowd dispersed; the elite posed for the annual
photograph; everyone soon went home to enjoy the day off, many wondering if there would be a parade next year and, if so, why.

■   ■   ■

Among those who, like Valentin Serzhantov, were important actors
in the Magnitogorsk of the 1930s and were still alive, was Rafael Fa-
deevich Shneiveis, who under the pen name N. Kartashov served as the
Magnitogorsk city newspaper's chief political correspondent during the
terror of 1937. He wrote several sharp pieces on supposed wrecking and
sabotage, pointing fingers and naming names. Unlike Serzhantov,
Shneiveis, who also lived in Cheliabinsk, welcomed the chance to meet
me.

Born in 1910 in a part of the old Jewish Pale of Settlement that later became Belorussia, Shneiveis, upon completion of the local seven-year school, went to the town of Smolensk and then on to Moscow in the 1920s. There he took a factory job and joined the Komsomol. As part of the big drive for industrialization, Shneiveis was "mobilized" to the construction site at Magnetic Mountain in the spring of 1931, arriving about the same time as tens of thousands of dispossessed peasant prisoners. In 1932 he was accepted into the party.

Shneiveis organized and became the first editor of the agitational newspaper *For Metal* (it continued as the newspaper of the steel plant and was called *Magnitogorsk Metal*). Along with a select group of favored youth, he studied at the fledgling Magnitogorsk Mining Institute. In 1933 the fast-rising "proletarian" Communist became a deputy editor of the *Magnitogorsk Worker,* a position he held until December 1937 when, after being graduated from the Mining Institute, he was sent to another steeltown, Kerch, to replace a top journalist who was arrested.

Shneiveis did not remain long in Kerch. In 1939 he was summoned to fight in the Finnish winter war and then in the Great Patriotic War against the Germans. Demobilized in 1946, he returned to Magnitogorsk, only to be posted by the *obkom* to Cheliabinsk to take up the post of deputy editor of the *obkom* newspaper, where he worked for the next twenty-five years, retiring in 1972. Since then he had published nine books, including four dealing in whole or part with Magnitogorsk. As an entry into the problem of individual responsibility, I asked about Lominadze.

"Lominadze," Shneiveis explained, "was a real party worker, not an office man or an apparatchik. He valued the newspaper, considered it vital, suggested articles, and followed what we wrote very closely but without commanding us. Lominadze spoke often among the people. He was always in view. A superb propagandist in the best sense of the word, he spoke with passion, with utmost concern for the needs of the people, whose interests he defended at every turn.

"We did not know the details of what he had done, of what he had been involved in, before he arrived. Nor were we, even as party members, privy to the inner workings of the party of Magnitogorsk. The city committee bureau decided against a solemn burial. His associates, including Bezbabichev, the editor of the newspaper, were arrested. We were all in shock until Rafael Khitarov, the new first secretary, arrived.

"They didn't explain anything to us. And the people understood nothing. I was twenty-five years old in 1935, struggling to become a professional journalist, studying at school. When in 1937 they arrested my closest friends—the poets Boris Ruchov and Mikhail Lugarin—I knew them very well and trusted them utterly.

"In my soul there was fear, alongside a secure belief in the righteousness of our overall goal. I could not believe they were guilty of spying and wrecking, but thought that because they were arrested, they were probably guilty of something. Think of us! We were so young. What could we know?

"The feeling of protest did not arise. We believed completely in Stalin, Voroshilov, Molotov. I was studying, learning, working at the newspaper. I had a young wife, a daughter who was just born to us. In fact, I was angry at my arrested friends. How could they have done what they did? How could they have made a move against Soviet power? Against the party?

"If your friends were arrested, to whom could you go to discuss and try to understand the events? True, party and Komsomol members, journalists—people we respected and trusted—were arrested. But in order to have really understood the situation, we would have had to have known the facts. If Lominadze was innocent, why did he shoot himself? It was difficult to figure things out, knowing only what we knew.

"I was not afraid. I knew I was not guilty. At a party meeting in December 1937, Pechenkin, the new editor of *For Metal*, [in my absence] accused me of being an enemy of the people, of being Lominadze's right-hand man. He was trying to save himself. But they wanted to know why, if I was an enemy, Pechenkin had allowed me to leave the city [for Kerch].

"Not fear, but pain. Something is happening, we felt. But remember the threat of war! We were engulfed by preparation for war. Even after the arrest of Marshalls Tukhachevskii and Bliukher, who for us were saints, we did not question the correctness of our path, the justness of our cause, the farsightedness of our leaders. For you, all of this is difficult to understand.

"Did anyone at the time undertsand? Maybe those who were older and more experienced. I was twenty-six! 'Build, build Magnitka'—this was what I knew. I had no political ripeness. A young man, dizzy times, a sacred goal in which I, we all, believed." His memory was crystal clear. He recalled events, places, names with great accuracy. He spoke of the prison laborers he knew, the injustices he saw, the hardships endured by all, although not by all equally.

"It is a big mistake to analyze the 1930s with what one currently knows. They were years of tremendous deception. They told us we had lots of rights; we had none. That we lived in a democratic country; our democracy was not real. We now know that Stalin did not simply make mistakes. He was purposefully evil; he acted maliciously.

"We were told and were convinced that we were building socialism. Now we see we haven't built it at all. But I want to emphasize that the people performed a miracle precisely because they deeply believed in tomorrow, in the task of the party. Today I remain very proud that I took part in the construction of Magnitka. Magnitogorsk is a monument to heroism, integrity, and glory.

"I am a Magnitogorskite. I am proud. I have nothing on my conscience. I am not guilty because my comrades died. My generation is guilty of nothing. Everything we could do, we did. When my grandson asks me, why didn't I resist, why didn't I feel it was wrong, I look at him with a smile. How can he understand? How could I as an editor have criticized Brezhnev in the newspaper? Why would I have wanted to?"

■   ■   ■

In addition to telling the story of the 1937–38 terror, the newspaper sought to fill in the memory hole surrounding the identity and fate of the peasants who were dispossessed and exiled to Magnitogorsk. "Special resettlers—what kind of people?" asked the newspaper in a long article in 1988. In answer, Iurii Bakker quoted testimony about the arrest and deportation of the Malykhin family.

"In the summer of 1931 we were holed up in the prison courtyard. There we found father. They fed us only cabbage soup and a piece of bread. We sat for a week under the open sky. It rained the whole time. . . . The convoy guards came at night. There was a loud boom: 'Everyone up!' . . . Everyone headed for the train station. As many as forty families were squeezed into a single freight car with barred windows. It was possible only to sit, not to lie down. For the necessities of nature there was a wooden bucket. For three days, while the train was under way, there was a heat wave. In the wagon it was stuffy. For a day and a half the door was not even opened.

"When they finally opened the door, we got clear soup and small chunks of horse meat. And again there was darkness, punctuated only by the ray of light through the bars. And again it was unbearably stuffy. Screams. And there was something to scream about. Mothers had children die in their arms.

"When we got to Magnitogorsk there was a cart by the tracks. We guessed—it wasn't for the living. From only the wagon in which we traveled, four little corpses were removed. More were carried out from other wagons. It's unknown where they are buried.

"We climbed. They put us up in canvas tents, six families to a large one, two to a small one. Each tent was numbered. The first months we all lived in that tent, and, of course, water penetrated the canvas. The ground underneath was frozen. People wrapped themselves in fur coats, animal skins, rags, whatever was brought from the village."

By late November 1931 they had moved into a barracks, which housed forty to fifty families. "At 6 A.M. they came to get us for work. The elder of the barracks, an employee of the NKVD, went around waking everyone up. We gathered at the headquarters building. Here they doled out the assignments. Who was sent to work on the blast furnace, who to the brick factory. Sometimes they took people directly to the site's labor power department. There people were directed. It was all difficult physical work—unloading coal, ore, and coke and digging foundation pits. Some worked in the smithy shop; others built barracks. To work and back we went with an armed guard. Our arrival back at the camp was registered."

Bakker's meaning was clear: not only was the city's history sullied by the use of prison laborers, but these "criminals" had not even been guilty of anything and had made what seemed to be a decisive contribution to the construction of the city. But all the monuments around Magnitogorsk were dedicated to the thousands of youthful idealists who supposedly built the city. Bakker's presentation required further clarification. Thus, if one goal of the inquiry into exiled peasants in Magnitogorsk had been to establish that these people ought not to have been stigmatized, another became to determine the extent of this prison labor and evaluate its precise role. These were issues that oral accounts, however moving, could not settle. Accordingly, V. Bakanov, a retired militia officer and amateur historian, was sent by the party's committee on history to investigate the archives in the provincial capital, Cheliabinsk. He published his findings in the Magnitogorsk newspaper.

On the basis of his research, Bakanov disclosed that there had been more than thirty thousand prisoners at the construction site in the 1930s. Such fantastic numbers, which elicited a barrage of letters, led to speculation on the question, as framed by the newspaper, "Who built Magnitka? Prisoners or enthusiasts?" Providing no data on the size of the Magnitogorsk work force in the 1930s with which to judge the number of prisoners, Bakanov blithely insisted that Magnitka was built by Komsomol enthusiasts. "It was," he wrote, "that boy or girl, called by his or her heart to build, every fourth or fifth Komsomol in the country. And those who didn't have a Komsomol card envied those who did." But the data themselves, later revised upward by Bakanov himself, argued for exactly the opposite conclusion.

Despite the apparent success of Bakanov's research in the party archives, the matter remained unresolved. That any modern city in only its sixtieth year of existence did not definitively know who had built it seemed to many people of Magnitogorsk extraordinary.

■   ■   ■

Accepting an invitation to meet with the full staff of the *Magnitogorsk Worker*, I could not help but notice that almost all the journalists present were old enough to have been employed before the advent of Gorbachev. How did they look back on their lives and actions?

"Today it is clear we could have and should have done more," admitted Elena Karelina. "Journalism is politics. We couldn't be free from that. Some consciously lied; others did what they had to do. This is our tragedy. It was not a question of some bureaucrat standing over us all the time. We simply did not have the information. The atmosphere itself hindered us; it did not encourage independent thought. We did not appreciate the full drama of our situation until later."

"Stagnation, stagnation—all one hears is stagnation," interjected Iurii Balabanov, correspondent for industrial affairs. "All those years at the steel plant Valerii Kucher and I fought for good things, for just causes. We fought with all our strength, and we brought good to many people." Others nodded their heads gently in agreement, yet no one seconded Balabanov's sincere, although perhaps untimely, remarks.

" 'What did you do before 1985?' " Vladimir Mozgovoi spoke out. "This currently popular question, modeled on those of our classic questionnaires ('Do you have relatives abroad?' 'Were you located during the war on enemy-occupied territory?'), usually arouses great laughter. I can't speak for everyone, but it is not entirely a humorous question." Later, in his apartment, Mozgovoi insisted on returning to the discussion.

"Today I'm thirty-five years old, the father of two children (twelve and ten). I grew up in a small Urals town, attended the Urals University in Sverdlovsk, and thirteen years ago began a career as a journalist in Magnitogorsk, rising from apprentice to columnist. Most of my classmates live in bigger cities; many have achieved high positions (some are already editors); some work for the central press.

"By Soviet standards, I'm middling: neither a country house nor a car; no VCR, no savings account. There are some books; the family is clothed and shod and relatively satisfied. I had good—that is, simple—parents, representatives of the middle level of the engineering and technical stratum, without brilliance but fully normal people. My grandmother, herself semiliterate, taught me how to read.

"I attended all the various stages of typical Soviet schools but did not become a dogmatist. The infamous 'short course' history of the Communist party did not serve as the essence of my grammar school or university education. I read *Ivan Denisovich*, the notebooks of Dovzhenko, *Master and Margarita*, and all the 'confessional prose' of [the journal] *Yunost* published in the 1960s, not to mention everything that was available from other channels (crumbs, by today's standards, but then it was not insignificant). My heart skipped a beat in 1968 [Czechoslovakia]. But in fact I really hadn't woken up (only one question, that of Stalin, was definitively settled).

"I lived without contemplation and sufficiently happily, enjoying the familiar joys of youth. I did well in school. There was no cause for conflict with the system. More precisely, I didn't think things through to the end, although I was far from embracing the guiding editorials, and not for a second did I believe in the rightness of the educated calf who pronounced judgment on the 'literary Vlasovite' [Solzhenitsyn].

"I entered university on the day of the opening of the Twenty-fourth Party Congress (1971) and was graduated on the day of the twenty-fifth (1976). Nothing really changed during those years, and in any case no change was promised. I was in line for a reporter's career.

"In Magnitogorsk I began in the news department, covering sports and more or less interesting events and people. Sports became in the years that followed the 'hunk of bread' that preserved me during Brezhnevism. Somehow, I sought to remain outside of 'big politics,' staying clear of page one (production) and two (party matters). I wrote about the 'unserious,' and as a result, during the so-called stagnation period, I wrote almost nothing of that kind. This was done instinctively.

"By the end of the 1970s I began consciously to make sure to preserve myself. Meanwhile, under the influence of various factors I became a different person. My profession pushed me in the direction

where 'my spirit could breathe as it desired.' I found folk song aficiona-
dos, songs of Okudzhava, Vysotskii, Galich, that formed a special world
of sincerity, truth, and right-side-up values.

"Then there was the Mining Institute's student philharmonia, dedicated to bringing culture to the dark masses. Also, the puppet theater
Buratino, a high example of civil and artistic courage. During the apex
of the stagnation they put on *The Dragon,* by Evgenii Shvartz, a
breakthrough that unmistakably, for us, broached the issue of the total-
itarian state and Brezhnev's misrule. A bolder play probably could not
have been found in the country at the time. Or such a play might have
existed but would have been suppressed.

"This was my world. I wrote about it for the newspaper, cultural
events, matters for the soul. I didn't write about it as I would have liked,
but I managed to say quite a lot, having mastered the language of innuendo, fully comprehensible to the intelligentsia (and not just them).

"Today I can say that this was a method of struggle, but back then I
didn't formulate it thus or decide upon a strategy and tactics. I just grew
intellectually and in the process hit upon the method of indirect speech.
I found a milieu, and it helped me to come to grips with Magnitogorsk,
to fall in love with this very difficult city."

During these years Mozgovoi, like most but not all of his co-workers
at the newspaper, joined the party—a decision guided, he assured me,
by career rather than ideological concerns. "Some made high-level careers; others knowingly brought on the barbed wire," he remarked. "Between these two extremes lay dozens of other options by which to separate oneself from (and ultimately make peace with) the 'stagnation':
internal emigration (the celebrated generation of doormen and jani-
tors), withdrawal from thinking (even from life), the 'fig in the pocket'
[never saying what one really thinks while crossing one's fingers concealed in one's pocket].

"A small percentage of people—it is probably the same in all soci-
eties—are ready to offer up their bodies for principle, to sacrifice themselves and their families. Our society is no different in that regard. For
me an open struggle with officialdom would have had an unfortunate
impact on my family. It would have been necessary to part with everything, even the children. Responsibility for them was (and still is)
greater than any ambition.

"Of course, this is conformism, one of its forms, an attempt to accommodate oneself and at the same time not to participate in the more

egregious hymns and prevarications. I am not ashamed of what I wrote those thirteen years. I'm ashamed of what I didn't write."

■   ■   ■

In Magnitogorsk, as in the rest of the country, the 1930s marked the dramatic rise upward in society of an enormous number of people. Most of the higher positions in local industry and government remained filled for many years to come by those promoted in the heady upsurge under Stalin. But others of Serzhantov's, Ruchov's, and Shneiveis's generation were less fortunate, having lost their lives in the great era of construction. Few stories of that first Stalinist cohort were more poignant than that of Viktor Kalmykov.

In 1931 Kalmykov, an unskilled recent migrant from the village, was recruited at the Stalingrad tractor construction site for Magnitogorsk. One year later Kalmykov was being featured in a photographic essay in the high-profile publication *The USSR in Construction,* which was then issued simultaneously in four languages. Kalmykov was shown arriving at the site with all his worldly belongings, wearing *lapty,* or peasant bast sandals. His communal barracks, where he lived with his new co-workers, was depicted, as was a reenactment of his marriage at the civil registration office to an unidentified woman. "Just as the construction site grows," the article intoned, "so people grow." As the newspaper photographs of 1932 showing Kalmykov in his fashionable new coat and cap deliberately testified, here was the new man. In 1937 Kalmykov was arrested and disappeared.

Every subsequent scholarly and popular account of Magnitogorsk history singled out Kalmykov and his meteoric rise from humble origins, only without mentioning his arrest and disappearance. When it was learned in 1988 that his widow, Emilia Bakke, was still alive, Kalmykov's fate became another memory hole the newspaper thought it could fill.

"Nineteen thirty-seven was a scary year," Emilia Bakke explained to a Magnitogorsk reporter. "My husband, Viktor Kalmykov, was working as the chair of the city's physical culture committee. He knew well many Komsomol workers. All of a sudden, rumors began to fly that the Magnitogorsk Komsomol was preparing to do something against Stalin. . . . Viktor was expelled from the party. He went to work as a fitter in the mechanical repairs shop. On 21 December he was arrested."

Emilia asserted she was saved because she had not adopted her husband's family name upon marriage. Thus, she was able to find work, as employers did not associate her name with that of an enemy of the people. And her good luck did not end there. Because Kalmykov's interrogator took a fancy to Emilia's sister, Emilia was able to see her husband after his arrest as long as she brought her sister Nina along.

Emilia claimed that she last saw her husband in July 1938. She had heard a rumor that a trainload of prisoners was headed out of the city. She climbed a hill and from there saw a group of men sitting naked on the floor of a flat car. One of them was later released and confirmed, "It was us. We saw you [on the hill] and we shouted." After her husband's arrest, Emilia, too, was interrogated. She stated that they tried to make her sign a statement that Kalmykov and others organized a rebellion. "Before I went to the interrogations, I bid final farewell to mama and the children. I would return at 2–3 A.M. No one was asleep. Everyone was waiting for me."

Few of her friends would speak to her anymore. Those who would urged her to go along with the police. "Sign, you can't help him anymore, and you'll only make things worse for yourself and the children. Everything is already concocted," they advised her. "And so I signed," she confessed, "only one paper I didn't sign—the one about disowning my husband." After the Twentieth Party Congress in 1956, Emilia was told that Viktor had died 15 September 1944. Neither the cause nor the place of death was given. Kalmykov was posthumously reinstated in the party in 1958.

An editorial comment followed Emilia's testimony: "For fifty years she was silent. And now this story. Perhaps something has been erased from memory; perhaps there are certain inaccuracies in her remembrances. How many years have passed. A whole human life. But we decided to print the story as we heard it, an authentic human document, drenched in tears and blood, full of suffering, and therefore invaluable." True enough, but could that be all?

Unlike Lominadze, Kalmykov was no old Bolshevik with whom Stalin had a score to settle. On the contrary, he was the quintessential new man of the Stalin era. How could such a person have been victimized? Who carried it out? And why? Many more questions were raised than were answered by the newspaper's attempt to color in yet another blank spot.

Moreover, further testimony from survivors of the 1930s published in the newspaper spoke of numerous arrests and disappearances that took place in the Mining Institute, the city health administration, the pressing shop of the blooming mill, and the factory autopark. It seemed that few, if any, organizations and institutions escaped the nightmare of the terror, understood to be far more extensive than previously imagined. But exactly how extensive it was and, more important, why it all occurred no one could say.

■ ■ ■

Igor, an educated young man at the beginning of a promising career, was asked what he believed in during a series of interviews in the spring of 1989. If Shneiveis sought to speak for the generation sixty and older and Mozgovoi that of forty, Igor represented the next generation down. He spoke with a politeness and a sincerity rarely encountered, let alone among people in their mid twenties.

"When I entered the party (three years ago), when I wrote the formal request, when I was accepted at the party meeting, basically I believed. Of course, I didn't believe everything; it was far from the time when absolutely everything was taken on faith. Certain things I didn't know— partly because of the lack of information (as I now see it) or the lack of a need to subject everything to critical appraisal.

"These past three years, a significant portion of the ground has been removed from under my feet. This takes its toll. But for me, at my young age, this has been much easier to comprehend than, say, for my parents' generation or for still older people. (Unfortunately, my grandparents did not live to witness these times.)

"My grandfather and grandmother arrived here in 1930. Grandpa came from Odessa, grandma from the Ukraine (she was the daughter of a white-collar railroad employee). They struggled to build this city from scratch. They came as Komsomol enthusiasts, voluntarily. They lived (as is described in the history books) in tents, then barracks. My grandpa began at the steel plant, traversing a path from simple worker to one of the bosses, eventually making it to Moscow. A real-life fairy tale.

"These were truly unusual people. Semen Borisovich (my grandfather), even after he began working for the Ministry of Ferrous Metallurgy in Moscow, was in consultation with the leadership of the Magnitogorsk steel plant and did a great deal for its reconstruction. He knew—without a computer, simply from memory—the profile of each metallurgical factory in the country. He was well educated, widely read, a cultured and extremely dedicated man.

"I was raised on these legends, on this faith. It is an extremely powerful, profound thing. Some have it, others don't; some to a lesser degree, others a greater. I have it, and I'm glad. This is the foundation with which one begins one's moral and spiritual life."

I asked Igor about the contradictions of the era. People read the newspaper, it did not correspond to what they saw with their own eyes, but they did not speak out; in the first place, it was not permitted to speak out, and in the second, even when it was allowed, they kept quiet. Did not such people who started with nothing in life but became successful pay for their rise with their integrity and freedom?

"I think it's more complicated. I had a hard time understanding it myself. I spoke with my grandpa about Stalin and all these matters, although by then it was 1985 (he died at the end of the year). I wonder if it is even possible to understand what happened simply from documents if you didn't live through those times.

"I am convinced and will never change my mind: my grandpa and grandma lived with integrity. They didn't do evil deeds; they didn't violate their principles. (It is a different matter that their principles from our point of view today were one-sided or even, in our minds, a deceit.) Back then there was honest and enthusiastic belief.

"The way you characterized it, I can't say that things were not at all like that. Yet for the most part, they were not. That my grandparents paid for their success with something . . . well, there no doubt were such occasions when they had to choose. Choices had to be made. But it is wrong to think that everyone who lived during the Stalin era and achieved something must have been a dishonest person with a heavy conscience.

"I don't feel the need to preserve the faith my grandparents had. We've all learned a lot since then. Their last years I lived with them in Moscow and had a chance to observe what kind of relationship they had with other people, how they treated others and were treated in return. I saw the deep respect accorded them by relatives, friends, neighbors. If only I could command such genuine respect from others when I reach their age, I would be satisfied that my life was not in vain. This is not an ideological matter; it is a human one.

"When I studied at the institute I got involved with Komsomol work. I was an activist. There was much that I was not satisfied with. But when I posed the question, What would be better, to do this kind of stuff, to try to change something for the better, to achieve something and learn, or instead to move to the side? I decided to be active.

"One must be active, one must work to change things, one must in the end simply gather strength to change something for the better in this life. Now my Komsomol days are over, and I ask myself, Was I right? Probably I was, for upon graduation from the institute, I had trustworthy friends, a sense of right and wrong, and something I believed in, principles. Again, these are human, universal issues, not ideological ones.

"Therefore, in answer to your question, What do I believe in? my answer is: in myself, in my own capabilities, in the possibility of change, in the dependence of positive change on our own efforts. It is not a matter of simply changing one's beliefs from yesterday's wrong ones to today's correct ones. You are right. It is not possible to live without faith. But faith is internal."

After graduation Igor chose not to remain in Moscow or to seek employment in other more comfortable places; rather, he chose to return to Magnitogorsk, to his parents and his roots, with neither illusions about the present nor regrets about his past.

■   ■   ■

In his memoirs, *My Century*, Aleksander Wat, a Pole who, like many of his compatriots, crisscrossed the vast archipelago of Soviet prisons and camps, related an encounter with Jan Hempel, a Polish editor, in the 1930s inside the infamous Lubianka prison: "Once during the night Hempel woke up—he suffered terrible stomach pains; he had a stomach ulcer—and he said, 'Two blast furnaces have just been fired in Magnitogorsk.' He really would sit in that stinking cell and talk about Magnitogorsk with a sort of quiet passion. A dreamer . . .

"We really did dream of the blast furnaces there. At that time we did not know—a little later the party found out, especially the higher spheres of the intelligentsia—but we didn't know then that Magnitogorsk had been built on the corpses of peasants herded there from the Ukraine, from all over Russia.

"We didn't know about that, but even had we known, I don't think it would have changed things much in that period. We had our answer ready: the price of revolution. We had entered that circle; I at least was already in that terrible circle where people are human material and abstraction. People are ideas; they serve the idea, are part of the idea, are the instrument of the idea."

As Wat's conversation shows, Magnitogorsk and its blast furnaces, while standing for an entire historical epoch, provided a symbol of hope for the future and a sweeping justification for all the senseless injustices of the present, even for those who experienced injustice. What, we may ask, after the well-meaning and strenuous efforts to fill in the blank spots, can Magnitogorsk be said to represent today? That is a difficult question.

A trip to an elementary school history class revealed disarray. Old textbooks had been recalled; no new ones had been sent; exams had been canceled. "History," one tenth grader remarked, "you want to know about history? No one has a clue. It used to be we got sick of hearing the same old lies; now we're angry because they have nothing to say." The teacher threw up her hands.

"I have always been dedicated to teaching them the truth," she insisted, "but now I read and I read, yet I don't know which truth is the right one. At home we get together with friends, sit around the table. All we do is talk about our problems and insufficiencies, endlessly, until someone bangs the table and shouts, 'Enough. No more about that.' But what else can we discuss?

"We try to evaluate the crisis. How deep is it? How serious? Is it possible to crawl out of the abyss? We want to believe; we have such hope. But the younger people, they don't believe. They say, 'That's your problem, not ours.' It's become impossible to deal with them. I want to do my job, but how can I teach them about our past when I myself don't even know what I believe anymore?"

■　■　■

When preparing his speech for the city's sixtieth anniversary celebration, Mayor Mikhail Lysenko asked if I would pick large sections of my work on Magnitogorsk's past to be translated so he could "put an end once and for all to the damned silences." His request seemed strange, for he could have simply asked me questions directly. It seemed that he really wanted to know what I had made of the perplexing place. Even though I know he found the information he was looking for, I doubt if he saw it the same way.

From the day the first party of settlers arrived at Magnetic Mountain in the late winter of 1929, they were imbued with a sense of history. It had fallen to them to create a new world. Filmmakers, novelists, and adventurers descended on this Soviet miracle in the steppe. Those taking part in the grand crusade felt that they were making history and that their efforts ought to be recorded every step of the way.

Beginning in 1932 teams of researchers collected enormous volumes of scattered documents, interviewed and surveyed great numbers of workers, took and gathered countless photographs, and wrote dozens of manuscripts for what was to be a gigantic, definitive history of Magnitogorsk. Although none of these specific works was ever published and in 1938 the entire project and some of its proponents were liquidated, the materials and plans assembled were deposited in the state archives in Moscow. There they remain today, having been examined over the years by a small number of scholars.

Looking through the files, I was struck by the unspoken assumptions that guided their origination: the elision of life and work, the understanding of work as heroism, the elevation of heavy industry as the apex of existence. Yet in the end, not only what contemporaries chose to leave for posterity but that they expended so much effort in the process held the key for understanding what happened at Magnitogorsk.

Well before the Bolsheviks came to power, there was a widespread sense in Russia of a special mission for the nation. Within educated society people disagreed on how closely Russia ought to imitate the West, but even the strongest advocates of Westernization felt that Russia must somehow maintain its distinctiveness.

Socialist revolution offered an answer. Russia would industrialize, would catch and even overtake the West economically and militarily, yet would do so in its own way, more justly, retaining its supposed moral superiority. None of the Bolsheviks knew what socialism really was, but they all knew, or thought they knew, capitalism, and it was on the basis of the rejection of capitalism that socialism took shape: Capitalism had private property; socialism would have state-owned property. Capitalism had markets; socialism would have a plan. Capitalism had bourgeois (parliamentary) democracy; socialism would have councils (soviets).

Socialism, however, would not come about naturally. To bring about the unprecedented undertaking of noncapitalist transformation required a special instrument, "a party of a new type" (in Lenin's phrase), which amid the chaos of a war-torn country managed to seize power in 1917, precipitating a ferocious civil war that lasted until 1920. Bolshevik victory was followed in 1921 by the "strategic retreat" known as NEP, which gradually revived the decimated country but promised an unsure prospect for bringing about "socialism."

When Stalin launched the country on the Big Drive, the scale and speed of the program, combined with its noncapitalist character and intense purposefulness, conveyed a clear message of the world-historical singularity of the USSR's undertaking "to build socialism." But the party, in trying to realize this noncapitalist utopia without relinquishing its monopoly on power, or "leading role," led the country not to paradise but to a sui generis political system, economy, and society from which some seventy years later it would struggle desperately to escape.

Symbolizing and encapsulating this wholesale transformation of

Russia under Soviet rule, Magnitogorsk was to be a city in which all the problems of cities known up to that time would be eliminated. The socialist city was a dream for a better way of life, for literacy, health, justice, happiness. But in addition to being a utopian city of the future, Magnitogorsk was a settlement attached to a huge and important industrial center. That center was also a dream, a dream for a technological and industrial revolution, a leap from wooden ploughs to automated steelmaking shops. This dream was somehow more urgent and perhaps more fundamental than the dream for a better way of life; indeed, paradoxical as it might seem, the better way of life was supposed to result from the building of the automated steelmaking shops. The revolution was a blast furnace, not a garden.

"Magnitogorsk is not a city built for people," remarked Viktor Shraiman, with a touch of sadness, during a conversation while we watched videos on his imported VCR—a coveted prize obtained on a trip abroad with the theater—in his otherwise spartan apartment. "It is not organized in such a way as to allow people to live. Life here is a desperate struggle where a feeling of great triumph comes from obtaining some pathetic item you in the West simply buy at the store when the need arises."

"But," he continued, as we looked from his balcony at the rows of fourteen-story prefabricated apartment buildings stretching into the distance along the badly decaying but unfinished boulevard, "Magnitogorsk is a paradoxical place. Completely without roots, it nevertheless is a city possessing very strong traditions. It grew exceedingly fast, very recently, and with much trauma. This hectic and cataclysmic birth and growth have conveyed a special status on those who lived and live here. It will take a while to sort this all out."

As we sat there, both moved to silent reflection by our conversation, all the talk about *perestroika* came to seem ultimately irrelevant, failing to capture the profound psychological experience of having had so many fundamental beliefs and traditions lose their meaning or even acquire an inverse significance almost overnight. Celebrations of International Workers' Day on 1 May and Victory Day on 9 May, two of the three biggest state holidays, had either become awkwardly hollow (1 May) or strangely ambiguous (9 May). (A similar fate had no doubt befallen the third, Revolution Day on 7 November, but I was not in Magnitogorsk at that time.) Newspaper articles about a once glorious history spoke almost exclusively of prisoners, arrests, and betrayal. People were wondering where to turn for a sense of collective identity.

The very training and practice of the craft of history had not been passed on to the present generation, and the disjointed, often slipshod attempts by journalists to eliminate the blank spots in Magnitogorsk's history through the unedited publication of recollections freely acknowledged as faulty engendered great confusion. Moreover, filling in the memory holes of the old historical view went hand in hand with the near total dismissal of the previous version of historical understanding, thereby leading ironically to the creation of different but even larger holes than before.

In Magnitogorsk, as the city finally began to mourn the multitudes unjustly murdered and acknowledge the suffering of those long tormented, de-Stalinization of the October Revolution still seemed profoundly necessary, although scarcely achievable. From the ceremonial day in 1936 when it was finally unveiled, an oversized statue of Stalin, placed on top of a raised pedestal with a platform, presided over the entrance to the Magnitogorsk Works. On state holidays, the air filled with the triumphal sounds of a military orchestra, and the local leadership, standing alongside Stalin's likeness, waved to the passing crowd, which marched in step bearing aloft portraits of the Great Leader and Father of All Peoples. Socialism, as everyone in Magnitogorsk knew, had a human face; that face was Stalin's.

In 1961 when Stalin's body was removed from the mausoleum on Red Square he had shared since 1953 with Lenin, all statues of the Man of Steel in Magnitogorsk were also removed. The main Magnitogorsk thoroughfare, Stalin Boulevard, was renamed Lenin Boulevard. The steel plant, which used to carry Stalin's name, bore the name of Lenin. No visible trace of the once ubiquitous name remained. There was, however, one monument to Stalin, no matter whose name it carried, that was not removed. Just as Stalin left behind a permanent monument to his rule in the layout and architecture of Moscow, which was reconstructed during his reign, so he left a permanent monument in Magnitogorsk: the great steel plant itself.

In Russian the word for steel (*stal'*) recalled the name of Stalin. As long as steel was produced in Magnitogorsk, Stalin would live on there, a symbol of the force that called forth the great steel plant, that very steel plant upon whose shoulders the victory over the Germans and the survival of the revolution were secured. Magnetic Mountain was locally known as Hitler's grave. But the Magnitogorsk Works and the civilization created with it were in fact a kind of Stalin mausoleum.

A bizarre centralized economy, the preponderance of steel amid complaints of inadequate supply, the virtual absence of a consumer or service industry, a nation fully employed yet unable to feed or clothe itself without resort to connections and side deals, the chronic housing shortage, the warlike nature of everyday life, the unlimited mandate yet utter incompetence of Communist party rule, and the extensive police surveillance—all were in large measure legacies of the Stalin era. Even the treatment of the city's past as a series of gaps to be filled and personal tragedies to be heard reflected the abiding presence of an era current reformers would like to put behind them. Moreover, Stalinism as a civilization was not simply imposed on people; it required and received their participation. Its deep roots were consolidated in the creation of an entire social system. Moreover, not one but several generations were reared in Stalinism, the social system, and many of the values it entailed, even beyond the dictator's death.

Although Stalin's image at long last was tarnished irrevocably, discrediting Stalin simultaneously cast a shadow over the entire history of this muddled city. In the process, questions of individual responsibility for past actions began to press upon the consciences of many, not just upon those old enough to have lived through the 1930s. Who was responsible? What was the difference between actively collaborating in someone's downfall and failing to intercede to save that person? What should be done with the surviving torturers and murderers? If the system was inherently bad, was everything one did in the past necessarily evil? Was it possible to commit evil unintentionally? And finally perhaps the largest question of all, were the sacrifices in vain?

If in Magnitogorsk the past began to loom large in the present, the past came to seem even more important for the future. Magnitogorsk needed to solve a number of pressing problems, from housing and water supply to clean air and health care. At the same time, the city needed new economic and political structures that could produce greater wealth while fostering democracy. Solutions to these enormous challenges were not easy to envision. In the meantime, the city struggled not only to feed and clothe itself but to teach its children who they were and where they had come from.

An exhibition of children's drawings covered the walls of the art studio at the Magnitogorsk Palace of Pioneers. It was the forty-fifth consecutive year such an exhibition had been mounted in the building built to serve as an instrument for socializing youth. Lina Demianova, for ten years the studio's dedicated instructor, traveled around city schools to sign up promising pupils. Her students had won all sorts of awards, including some in international competition, and their works had been published in children's calendars.

Five-, six-, and seven-year-old artists were first taught by Lina to copy drawings of world masters before being encouraged to create on their own. For inspiration Lina took her charges on trips to Leningrad, Riga, Kiev, and other older cities of culture. When the time came to experiment, the children were asked not to picture their country in the year 2000, as the state instructions suggested, but to visualize their dreams for the future.

"Socialization [*vospitanie*] begins early," Lina explained, as she gave me a tour of the exhibition. "Children have many fears, but they also have dreams. It is very important to be able to help focus those dreams, to give them a healthy, expressive content. Too often we box them in. Their minds can become trapped so early in life without them even knowing it." Of the several dozen drawings on display, almost all portrayed neat houses, green trees, and bright sun. Not one depicted steel-making or a steelworker.

Afterword

"The garden city, about which the first settlers of Magnitka dreamed, was, to put it mildly, never realized," wrote Vilii Bogun, the city's long-time architect, on the eve of Magnitogorsk's sixtieth anniversary. Bogun's first name, derived from the initials of Vladimir Ilich Lenin, serves as a reminder of the hopes of that earlier epoch, hopes now thought to have been cruel delusions.

"It really makes you appreciate being American," I was repeatedly told when relating Bogun's words and the story of contemporary Magnitogorsk to American audiences. So, to put in perspective what happened in Magnitogorsk in the second half of the 1980s, perhaps the best place to start is here at home. And if there is one American city that can be likened to Magnitogorsk, it is Gary, Indiana.

In 1906 U.S. Steel broke ground, on the shores of Lake Michigan just south of Chicago, on what was to be the world's most modern steel plant. Along with the plant a town arose, named after Judge Elbert H. Gary, then chairman of U.S. Steel. Built from scratch at a previously almost uninhabited site, with a certain haste and on a large scale, Gary caught Stalin's fancy. Magnitogorsk, in Stalin's eyes, was originally conceived as the Soviet Gary.

Indeed, the development of Gary and Magnitogorsk showed certain parallels. Gary too was a company town. U.S. Steel built most of the housing, ran many of the stores, and contributed the overwhelming bulk of revenues for the city government. As in Magnitogorsk, in Gary few resources were devoted to social concerns or the people's welfare.

The Gary labor force, much of it consisting of poor immigrants, lived in shanties "on the other side of the tracks" in a part of town colloquially known as "the patch" for its rows of bars, frequent fistfights, and supposed moral laxity. In Magnitogorsk, a similar residential territory imagined by the authorities to be an exclusive breeding ground of evil was called "Shanghai."

To be sure, in stark contrast to the experience of the people of Magnitogorsk, Gary's inhabitants were not systematically victimized by state-sponsored terror, and they could move elsewhere if they so desired and possessed the means. And yet a majority of the people in Gary lived materially on the edge, under the constant threat of unemployment and with little possibility for social advancement.

Magnitogorsk was distinguished for, among other things, its emblematic role as a device to inculcate a new set of values in generations born after the revolution. In Gary a deep commitment to education, especially to socializing the younger generation in "American" values, combined with an innovative program to make Gary schools among the most famous in the country. And although Gary, unlike Magnitogorsk, did not play a dramatic role in its country's history, nevertheless Gary's elite was imbued with a fervent sense of missionary zeal. Just as its Soviet counterpart would be, the frontier town on the southern shores of Lake Michigan was billed as the "city of the century." But in Gary, as in Magnitogorsk, things turned out differently.

By the early 1980s, when demand for steel plummeted, layoffs at the Gary Works led to a city unemployment rate in excess of 20 percent for four consecutive years. Although by 1989 unemployment in Gary had fallen to 11 percent (still twice the rate of the surrounding suburbs), employment at the Gary Works, which once exceeded twenty-one thousand, had fallen to seventy-five hundred. Beset by ever-higher indices of "structural unemployment," Gary also suffered from a litany of social problems familiar to residents of American cities, including widespread drug abuse, adult illiteracy, "hereditary" poverty, homelessness, inaccessible medical care, and a truly astonishing level of violence. In the 1970s and 1980s on average more than sixty murders a year were committed in Gary. In 1987 Richard Hatcher, then the country's longest reigning black mayor, was defeated in the city's Democratic primary after twenty years in office. The victor and city's new mayor, Thomas Barnes, who was also black, skillfully exploited the pervasive fear of crime in his campaign.

Nor has Gary been immune from the racism that troubles American cities generally. In 1970, when the city had a population of 175,000 people, Gary was about 55 percent black. Today, fewer than 140,000 people are thought to be living in Gary, of whom 85 percent are black. In other words, whites have been fleeing, especially to "less threatening" surrounding communities. As a result, even mundane municipal disputes between Gary and neighboring suburbs take on explicitly racial overtones.

Urban renewal—a catchword for a variety of policy measures designed to revitalize America's cities that has often meant simply evicting the poor from "gentrifying" neighborhoods only recently abandoned to them—has yet to be tried in Gary, whose downtown remains a desert of boarded-up storefronts. A promotion in 1988 to attract new business to Gary, which was attended by some three hundred companies, had no place to convene. Instead, the executives met in nearby Merillville. Meanwhile, a three-hundred-room high-rise carcass, which opened in 1969 as a Holiday Inn and closed six years later, loomed menacingly over city hall. Plans to lure tourist dollars to Gary by building casinos on the lakefront have yet to be acted upon, perhaps in part for fear of reproducing the debacle of Atlantic City, where runaway municipal corruption rather than urban revitalization rode in the high rollers' wake.

Gary's myriad woes have not been caused by the decline of its steel plant, where an aggressive program of technological renewal brought about a remarkable turnaround. Operating at close to its full capacity of nine million tons, the Gary Works accounts for nearly half of the successor USX corporation's output and remains by far the nation's largest mill. Pretax profits in 1988 were thought to be considerably more than $300 million on revenues of $2 billion. But modernization of the factory has meant consistently less employment. And although some mills like Gary have bounced back, many others have been shut down.

In 1984 the Bethlehem plant in Lackawanna, New York, closed all but a small portion of its once huge complex, capping two decades of decline from a work force of 11,700 to one of a few hundred. The Homestead Works in Pennsylvania, for decades one of America's premiere mills, employed 20,000 workers in 1945, 7,000 in the late 1970s, 3,500 in the early 1980s and 23 the day the mill was shut down in July 1986. At its high point (1950) the American steel industry accounted for nearly 50 percent of world production. By 1988 the U.S. share of world output was a little more than 11 percent. As late as 1981 the steel industry employed 560,000 people; in 1989, it employed fewer than half that number.

Against the background of the decline of the American steel industry, the Gary Works stands out as an unqualified "success," although residents of the city may rightly feel they have much in common with the people of Homestead or Lackawanna. And Big Steel's fall—Gary notwithstanding—is only one aspect of a larger pattern of American deindustrialization affecting hundreds of communities across the nation. This turn of events has been described as the "transition" to a "service economy" signaling the end of "Fordism" (a model of industrial development founded on the use of product-specific machines and of semiskilled workers to produce standardized goods at huge assembly-line plants). Such a characterization implies an air of inevitability and conveys the stamp of approval.

Looking at Magnitogorsk from this American perspective, one is tempted to see the current predicament of the Soviet steeltown as a manifestation of the structural economic crisis experienced by American industry—in the fashionable expression, as one more example of the end of Fordism. Indeed, nowhere else in the world was Fordism carried as far as in the USSR or allowed to last so long. Magnitogorsk is part of a Soviet rust belt yet to undergo the wrenching "adjustments" already inflicted upon cities of the American rust belt.

But there are at least two problems with the notion that Magnitogorsk is essentially an unmodernized Gary. First, Gary is an exception by American standards. America, which instead of refurbishing outmoded industrial plant has for the most part simply abandoned it, ought not to be used as a benchmark. Every industrialized country has produced a rust belt; not every one has dealt with its rust belt the same way. As the examples of Japan and Germany, among others, have shown, that some industrial plants are obsolete need not serve as a pretext for letting an entire country's manufacturing base evaporate.

Second, Magnitogorsk's crisis goes much deeper than any in American industry. In Magnitogorsk, alongside technological obsolescence and social distress, political and economic structures put in place under Stalin have been coming apart, an unraveling that has impinged directly on the great-power status of the Soviet Union. Gary has its share of profound social problems, but they have not provoked a societywide reconsideration of the political and economic order. In Magnitogorsk not just Fordism but Stalinism has been dying.

■ ■ ■

Stalinism signifies more than the rule of Stalin; it connotes the entire "system" that arose during the 1930s. Its main economic features were a strong emphasis on heavy industry and the military, extreme centralization, fixed prices, and a taboo against markets and private businesses. Culturally, Stalinism entailed a thoroughgoing censorship, rigid orthodoxy in intellectual matters, an ethos that championed labor, and patriotism. Socially, it involved elaborate privileges for the loyal, pervasive police power, surveillance and informing, repressive laws, and a disregard for all laws when expedient. Politically it combined a reliance on commands and threats with tight control over appointments and rewards.

Stalinism was also distinguished by the widespread use of terror and the personal dictatorship of Stalin. Many commentators interpreted Stalin's death and the "relaxation" of the terror to mean that Stalinism had ceased to exist. Nevertheless, long after the mass terror and Stalin's personal despotism had ended, the Stalinist order lived on, modified but not transformed. Mikhail Gorbachev himself characterized *perestroika* as a deliberate attempt to overcome the legacy of Stalinism, which, he argued, still survived throughout society, the economy, culture, and politics.

When Gorbachev became general secretary, the Soviet Union was still a society with a fully state-run and almost wholly state-owned economy and with a clumsy but omnicompetent political machine that maintained a presence in all societal institutions it permitted to exist. He and other top reformers eventually came to believe that these two pillars of the hollowed-out Stalinist order—state control over the economy and party control over the state—had to be shattered for the country to "modernize."

Although only a top member of the Soviet leadership could begin *perestroika,* responsibility for the breakthrough belongs not just to Gorbachev, or high-level party "liberals" such as Aleksandr Yakovlev, but, as the British scholar Geoffrey Hosking has reminded us, to certain scientists and writers, religious practitioners and human rights activists, of whom the most renowned was Andrei Sakharov.*

Sakharov and a few score courageous individuals, asserting the universality of human values, campaigned at great personal risk for radical structural reform of the Soviet Union long before the adoption at the

* *The Awakening of the Soviet Union* (Cambridge: Harvard University Press, 1990).

Twenty-seventh Party Congress in 1986 of the Communist party's plan for *perestroika*. Most of these individuals were branded "dissidents" for their principled insistence that the Soviet Union observe its own laws, and they were subjected to constant harassment, criminal trials, and forced emigration or internal exile. Some, like Sakharov, survived to see the fruits of their tireless efforts (and even to shape the course of subsequent events once the party decided to follow their lead); others did not.

The impact of dissidents was greatly magnified by the attention paid to them by the outside world, but to appreciate why a few score individuals armed with nothing more than their uncaptive minds could pose a challenge to the Soviet state it is necessary to recall that the regime grounded itself in a set of questionable propositions that claimed to be the One True Theory. To prevent the unmasking of its ideology, the state did all it could to suppress alternative ideas. But in the end the regime's ideology, a major source of its legitimacy, would prove to be one of its fundamental weak points as the state's desire to enter the computer age came up against the brick wall of its own censorship and secrecy.

Pressure from dissidents alone, in other words, did not compel the Soviet authorities to rethink the nature of the Communist order. To explain why the staunch Communist leadership recognized an urgent need for potentially destabilizing reforms, commentators have rightly focused on the formidable pressures exerted by international competition and the diminishing capacity of the Soviet Union's industrial and military infrastructure to compete effectively. But as the preeminent Soviet specialist Moshe Lewin has argued, domestic developments associated with urbanization, especially the spread of education and the rise of professionals, exerted pressures of their own and created a large potential constituency for reform, both inside and outside the Communist party, which, after all, drew its membership from society.*

In Lewin's long-term view, the basis for, and part of the driving force behind, the eruptions of the late 1980s was laid even before the Khrushchev period and expanded beneath the stagnant facade of the Brezhnev years. Thus, scientists and artists who clashed with the regime beginning in the 1970s were not as out of place as they appeared. Rather, they formed the leading edge of a massive social wedge that was poised

---

* *The Gorbachev Phenomenon: A Historical Interpretation* (Berkeley and Los Angeles: University of California Press, 1988).

to crack the "outdated" political structures and that in 1985 would even take command of those structures.

Left unaddressed by Lewin, however, was whether any large and important strata of urbanized Soviet society, far from having developed political interests different from those of the state or an "objective" need for a more modern political system, might resist efforts to alter the status quo. Moreover, what if those urban strata with a putative "objective" interest in "political" modernization did not act to realize their interest? These were the very dilemmas with which the Soviet leadership had to wrestle.

Seeking to demystify the seemingly miraculous appearance of a reform-minded leadership in the Soviet Union, Lewin demonstrated that a reform process was not begun out of the blue, even arguing that it was historically necessary; he did not, however, seek to examine what the new political structures would look like, what changes they would require in the underlying social structure, or how the transition would be effected. As a result, his analysis of the political consequences of urbanization could not explain why, if the social structure essentially "required" *perestroika*, the process nonetheless became so obviously bogged down. The experience of Magnitogorsk provides some clues.

■ ■ ■

Magnitogorsk had no famous "dissidents" of its own, but it did have a handful of local artists who drew inspiration from vague and incomplete underground reports of men and women who had summoned the courage to oppose individually the structures of oppression. Although the city was without the "space" provided by human rights campaigns, a movement for non-Russian cultures, or a strong church revival, Magnitogorsk had a theater that provided spiritual sustenance and a privileged realm of alternative thought throughout the Brezhnev years. Moreover, under Brezhnev Magnitogorsk society was exposed to the slow but cumulative corrosive effects of the war in Afghanistan, which claimed hundreds of lives and maimed many more even as it went unacknowledged by the authorities.

Long before 1985 Magnitogorsk had a large number of technicians, engineers, teachers, and other professionals who were increasingly frustrated by what they viewed as irrelevant ideological restrictions in their work. These men and women took the extraordinary time and bother to cultivate interests in Western ideas and practices, including reading everything published in the Soviet press about other countries, attending foreign films, learning languages, and, less successfully, seeking out foreign publications and—the rarest prize—foreign contacts.

But notwithstanding twenty years' worth of performances by the city theater, the effects of the war in Afghanistan, and the existence of an urban intelligentsia, the response of Magnitogorsk society to Moscow's call for fundamental change was characterized by exceptional wariness and, in some quarters, outright hostility. This should come as no surprise, however, given the strategy of reform chosen, a strategy tied to an understanding of social organization inherited from the Stalin period.

Stalinist industrialization created more than just factories; it created a new social structure composed primarily of Communist functionaries, engineers and scientists, and a huge pool of workers. Each principal urban social group was encouraged to develop a sense of identity, but within a model of social organization that did not allow antagonisms between groups and did not differentiate between society and the state. Society was thought to possess unitary interests, and these interests were supposedly embodied in the Communist party.

Perestroika was conceived as a party-led "mobilization" of "society" in which the "masses" would become "active" and in so doing demonstrate their support "from below" for the party's reform program "from above." Society's participation in the reforms was seen as integral to their success, but the relative proportion of input from above and below remained undetermined, as did the forms input from below would be allowed to take. The Soviet intelligentsia was appealed to as a distinct group and permitted to found discussion clubs, but workers—by far the most numerous of the three main urban groups formed under Stalin—were not singled out for a distinct role. It was taken for granted that Communist functionaries would be in the forefront of the entire process.

Ironically, however, of the three chief urban social groups, the battalions of party functionaries were the least interested in reforms precisely because they had the most to lose. The attempt at reform of the Communist order threatened the privileges of individual apparatchiks, provoking their resistance and revealing that the Communist party, far from being a reliable instrument for carrying out a bold new policy, was one of the major obstacles. The Magnitogorsk party apparat, careful not to repudiate openly the central leadership's reform program, was nonetheless "riding out the storm," a state of affairs only too visible to the rest of society.

Betrayed by their own forces, Communist reformers in the center reluctantly turned to emerging anti-Communist political movements composed of disaffected intellectuals and artists to provide the momentum for change and then even to articulate the program of what kind of change was necessary. Indeed, since 1985, the national republics and largest cities of the Russian republic experienced the rise of groups constituting themselves as a "civil society" on the liberal model (organized entities able to form and act independently of the state). But in Magnitogorsk groups claiming to constitute civil society did not emerge. Magnitogorsk's "informal" political movements were composed of marginal elements with ineffectual leaders and offered neither an alternative to stagnant apparat domination nor a stick by which to goad the apparat along the reform path. On the contrary, the existence of the informals came in handy as the recalcitrant apparat maneuvered to demonstrate a proreform posture.

Magnitogorsk intellectuals, to the extent they became politically active, did not found informal movements; they remained *wholly* within the existing power structure (witness the discussion club at the wire factory) and thus were incapable of affecting it, while students did little more than bemoan their fate. Meanwhile, members of the local theater made a conscious decision not to engage in direct political activity when the opportunity came. With the notable exception of the relationship cultivated by the city newspaper with the reading public—a fundamentally passive mobilization—societal activism, such as it was, remained within the boundaries of the party-state conception of social organization.

Even the remarkably active election campaign that energized Magnitogorsk's population in 1989 showed the weakness of society's mobilization there. Not simply the most effective but virtually the only organized force during the campaign proved to be the Communist apparat, which skillfully deflected an assault on its complacent monopoly power concocted by Moscow. Despite the coalescence of broad societal support for greater openness and accountability and for competitive multicandidate elections, in Magnitogorsk effective organization by society to secure these achievements did not result after a summons from the central Communist authorities or even after the image of Communist invincibility began to crack. But if in Magnitogorsk none of the groups that played so prominent a role elsewhere fought to create an enlarged political arena, one group did: journalists.

In sorting out how the newspaper staff was able to establish itself at the forefront of change and offer a rallying point from which to challenge the monopoly of the local Communist machine, one must give due attention to the importance in any modern society of information, the significance of which was only enhanced by the previous selectivity and ideologized nature of information under Communist party rule. *Glasnost* opened up wide political possibilities for all, but because of their vocation journalists were able to have an immediate revolutionary impact simply by doing their jobs—provided they had the capabilities *and* no one stood in their way. Events proved that the talent was there. The ruling apparat, however, did not approve.

To understand how, despite the opposition of the local ruling clique, the Magnitogorsk newspaper succeeded in becoming an independent locus of power one must recall the thirst of the reading public for truth, a thirst awakened and made widespread by *glasnost*. Yet even the thirst for truth would have meant little in Magnitogorsk without the presence of Valerii Kucher, an authoritative figure with a strong sense of social responsibility who, although not from outside the power structure, understood the importance of renouncing the power accrued from official status and securing a popular mandate to further the cause of progressive change.

In some ways, Kucher's political strategy recapitulated that of Mikhail Gorbachev. Following Gorbachev, Kucher chose to work for change inside and through the party. And like Gorbachev, Kucher sought to hold the center, remaining indispensable to "left" and "right" and using each to counterbalance the other and propel them both forward at the same speed. (A major difference was, however, that Magnitogorsk had no left. As a result, Kucher was compelled to play the roles of both the center and the left at the same time—something his mentor in Moscow also seemed to be doing, although not out of compulsion.) But the inherent contradictions of such a position eventually cost both reformers the political initiative.

In Magnitogorsk the apparat had few friends among the populace but only one substantial challenger, who was himself an apparatchik. Walking a delicate line, Kucher single-handedly carried the banner of reform for the party in Magnitogorsk and did more than anyone else in the city to bring about a mental revolution and moral regeneration with profound psychological consequences. Yet in the end he blunted the reformist edge of his own leadership. Bearing the weight of inordinate responsibility, Kucher crossed all lines but one, the line of Communist party rule, and this decision, dictated by both tactical considerations and conviction, ultimately restricted the progress of political democratization in Magnitogorsk and brought the city to an impasse.

At the newspaper Kucher did not act alone, but in concert with a handful of professionally trained correspondents who had attained their positions chiefly on merit and who, under his politically astute direction, were able to transform the formerly subservient mouthpiece of the city party committee into both a source of enlightenment and a powerful political instrument. Yet although the *Magnitogorsk Worker* attained an impressive dynamism and garnered widespread moral support for *glasnost,* its efforts to involve broad circles of society in the reform process were stymied, an outcome the newspaper attributed to the ingrained passivity of the populace.

People supportive of change were clearly waiting for change to happen *to* them rather than trying to bring it about through their own efforts, and in this they behaved as they had been expected for decades to behave. Factors other than "instinct" encouraged passivity as well. One was the inability of the reforms to deliver tangible material benefits in the short term (indeed, quite the opposite resulted), adding to the dismal legacy of previous reform programs that had promised much and delivered little. And in truth, it was not clear *what* the people were supposed to do, aside from faithfully reading the daily newspaper.

Calling for social mobilization, the Communist party nonetheless continued to assert its self-assigned prerogative to lead and to restrict at every turn the independent "cooperative" (that is, private) business sector. Meanwhile, faithfully reading the newspaper meant having one's worldview and self-identity turned upside down. Long accustomed to a particular understanding of their country and their lives, an understanding infused by a deep sense of their city's past, the people of Magnitogorsk had to contend with more than the discovery that the Soviet Union seemed to be a Third World country. More important, they had to confront the questions of who they were and where they came from after the language and concepts they had always relied on to articulate their collective and individual identities ceased to hold meaning.

Passivity there certainly has been—social paralysis would be more accurate—but behind *perestroika*'s failure to take hold lay more than ingrained or reinforced passivity among the populace. The party's reform program, doomed from the start, was an impossible attempt to overcome the inherent contradictions of the Soviet order without altering underlying structures. Still, whether the process could be moved forward after the discovery of the incompatibility between the goals and strategy of reform depended on the ability of non-Communist political groups to seize the initiative. On this score Magnitogorsk suffered from its social structure.

The successful new political movements around the country that arose to challenge the Communist party were overwhelmingly made up of representatives of the intelligentsia. Moscow is deceptive in that regard. Whereas the relative weight of the technical, scientific, and artistic intelligentsias is far greater in Moscow—home to government ministries, research institutes, and a flourishing cultural scene—the profile of Magnitogorsk, weighted in favor of industrial workers, more closely resembles that of the country's urban population as a whole. And industrial workers, as we shall see, for the most part kept their distance from *perestroika*. (It also must be kept in mind that unlike many industrial cities on the periphery, where national movements served as vehicles for galvanizing people of all social ranks, Magnitogorsk was home predominantly to Russians rather than, say, aggrieved Estonians or Georgians.)

Thus, in Magnitogorsk, as in most of urban Russia, a paradoxical situation arose. Even though one of the distinctive characteristics of the Gorbachev-era reforms was the rejection of a naive faith in the efficacy of solely administrative methods to effect large-scale change, "society" did not respond properly to its assigned role. And when it did respond, the results were not entirely welcomed by the top leadership.

In the largest cities and in the national republics, officials discovered, unleashed social forces pulled in unintended ways and gave *perestroika* a different, more radical, character based on a liberal model of societal organization; elsewhere, officials found, the country's basic social structure was no more ready for party-led *perestroika* than it had been for the onslaught of the Stalin-era transformation, when far different methods to effect a social and political revolution were used.

Moreover, even as the social structure inherited from the Stalinist revolution, notwithstanding the "modernizing" effects of urbanization, proved at least as much an impediment as a stimulus to change, the architects of *perestroika* were reluctant to alter that social structure. The ambivalence of the Communist leadership in Moscow toward cooperatives, when combined with the inclination of besieged local leaders aware of popular moods and eager for the rare chance to curry favor, obstructed the development of a "cooperative" or private sector at every turn. No "bourgeoisie" was encouraged to develop, although one did begin to take shape anyway (often in alliance with or even from among the managers and party functionaries). Nonetheless, for political and ideological reasons, even the most unambiguously proreform members of the Moscow leadership did not choose to tap this potentially vast reservoir of social support for change.

Events soon made clear that *perestroika* essentially rested on the thin social base of some (not all) intellectuals, some of the "marketeers" inside and outside the command economy, and a narrow stratum of proreform party officials. Nothing could have been more telling of the lack of social support than the constant preoccupation of these people with the "reversibility" of the process and the fate of one man, Mikhail Gorbachev, whose strategy of seeking his strongest backing abroad for change inside the USSR seemed simultaneously ingenious and absurd.

■ ■ ■

Since it has become obvious that Communism has been abandoned even by the Soviet leadership, it is easy to forget that *perestroika* was originally directed at saving that order, not destroying it. Conversely, with the Communist order openly repudiated by members of the top leadership, it is tempting to expect Communism to vanish overnight. But if successful reform has proved illusory, transcendence has shown itself to be an enormously complicated, contradictory, and long-term endeavor, and one that, if at all manageable, may not be so by centrally exercised authority.

At the all-union level and in many regions the party's monopoly has been revoked not merely on paper but at the ballot box. And although party cells persist in all institutions while continued state control over the economy furnishes the party with the means to run its powerful patronage machine, alongside the party machine new governing structures have taken shape—an executive presidency, the Congress of People's Deputies—while old ones, such as the Supreme Soviet, have been fundamentally transformed.

Before the advent of these institutions, the Soviet Union was not a one-party state (that is, a state run by a single party, such as Japan) but a party-state in which an unelected apparat operating beyond public view "shadowed" not only the nominal state structures but *all* the legal organizations of society and enterprises of the economy. With the Presidential Council, Congress of Deputies, and revamped Supreme Soviet, the country now has a free-standing state structure whose control has become a matter of open competition among opposing political groups. All the mechanisms of political democracy, with the important exception of an independent judiciary, are in place.

At the same time, the country has undergone a fragmentation of power that has rendered the location of ultimate authority ambiguous and raised questions about the continued governability of any constituted authority over its nominal jurisdictions. Declarations of political *and* economic "sovereignty" by national republics have been matched by similar proposals put forth by smaller political units such as provinces (*oblasts*), districts (*raions*), cities, and even urban wards. Each breakaway block of the old administrative pyramid discovers itself challenged from within by still smaller blocks and at the same time up against the might of gargantuan enterprises breaking loose from parallel ministerial hierarchies.

The example of Magnitogorsk verifies the trend not toward decentralization but toward a splintering of centralism, as regions reject Moscow's "colonialism" and seek to establish their own centralized control over everything in their territories. In Magnitogorsk the devolution of power from the center gave impetus to a struggle between the city's largest enterprise, the steel plant, and municipal authorities for "all power," only without the proliferation of groups from across the political spectrum to contest for seats on the municipal council. Unlike the situation elsewhere, within the Magnitogorsk fief the hierarchies of old remained intact.

For any municipal government in Magnitogorsk, "freedom" from the central Ministry of Ferrous Metallurgy could just mean domination by the local "ministry," that is, the steelworks. And even if the balance of power shifted in the city's favor, city leaders of any stripe would face the problem, given a glut in the international steel market for *modern* product, of what to do with this industrial dinosaur aside from dividing it into smaller pieces that could perhaps be retooled and salvaged for other purposes.

On the face of it, none of these developments appears able to provide the conditions for stable economic growth, let alone prosperity. It may be, however, that radical economic restructuring would be better attempted on a "grass-roots," region-by-region basis, from the inside out. Amid the growing chaos resulting from the dissolution of the command economy, firms have had no choice but to seek "market relations" with other firms; that is, to expand those connections developed clandestinely inside the womb of the old command economy. In the absence of a credit and banking system, not to mention reliable transportation and communications, these relations cannot be said to constitute an effective market economy. But they do foreshadow, at least in some places, the re-formation of the very interregional ties that are coming apart at the political level.

■   ■   ■

It has often been observed that the Soviet system politicized everything but politics. As that order gave way, newly "politicized" politics has managed to all but consume the energies of the country. Ordinary people formerly indifferent to political developments have found their simple interactions with friends and family completely dominated by discussions of the latest political events and the state of the country. Most striking of all, the Communist order itself became the overriding political issue, as have the various proposals for a new order.

Not even the elasticity of the term *perestroika*—which has stretched to encompass the aspirations of virtually everyone, conservatives and liberals, party and antiparty—can disguise any longer the prospect facing the Soviet Union of adopting what it used to deride as "capitalism," even if the process may turn out to be less a centrally introduced transition than a regionally based one. In any event, within the framework of an economy founded on markets and private property there is wide latitude for differences of social policy, as the battles among proliferating political groups in Moscow and elsewhere have reconfirmed. Although much of this wrangling seems to take place at the level of abstract argumentation, social constraints are making themselves felt and will continue to do so. And perhaps the greatest social constraint on would-be reformers is the status of workers, a group thought to be developing a sharper sense of separate interests and an increased capacity to defend those interests collectively.

During my 1989 trip to Magnitogorsk I expected the steel plant to burst into flames at any moment, given the palpable atmosphere of social tension and the sheer number of workers. Nothing of the sort occurred. Even when huge strikes broke out in coal-mining regions of the Ukraine and western Siberia in July 1989, workers in Magnitogorsk remained docile, engaging in neither work stoppages nor organizational activity outside the party-dominated trade unions. On the surface, it seemed that nothing could prevent sixty thousand Magnitogorsk workers, if they so desired, from toppling the ostensibly all-powerful triad of factory management, trade union, and party committee (if events in Moscow did not perform the deed first). But the reality was far more complex.

Unlike the miners—workers in a declining industry who, amid all the talk about renewal, experienced a sharp decline in living standards in the two months before their uprising—workers at the Magnitogorsk steel complex reaped uninterrupted benefits from their employer's huge stock of scarce goods. "The most influential workers at the steel plant are well taken care of [*prikormleny*], especially in relation to the general Magnitogorsk population," explained Evgenii Vernikov, the managing editor of the newspaper, when asked about their quiescence. "They have better food, lots of meat, and a chance to obtain some of the many spoils that 'fall' the factory's way, from imported cassette players to one of our better domestic-make automobiles. They may not be happy with everything, but why should they strike?"

Like the apparatchiks, workers retained a strong stake in the prevailing system. Indeed, a majority of Magnitogorsk workers scoffed at the hoopla of party-led reform, and not only because of their well-honed skepticism toward thunderous official proclamations of impending improvements. Many workers already had apartments, for which they paid next to nothing in rent. Ration coupons did not overly concern them, given the open sale of meat, butter, and other goods on factory grounds, where substantial lunches were also available at modest prices. And although the availability of goods at the factory declined during *perestroika,* the difference between what workers at the Magnitogorsk Works could obtain and what those in the city could get increased.

Anger at officials' corruption and incompetence was palpable, however, and some workers—far from all—did express an interest in a radical reordering of power. But to organize, become active, and take risks one must have faith; at the least, one must believe that positive change is not only necessary but *possible.* Most disgruntled workers commented that they had witnessed the removal of the slogan "The people and the party are one," but they also noted the lack of resultant material benefits and the rise of "new" bosses who in some cases were even more demagogic than previous ones. And all remarked that the authorities' careful attention to "favorites" strongly inhibited the development of worker solidarity. Despair and cynicism weighed like stones around angry workers' necks.

One steelworker, whose comments were echoed by many others, tried to justify workers' inaction. "What would we get with a strike? If we walk out, make demands, and obtain concessions, someone somewhere else loses. A strike cannot create more, it can only redistribute the little we have. In fact, strikes mean less productivity. That is why we are against them. We should not become parasites on other workers." Such reasoning constitutes a sincere sense of collective responsibility, a guilt-ridden justification for passivity and fear, and, above all, a reflection of diminished expectations.

To be sure, strikes are an extreme option, even for highly "conscious" workers. In interviews, those Magnitogorsk workers weighing the pros and cons of militancy claimed to be afraid to make the first move, to test the waters and see whether they would be arrested if they held a strike. They pointed out that both management and the party agitated vigorously on the shop floor against "militant" (that is, independent) worker activity and, moreover, that the authorities were by no means limited to agitation, surveillance, and the threat of repression for discouraging independent worker organization. Workers were only too well aware of how the trade unions, the Komsomol, and the party retained control over the distribution of goods and services, favors and rewards, at places of employment. Indeed, with all workers dependent on the authorities for everything from their housing to their daily bread, there was less a sharp line differentiating "favored" workers from the rest than a continuum of the slightly greater and lesser rewarded. Everyone had something to lose.

Moreover, forming and maintaining representative and effective organizations is an achievement not to be taken for granted, as the striking miners discovered when their strike committees faltered from bad leadership or simple exhaustion, or when the committees were in some cases easily coopted by the authorities. The more contact I had with Magnitogorsk workers, the more I saw that they were especially well schooled in questions of power. Yet they demonstrated a deep mistrust of politics and political parties and a hypersensitivity to demagogy, which inhibited their willingness to link up with other social groups, such as intellectuals and students. Cleavages among the various subgroups of workers, young and old, skilled and unskilled, could place additional strains on movements for solidarity.

And in the name of what should workers revolt? Workers did express near unanimous disgust at abominable working conditions and meager pay and resented management's patronizing treatment. They were justifiably concerned about their health, about their standard of living vis-à-vis the West, and about opportunities for their children in the future. But they did not necessarily see the solution to these problems in the market system, with private ownership, fluctuating (that is, rising) prices, and "socially beneficial" unemployment, even though as a result of *perestroika* they came to doubt the viability of the protective command economy and to scorn appeals to socialism.

But in the end, if *perestroika* means anything to workers, it means dignity and a chance to decide their own fate. Because of the muscle workers could potentially muster if organized, the prospect of a protracted transition to "capitalism" could well pose as big a political challenge to an industrialized Soviet Union as the building of socialism did to an agrarian one.

■   ■   ■

It is striking how much of the political debate in the Soviet Union is taken up with social questions, from the crisis provision of bread and meat to the potentially devastating consequences of unemployment and the perceived necessity of cushioning the expected blow of any transition for low-income groups. By claiming to provide for all the needs of its people, the Soviet system made living standards one of the most important barometers with which to gauge the system itself. *Glasnost* brought a flood of devastating information to bear on the question, yet *perestroika* seemed only to make matters worse. But through it all, the articulation of political programs in social terms remained as strong as ever.

By contrast, national considerations were completely absent at the outset of the reform process in 1985, yet they have risen to a place of importance alongside, if not above, social considerations. As a result, central authorities, already overwhelmed trying to contain the damage caused by each new economic or natural disaster, are now compelled to contrive a workable framework for the delegation of responsibilities to the center that the newly sovereign republics can be cajoled into accepting. Republics, however, may turn out to have the flexibility and public confidence to achieve what the all-union authorities have been unable or unwilling to do.

Yet if the administrative sovereignty of national republics is a welcome development, ethnic conflicts between and within republics have demonstrated the dangerousness of nationalism, especially with 65 million people living outside the republic of their nationality. Nuclear warheads positioned on the territory of the national republics are reportedly being moved to the Russian republic. Rumors of impending army or KGB intrigue, once feared as the worst possible turn of events, remain disturbing in the eyes of most people but lately have begun to look less menacing than some alternative scenarios.

With central government authorities still enamored of half-measures and increasingly at cross-purposes (not to say irrelevant), reactionary forces, especially in the party's countrywide apparat, have gone from biding their time to taking the offensive. Even as the authority of the top layers of the party, including the Central Committee and Politburo, was subverted in June 1990 at the Twenty-eighth Party Congress, the power of local party organizations was on the rise. The apparat turned out to be no less "activated" in the politicization brought on by the competitive elections than democratic forces. Reasserting command over substantial financial and organizational resources, the apparat became determined to take even greater advantage of its privileged position.

Despite having been irrevocably discredited before the public, reactionaries have been able to induce a paralysis of "dual power" in cities where the Communists have lost control over soviets to anti-Communists and to exercise de facto veto power over national policy in those cities without anti-Communist administrations by means of their enduring dominion over the command economy. Here antidemocratic forces have given a preview of what the country can expect from any large-scale privatization effort: the old economic and political elites remain by far the best positioned to influence the process and extract a bonanza.

Disillusionment continues to deepen as the bulk of the populace, encouraged to believe that a "regime" change would at long last solve the country's problems, watches in disgust as politician after politician speaks, one bolder than the next, but nothing positive seems to result. Instead, the torrent of speeches and legislative acts has been accompanied by a swelling refugee population, near hyperinflation, the disappearance of even those goods regulated by rationing, and a variety of "bandit" capitalism and profiteering from the malfunctioning of the state-run economy that has made the already worrisome notion of a market economy that much less reassuring.

Ominously, KGB and journalists' investigations have reported instances of large stocks of goods deliberately withheld from distribution with the apparent aim of exacerbating the economic disorganization and sowing panic. The struggle for power has assumed all forms, it seems, except traditional civil war. Meanwhile, radical economists and democratic politicians steadfastly champion a "transition" to the market as a kind of chain ready to be pulled at any moment on the flush toilet of the country's ills. But an angry and uncertain public mood and a dangerous level of social tension have persisted for years, with little relief in sight.

■   ■   ■

Straddling the great Eurasian landmass, Russia has always exerted great influence on its many and varied neighbors and in turn has been subjected to influences from the Near and Far East and from Europe. But with the reign of Peter the Great in the seventeenth century, Russia's rulers turned their attention increasingly to "the West," which seemed to present at once a grave threat to, and an important source of, Russian aspirations.

For centuries after its formation under Peter, the Russian Empire had its great-power ambitions challenged politically, economically, and militarily by the West. The Soviet Union, successor to the empire, took up and even expanded those ambitions and drew an even greater response as Soviet propagandists proclaimed their system's superiority to that of the West. Rapid industrialization during a time of Western economic depression substantiated Soviet boasts, and the eventual rout of Hitler on the Eastern Front brought extensive territorial gains, a sphere of satellite states in Eastern Europe, and increased international stature. Postwar triumphs in science and technology conferred still more luster on the USSR.

Thus, despite many setbacks and embarrassing moments along the way, the Soviet Union reached apparent parity (at enormous cost) with the West in the period following World War II. But in the eighth decade of the twentieth century, the USSR suddenly collapsed, weary from a competition it could no longer fight in a world still dominated by Western ideas, technology, and economic and military might. These were the stakes *perestroika* entailed and the eventuality *perestroika* could not forestall. In that sense *perestroika* has meant decisive defeat.

Moreover, internally *perestroika* has been characterized by severe economic dislocation, bloody ethnic strife, increased lawlessness, profound psychological disorientation, a seemingly irreversible political fragmentation, and a near loss of governability for central authorities. For all these reasons the term *katastroika* (a pun on *katastrofa*, or catastrophe) has come to serve as a derisive substitute for and statement on *perestroika*. But no one familiar with the condition of the country just before 1985 could doubt, even in hindsight, the long overdue imperative for radical structural change, not to mention the magnitude of the difficulties, internal and external, that such an undertaking would unavoidably involve.

Perestroika demonstrated that the order planted with such suffering under Stalin mercifully contained the seeds of its own destruction, seeds nurtured from without as well as within. Whether that misbegotten order also contains the seeds of a future order of greater justice, prosperity, and stability and whether vigorous external involvement will again be forthcoming remain to be seen. For now one thing is clear: the epoch opened in 1917 by the October Revolution and symbolized since 1929 by Magnitogorsk has drawn to a close.

The story of Magnitogorsk resembles nothing so much as the narrative on a flight recorder discovered amid the wreckage of an experimental political and social machine whose flight was equally as turbulent in its descent as in its ascent. Arising as it did in the 1930s, Magnitogorsk was a concentrated form of the Soviet system, a Stalinist "success" story without even a pre-Stalinist revolutionary past. When the wholesale de-Stalinization of the revolution began under Gorbachev, there was no Leninist legacy for Magnitogorsk to try to reclaim as a substitute. In this sense, Magnitogorsk could ironically claim to be in the vanguard even as it was so obviously a political backwater. But after Stalinism was finally and irreversibly discredited, Magnitogorsk seemed left without any reference point at all.

For a sense of direction and orientation Magnitogorsk looked, as in a way it always had, to the West (now thought to include the Far East)—only this time not to "catch and overtake" the powerful though immoral civilization of capitalism. Having tried to do the West one better by acting upon the West's most radical notions, Magnitogorsk, the quintessential emblem of supposed Communist supremacy, now bowed before the burnished image of an apparently superior rival, a civilization that this chastened Soviet steeltown hoped to study and emulate. One can only wish the people of Magnitogorsk extraordinary powers of analysis and good fortune. *Caveat emptor.*

Index

Compositor:	Princeton University Press Printing Division
Text:	10/13 Galliard
Display:	Galliard
Printer:	Princeton University Press Printing Division
Binder:	Princeton University Press Printing Division